CHRISTINE ... for ... 938 and
began her working lit ... a n ... training at the Royal
Berkshire Hospital in Reading alongside her sister Jennifer
Worth. Now a renowned figurative sculptor, she is best
known for works such as the remarkable Commemorative
Fountain outside the Royal Shakespeare Theatre in
Stratford-upon-Avon. She lives in Devon.

The Midwife's Sister

CHRISTINE LEE

PAN BOOKS

First published 2015 by Pan Books
an imprint of Pan Macmillan, a division of Macmillan Publishers Limited
Pan Macmillan, 20 New Wharf Road, London N1 9RR
Basingstoke and Oxford
Associated companies throughout the world
www.panmacmillan.com

ISBN 978-1-4472-8264-8

Copyright © Christine Lee 2015

'Give Time' reproduced by permission of Richard Burns

The right of Christine Lee to be identified as the
author of this work has been asserted by her in accordance
with the Copyright, Designs and Patents Act 1988.

All photographs are from the author's own collection apart from
p.8, bottom, which is © David Keith Jones/Alamy.

All rights reserved. No part of this publication may be reproduced,
stored in a retrieval system, or transmitted, in any form, or by any means
(electronic, mechanical, photocopying, recording or otherwise)
without the prior written permission of the publisher.

Macmillan does not have any control over, or any responsibility for,
any author or third-party websites referred to in or on this book.

3 5 7 9 8 6 4 2

A CIP catalogue record for this book is available from the British Library.

Printed and bound by CPI Group (UK) Ltd, Croydon CR0 4YY

This book is sold subject to the condition that it shall not, by way
of trade or otherwise, be lent, hired out, or otherwise circulated without
the publisher's prior consent in any form of binding or cover other than
that in which it is published and without a similar condition including
this condition being imposed on the subsequent purchaser.

Visit **www.panmacmillan.com** to read more about all our books
and to buy them. You will also find features, author interviews and
news of any author events, and you can sign up for e-newsletters
so that you're always first to hear about our new releases.

Dedicated to the memory of my sister Jennifer,
whose courage and fortitude led to me
writing this book

RENFREWSHIRE COUNCIL	
194779121	
Bertrams	14/03/2015
941.084	£7.99
JOH	

GIVE TIME

So take your time, enjoy it at your leisure,
Relish your hours, yet watch them pass away,
Or save time, and relinquish every pleasure
In mourning for a morning or a day,
Or, keep time, and tap out its subtle measure
Dancing in rings until steps go astray –
But give time, and receive time's finest treasure,
Visions of stars and galaxies at play.

Move through time's inner rooms and corridors,
And die imprisoned behind solid walls,
Trace each of time's results from its first cause
And hear time's hidden echoes and footfalls,
Then listen to time clapping its applause
And beg for time for extra curtain calls.

RICHARD BURNS

PROLOGUE

The moment we went into the house we knew something was wrong. We stood in the hall, my sister and I, listening, hearing nothing but the ticking of a clock in the distance. It was the quiet that was peculiar. Ours was a house always filled with life – laughter, singing and the sound of the wireless. It was as if we had come to the wrong place. Seconds passed while we absorbed the unfamiliar, unsettling atmosphere. I looked up at Jennifer. She was the eldest and biggest. Her expression was serious, her face a picture of concentration. I slipped my hand into hers and stayed silent, waiting for her to make a move. Without a word we headed up the stairs and crept from room to room looking for our parents, even though we both already sensed that we would not find them. Still, we went on searching, finally returning to the landing on the first floor and sitting at the top of the stairs. I hung on to Jennifer's hand.

In the hall, just inside the door, were the bags we had brought back from our holiday at the seaside. We had been dropped off by one of our aunts. Our mother, Elsie, had been with us for the first few days, but Gordon, our father, had not come down as he was working. Mother, missing him, had decided to return home early to Amersham and surprise him, leaving us behind with our aunts. I didn't mind her going and neither did Jennifer. It was not as if we were abandoned, as the house in Jaywick Sands, near Clacton, we knew well and loved and, anyway, we also loved our aunts.

The day our mother left she looked wonderful, her long dark hair newly washed, her favourite lemon-coloured dress swishing around her legs. She was full of joy, elated, effortlessly casting bright sunbeams as she kissed us goodbye.

That day was the last time for a long while that we saw her like this.

Jennifer got up and tugged me to my feet and we left the house. We went to see our grandmother, who lived opposite. She was a reassuring presence and explained that our mother was ill, but not what had happened, or where she was. We didn't ask. Later, our father returned and took us back to our own home. He seemed his usual affable self and pleased to see us. He made us something to eat and put us to bed but told us nothing about our mother and, again, we wondered but didn't ask.

I think we were too afraid of what he might say.

It was the autumn of 1945. I was seven and Jennifer had recently had her tenth birthday. We knew that whatever had occurred had to be serious. What we didn't know was that our childhood as we had known it was over.

PART 1

When I Was a Child

Gordon aged ten on his mother's farm.

My mother at her sister Doris's wedding,
sitting on the front row, the second on the left.

Beginnings

From a very young age I did everything with my sister, Jennifer. We had huge freedom and enjoyed great adventures together, just the two of us. I don't ever remember our parents being anxious about our exploits or trying to stop us from going off on our own, exploring. They encouraged us to be strong and independent and probably knew little of what we got up to. We more or less did as we liked.

I was born on February 1, 1938 and brought up in Amersham, in Buckinghamshire. My father was sent off to register my birth, under instructions from my mother that I was to be called Rosemary Elsie. He preferred Christine Mary, registered me as such, and Mother had little choice but to accept it. Christine was soon shortened by most people to Chris, although my father always called me Christabel. By the time I came along, Jennifer was a determined child of two and a half. One of my earliest memories when I was perhaps three years old was of us going for cycle rides as a family; my father in front, me on the back of his bike, then Mummy, and behind her, Jennifer. Seeing my sister pedalling like a mad thing, I felt very proud to be sitting in some comfort behind my father. We went for walks, too, which I loved and hated in turn, since my legs were shorter than theirs. I would struggle on, often arriving at our destination to find half the picnic had already gone.

7

We often went to the seaside, to the house at Jaywick Sands, which my father had bought at the beginning of the war. He had an open-top car and Jennifer and I would stand on the back seat regardless of the weather. Wind and rain were nothing to us. We laughed, tipped back our heads, and caught droplets of rain in our mouths as we sped along. In the 1940s, there were few other cars on the roads and no seat belts or laws about children being strapped in – and cars did not go at the speeds that we drive at today. We found it exhilarating. If the rain came down, it was not my father's habit to stop the car. He drove on, and we sang at the top of our voices. Jennifer and I loved 'Two Little Girls in Blue' from the Broadway musical of the same name: 'Two little girls in blue, lad / two little girls in blue / They were sisters, we were brothers / and learned to love the two / And one little girl in blue, lad / who won your Father's heart / became your Mother / I married the other / but now we have drifted apart.' We thought this very beautiful and sad at the time.

In 1942 the country was at war, but for us as a family the conflict and its horrors seemed a long way off as we escaped to our house by the sea, where friends and relations gathered during the holidays and an atmosphere of fun and goodwill prevailed. Jennifer and I would run onto the long, wide, empty beaches, braving the mountainous seas, with their huge waves; we made ever-larger sandcastles, and buried each other up to our necks in cool, damp sand. We laughed as we danced with lengths of seaweed, tossing them around, and collected exquisite shells and debris from ships, brought in on the tide. I loved catching in my hands the tiny crabs inhabiting the rock-pools – and in doing this I thoroughly enjoyed the only power I ever had over my big sister, for she hated these tiny creatures, and I loved to chase her unmercifully with them. She would then reciprocate by pinning me down on the beach, and tickling the soles of my very sensitive feet. As for her own feet, Jennifer always seemed to have them bare whenever she could and even in adulthood would walk around without shoes, even on roadways. It didn't seem to bother her. She was tough.

I was four, Jennifer almost seven, two very different little girls with a shared sense of fun and a strong bond. Jennifer, tall and skinny, very short-sighted, requiring pebble glasses; me, shorter and plumper with curly hair and, it was said, an angelic smile.

I can still picture us sitting on a deserted beach of sand and pebbles. It is summer, and a breeze blows on the south coast. Always, there seems to be a cool breeze coming in from the sea. We hug our knees and look into the distance. Seagulls swoop and screech, and the pale sun comes out from behind white cotton-wool clouds. The smell of seaweed and salt is in our nostrils. We are at one with our surroundings. There is not another soul to be seen. Behind us loom huge rolls of barbed wire, put there to keep out the Germans. We find a gap in these defences and creep through it, into our own little Eden.

The greatest excitement from those beach days was when we discovered on one of our excursions a disused roller-skating rink, abandoned at the outbreak of war. The rink was at least the size of a tennis court, and there were rusty skates of various sizes still hanging out of open metal cupboards. No one was there, no one to stop us taking over. On these old, disused skates we tried to move about the rink, and fell and fell again, grimly holding on to each other. With bloodied knees and hurt hands, we returned home. Our mother, ever cheerful, made nothing of our wounds, and we were told to try again until we got better. Alone, and without help from anyone, we did. Before long, with great pride, we flew around the huge expanse of the rink.

Our mother and father had the same relaxed attitude to rock-climbing, cycling and swimming. Jennifer was a wild child, reckless. She would balance on one leg on the very edge of the high cliffs, her other leg extending outwards over the drop. It seemed to me a certain death. I would beg her to stop and hold my breath as I watched, terrified, before running away, her laughter carrying on the wind behind me.

Free spirits, we ran and jumped and shouted to the howling sea. We were eager and aware of life all around as seagulls swooped and the wind gusted and almost blew us over. Along a footpath of pebbles and tufts of grass were many battered buildings with flat roofs and no windows. These old defensive forts, Martello towers, had risen up the century before. We peered through the narrow entrance of one into darkness. Gingerly, we crept into the gloom, smelling something rancid. I tugged at Jennifer's arm.

'I want to go,' I said, afraid.

'Oh no, Baby,' she said, shaking me off.

Jennifer always used the term *Baby* to describe a want of courage.

There was a hissing and a mewing. We froze, waiting for our eyes to grow accustomed to the dark.

'Jennifer . . .' I began.

'Ssh, don't be a baby,' she said, and took another few tentative steps into the dark.

Against the far wall, a great skinny black cat lay on dirty oil sacks. She pulled herself up to her full height, baring her teeth, eyes flashing. During the war there were many neglected cats, often wild and ferocious. Jennifer knew not to get too close. I huddled behind her.

At home we asked for food for the cat, but when we returned clutching our bounty, she had gone. We searched every tower, but there was no sign of her. In the end we left the food beside the dirty sacks where we had first seen her.

These seemingly endless holidays filled with adventure were magical to us.

The First Few Years

At the beginning of the war we had moved from a pretty little cottage into one of our grandmother's properties in Hill Avenue, above and behind one of her shops. It was quite spacious, although the garden was somewhat reduced in size by a huge, ugly air-raid shelter. Jennifer and I had to share a bedroom, which was large by today's standards, with a big open fireplace that divided her side from mine. It was in this room that we usually played, as there was plenty of space for our games. We had an enormous dressing-up chest, a wardrobe with all our clothes and an old Victorian chest of drawers. We liked this room and never considered that we would have liked to be on our own.

Sundays at home in winter were good. The fire was lit in the drawing room after breakfast. It was a fairly ugly room with large furniture and huge paintings of stylized ladies adorning the walls, but when the fire was lit and the room filled with music, it came to life. It was here that we learned to play cards. Mother, Jennifer and I would join in, and our father too – his favourite was whist, or there was rummy, snap or patience. I adored seeing the flames of the fire climb up the walls of the chimney and cast shadows in the evening light. We ate celery and cheese from a trolley, and crumpets which we toasted on a fork in front of the fire. The silver and pretty china came out on a Sunday and we sat there politely, eating off small tables.

I remember one snowy Sunday when we walked through the woods to Rectory Hill, Jennifer towing a large and magnificent toboggan Daddy had made us. He was dying to try it out, and so was Jennifer. He had built it from old oak planks and fitted metal strips onto the outriders. He was very proud of it and it looked amazing. When we arrived on the hill it was really wonderful to watch Jennifer and Daddy go off at tremendous speed all the way to the bottom. I was exhilarated just watching, and I was thrilled when it was my turn and I sat behind Jennifer clinging tightly to her waist. At the bottom we fell about laughing as we tumbled in the snow. But the toboggan was heavy, and by the time we had dragged it back up the hill this little girl was exhausted, and content to watch as Jennifer and our father continued with huge enthusiasm.

It may seem odd to see our childhood as idyllic in the midst of war, but in Amersham we were removed from the terrors of the cities. It is true we had food rationing – little butter, little meat, and only one egg each a week. But the black market was rife, and my father sorted out extra rations with a farmer friend. Each week during the war Jennifer and I were sent on a bus to Chesham to collect a shoebox filled with beautiful brown eggs. We knew it was illegal and were terrified in case we were caught, but always returned home safely to our mother, who opened our parcel triumphantly. Yummy! Boiled eggs for breakfast! Our mother was also very popular with all the tradesmen, who would keep her special treats when they arrived. A tin of peaches was certainly a prized possession, and would make us all terribly excited. We did not think that we were missing out on anything, yet we knew nothing of bananas, oranges or cream. Compared to many others, we were lucky.

The war played havoc with people's emotions; everyone was affected, and everyone helped each other. But despite the privations there were parties in our house: loud parties, dancing and singing to the latest sheet music played by my mother on the piano. So many faces, singing along, all the women in sexy clothes, lips all covered with Max Factor lipstick. Then hushed voices at night, talking of atrocities and death. We heard of the Germans, the Chinese, the Japanese. Fear see-sawed. Strangers were trying to kill us. Jennifer and I sat on the stairs in the dark and listened to the grown-up talk. So many people were dying. We did not like it.

We had few toys, but we didn't really need them or want them. My favourite doll, although she was pretty ugly, was called Lois. She was handmade from dull green cotton material left over from some worn-out garment. Jennifer liked a soldier doll, which was equally ugly and handmade from scraps of old material. We invented games, played shops with the contents of our mother's cupboards, and schools with paper and pencils – Jennifer was always the head teacher, and I was the child. And we played hospitals with torn-up bed linen. Jennifer was always the doctor and I was the nurse, and we would bandage each other and make slings.

Dressing up was our favourite game. Out would come our mother's amazing clothes, hats a speciality. An emerald-green silk doughnut snood with long, green, coarse netting that lifted up your hair was my favourite. Jennifer liked a theatrical curly wig. As for our mother's incredible long dresses, we had to be content to look at them and feel them because we were not allowed to play with them. Mother wore these when our parents went out in the evenings. They loved dancing, particularly at The Orchard, at Ruislip, always coming back with treats for Jennifer and me. I can still remember a wonderful dress our mother wore with a ruched fine silk bodice in cerise and a lavender heavy satin skirt cut on the cross so that it billowed out as she moved. Clothes were beautifully made then, with hand-stitched button holes, zips perfectly introduced, and hemming done by hand. In time, I learned to do all these things, and felt proud of myself.

Mother laughed a lot and flirted her way through life, making everyone she met feel good. She overwhelmed me with her huge kisses and clutching me to her ample bosom. Jennifer kept her strictly at arm's length. We both disliked these huge hugs; they were just too much. Mother was such a warm person, but we children were like her gloves, to be put on when necessary. While she had time for everyone, particularly her friends, she sometimes forgot us completely. We got lost at the zoo, on stations, in shops, theatres, cinemas and libraries. On many occasions I was found wandering unaccompanied and announcements were made for the mother of a lost child to report to such and such an office. Mother would collect me, never with the slightest hint of concern. Losing her children was a commonplace occurrence. I actually found these occasions when I was 'handed in' more thrilling than upsetting.

We did so adore our mother. We would watch her, mesmerized, as by a dragonfly. At bedtime she would tell us wonderful stories, all made up from her fertile mind, and they would continue, keeping us enthralled night after night. These stories of fairies, beasts and demons were a never-ending serial of excitement.

She loved to cook, and this was another time when we got her undivided attention. I loved sitting on the table helping to chop and stir and break eggs and lick spoons, as the fire burned in the range and music rang out loudly from the wireless. We were given the cake spoons to lick. Jennifer always adored cake, and she adored licking the big wooden spoons covered in fruit-cake mixture.

We would always have puddings and pies after the main course and I can still remember apple pies, crumbles and Charlottes, treacle pudding, spotted dick and rice pudding – absolutely delicious. And of course stewed fruit, which our mother preserved in large Kilner jars as it came into season: apples, pears, plums, rhubarb. We'd collect the pips on the side of our plates and count them out to see what our futures would hold: *coach, carriage, wheelbarrow, dung cart* – to be repeated as many times as there were pips. Or *boots, shoes, slippers, clogs*. Or *rich man, poor man, beggar man, thief*. Or *tinker, tailor, soldier, spy*. We pretended to dread the last one but found these games hilarious, and went on and on organizing and rearranging our plates.

As a family, we cooked. We stirred and tasted and laughed and hugged each other. Cooking was our play, our family play, and eating was serious business. My father's mashed potatoes were to die for. Our Aunty Doris used to make the most delicious sponge cakes and time herself for twenty minutes of hard hand-whisking with a fork to make these perfect confections. Our mother was far too impatient, and hers came out like biscuits. As an adult, Jennifer's cakes also came out like biscuits, to the delight of her children, who would play 'catch' with them in the garden.

As a child, I loved cooking and Jennifer loved eating, so all was well.

Every night we were given a dose of rosehip syrup and then cod liver oil and malt; Jennifer first, then me. We neither of us liked this great spoonful of sludge, which smelt very bad. We had all the childhood complaints, from mumps to measles and whooping cough and chickenpox. It was normal then – all children got these illnesses. We had to stay in bed for days, the fire was lit in our bedroom and trays of delicious food were brought in to us. It was really enjoyable being ill, as Mother would hover, and Grandpa come in to play draughts with us, and we had the wireless brought into our room. Before penicillin was widely available, M&B (sulphapyridine, an anti-bacterial drug of the 1940s) was the only drug used for these complaints. Jennifer and I were both fearful of getting scarlet fever with its horrific ramifications or, even worse, tuberculosis. We both had a great deal of tummy aches, for which we were given Dr J. Collis Browne's Chlorodyne, which we thought delicious. It certainly had a remarkable effect, curing our tummy aches instantly. They still sell it now but have taken out most of the morphine and it doesn't seem to work any more.

The most important garments in winter were liberty bodices, which Jennifer and I were buttoned into every year. These fleece-lined sort-of-vests kept us warm and safe from the cold – no central heating then. I also used to get really nasty chilblains every winter and was made to sit on a chair with my feet in a chamber pot of urine. Ugh! I felt it was so undignified, even though it was my own urine, and Jennifer would be delighted at my discomfort, dancing around and laughing.

My father's transport business flourished during the war, so weekends were times for shopping, buying sheet music and, on occasion, going to London. My mother loved clothes and nothing, not even Hitler or the restrictions of clothing coupons, was going to stop her frequenting her favourite shops. She could buy extra clothing coupons on the black market, which was what she and her friends did. We taxied through bombed-out London, seeing the effects of war, the devastated buildings, the poverty on the streets. My mother swept through it all, from half-ruined Oxford Street to Harrods in Knightsbridge, and we sailed along behind her in our matching clothes from Daniel Neal's, in Kensington, the two of us in our pristine white ankle socks and Start-Rite shoes.

Jennifer played the piano from a very early age, and I would recite poetry for our mother's friends, as this is what we did before the invasion of television. Every week there was ballet dancing at the Fabian School of Dancing at the Turret House, where I performed with enthusiasm while Jennifer bunked off. On Wednesdays there were piano lessons with Miss Goudie, a large, florid lady who lived down White Lion Road, some way from our house. She would teach Jennifer first, all smiles, while I sat and waited my turn. No more smiles.

'Why have you not practised?'

But how could I, when my mother and Jennifer were always on the piano? I hated these weekly lessons; I thought Miss Goudie was fat, and smelled. To make matters worse, we had to walk to her house alone. In the winter during the war all the streets were dark, lamplight forbidden, and the houses had blackout curtains at their windows. The wardens and police were about, looking for gaps of light. So Jennifer and I would creep along the pitch-dark streets, holding hands, fearful that at any moment something from within the wilds of our imagination would leap out at us.

At home, there was an air-raid shelter in the garden. Raucous sirens would ring out, warning us all to take cover and go into the shelter, but we never did. The air-raid shelter stank of damp, and we thought rats lived there. Anyway, our mother's fearless attitude prevailed over all.

'It's only bombs, dear,' she would say, and cheerfully carry on with her life. So my sister and I did the same.

Mother always ignored anything she found unpleasant.

Amersham may have been peaceful, but we found our own excitements. Our favourite was going off to play on the common. It was very safe, but Jennifer and I would secrete our pennies into our pockets and run to the stile that allowed access to the railway line. We would climb over it, place our pennies on the line and wait. We thought it was very, very dangerous. We held hands and were breathless. Trains would pass at speed, unaware of two small girls hiding in the grass. The noise of the wheels on the line was huge, and the wind even more so, throwing us sideways as the carriages roared past. Then we would run excitedly onto the line to inspect our pennies, and compare their size and shape – such fun, they were hot and misshapen. We told no one – somehow we knew it was not something the grown-ups would enjoy.

Christmas was a glorious time, with every year a wonderful tree to decorate on Christmas Eve, and under it so many presents from aunts and uncles, grandparents, cousins, and the best and last from Daddy and Mummy. The wrapping was very basic, as there was little pretty paper around at the time and my mother hadn't the patience to create anything superficially pretty, but we all made paper chains to put on the ceiling and brought in holly to decorate the room. There would be lots of delicious food, and an enormous bird, always a turkey or goose. Our father's arrival with it was heralded with shrieks of laughter. Where had he got it from? Our cousins joined us, and we played games until darkness took over. Charades was a favourite with our mother.

On Boxing Day, Mummy, Daddy, Jennifer and I dressed up to go to The Orchard, a large exclusive restaurant in Ruislip with a dance floor at its centre. There were balloons and crackers and so many wonderful things to eat – unheard of during the war. There were singers and a band, and Daddy took Jennifer onto the dance floor to dance with him, and then me, standing on his feet. What joy! Then it was off to London to see Bertram Mills Circus, where we held our breath waiting for the trapeze artist to fall. Every year we also went to London to see *Peter Pan* and every year we believed in Tinker Bell and shrieked at Captain Hook.

To School, Gently

Our first school was Kingsley House, where for the first time I recognized that boys had the best deal – they played the drums and large, crashing cymbals, while we girls were given triangles. With very bad grace, we hit them discordantly.

Jennifer and I would walk to school hand in hand, past the shops, to the other side of Amersham where our small nursery school was situated. We were aged three and five and a half, and our mother thought it perfectly safe for us to walk there alone, as was usual in those days. Everyone knew each other and there was always a policeman on the street with his high helmet to protect us if need be. One excitement I can remember was when Jennifer won a black china doll by naming her Dinah. Mother had schooled her not to say Diana, I've no idea why. I can't remember the name I gave. Jennifer won because the headmistress felt Dinah was the most suitable name. She was very proud of her prize, but we seldom played with her.

In 1942, when still only four and seven, we were sent to Belle Vue, a polite girls' school a few miles away. We travelled by steam train by ourselves to Little Chalfont, with the guard in charge of making sure we got off at the right station. We loved the train journeys, the smoke, the guard's whistle and jostling through the countryside. We wore black and gold uniforms, and black berets with darling little gold tassels. We dawdled to school from the station along winding country lanes, listening to the birds and picking flowers on the way, and in the autumn kicking up the dried golden leaves and collecting chestnuts. We were always late but no one minded, and we loved the old house set at the end of the long drive. We had stories read to us by the beautiful Miss Clarke and were told how special we were. Then the school moved to Hyde Heath, changed its name, and collected all the Amersham children by coach. No longer the joy of a steam train, and the walks down mossy lanes. The coach was smelly and I was always sick on the way, but everyone was kind, even if Jennifer ran away, for she heartily disliked the smell of sick.

In the summer it was different. We cycled to school along the leafy lanes, with the smells of summer and the sound of cuckoos in our ears. We loved it, except for the fact that Jennifer's bike was bigger than mine, and went faster, and I was always left behind. My wild, adventurous sister was always falling out of trees that were too high for her and making great holes in various parts of her anatomy.

At school, with great difficulty, we knitted coloured squares to make into blankets for the war effort. We collected ship halfpennies (ha'penny coins with sailing ships on one side, and the king's head on the other) so that presents could be sent to the sailors who were risking their lives for us every day. We also collected coloured pictures which were given away inside cigarette packets: Clark Gable, Greer Garson and Hedy Lamarr were our favourites. In those days, all packets of cigarettes had small photo cards of film stars, sportsmen and the like.

We also had pen pals and, with help, wrote simple letters

of encouragement to the troops off fighting in different parts of the world. The intention was to keep up morale. We collected the exotic stamps from their replies. It was all very exciting for us, except when some did not write back and we were left to wonder what had become of them. Had they survived?

We were read books at school – how I loved *The Wind in the Willows*. I particularly and secretly adored Toad – I knew he behaved very badly, but he was just so much fun. I have never changed.

Although dilatory and not particularly interested in homework, Jennifer was very bright, and was put in a class with children rather older than her. She fitted in, was happy enough, and made some friends. Molly Wilkinson was her very best friend. I, on the other hand, struggled to keep up.

'She does not seem to pay attention,' my teachers said, perplexed. 'Or do her homework.'

They were right. In the classroom, I would concentrate on the great outdoors through the windows, fascinated by the changing seasons, wishing I could escape to explore the countryside. I felt part of the countryside. I was the grass over which I rolled, I was the daisy and the bee. I was the big oak and the swallow. I was the sunlight and the wind and the rain. How I loved the rain – the splashing as I ran into it, opening my mouth to catch the droplets, sloshing about with bare feet in the summer and wellies in the winter. These were the things that drew me in. Many years later, I discovered I had a mild form of dyslexia, although growing up in the 1940s it was a term that was unknown to me. Undoubtedly, it affected my ability to read and write at an early age.

'Jennifer's the clever one, Chris is the pretty one,' was how our mother frequently described her daughters. She repeated this all the time.

'Your sister is much cleverer than you, you should be more like her,' I was told by my teachers on more than one occasion.

I remained silent. Did I really want to be more like her? I was uncertain. She would play with me and then discard me, tease me and run away. No, I decided, I did not want to be more like Jennifer. Yet, together with my mother and my grandmother, this headstrong girl brought me up, and I loved her fiercely.

Background Lives,
Fateful Consequences

Our parents seemed to adore each other. The love between them was apparent in the laughter they shared, the looks that passed from one to the other. Before things went wrong on the day that Jennifer and I returned home to an empty house in 1945, I never sensed the slightest friction or unhappiness between Mother and Father.

Our father, Gordon, was the youngest child of five, born in 1911 into a respected farming family on the North Wales border. His father died when Gordon was only nine, and soon after this tragedy, foot and mouth disease came to their farm and wiped it out, leaving a young widow with five children to struggle on with great difficulty. Any farm employees had to go, and the family took on all the work themselves. My father remembered seeing his mother being chased by a bull while carrying a bucket of milk in each hand and hurdling a five-bar gate. For him, from the ages of nine to fourteen, it was the local school during the day and then work on the farm – if he could be caught. He had been given an old motorbike and spent hours doing it up, escaping to the nearby town of Chester.

At fourteen, Gordon had to leave school. He was needed on the farm. But after four days of Grandmother's maxim, 'If you don't work, you don't eat,' and realizing that he was expected to hoe a field of turnips among other horrors, he said his goodbyes and left. The world was waiting for him. He hitched a lift on a lorry going south and enthusiastically sang all the way. He was dropped off at a garage on the outskirts of Amersham. He had no money, was hungry, and had no idea where to go. He looked around, strode up to the only man in sight and asked if there was any work about. Food was all he wanted in exchange for work, and he was taken on instantly. Could he drive a truck? He had driven tractors for much of his early life and reckoned that he could drive the garage beast, so was taken on to deliver tyres. He lived above the garage. This arrangement continued without dissent for some years, and as he watched and worked, he learned. He took on another job on his day off and somehow saved enough to buy a dilapidated milk float. With great pride he set up in business by himself, delivering tyres and undercutting the prices of his first employer. It was in this milk float that he arrived at a polite dance in the leafy district of the Chilterns, saw our mother, and fell in love.

Brought up in Amersham, surrounded by the gentle Buckinghamshire countryside, Elsie Gibbs was born in 1914, the youngest child of seven. She was very pretty and very bright and was loved and spoilt by everyone. She passed the exams into Dr Challoner's Grammar School, where her mother proudly paid her school fees, and flourished. At sixteen, eager to get on with her life, she left school, applied to take the Post Office exams and was accepted. In those days she had to do a two-year training. She was extremely conscientious and quickly became the smartest and, she thought, the best ever Post Office counter clerk. She was aware that Britain was in the grip of a depression, struggling with unemployment and poverty, but told me later that in leafy Buckinghamshire they danced and partied and enjoyed life to the full. They were alive and they celebrated.

Elsie was an extremely pretty dark-haired girl with bedroom eyes, a fabulous hourglass figure and great legs. She always dressed in pretty clothes and adhered to my grandmother's maxim: 'Fine feathers, fine bird.' She wore the latest fashions, danced a mean charleston, and was greatly admired by all. She charmed, teased and flirted in turn. She had a delicious sense of the ridiculous and this, mixed with her keen intelligence, made her unstoppable.

At least, that was, until Gordon set eyes on her.

She was dancing, surrounded by an admiring crowd, as he looked on. My Aunty Doris, who was there, told me she watched my father move in. There he was, a good-looking, dark-haired stranger. It was as if my mother's heart stopped. They danced and danced. Her brothers and sisters watched, and tried to stop her leaving with him, but to no avail; the two were magnetized.

He asked her, 'May I drive you home?'

She said he could and was completely undeterred when she set eyes on his form of transport, the milk float.

Christmas 1934 came, with all the festivities, and they escaped, telling nobody about their plans. This time they went to Folkestone, and did not return for two days, so involved with each other were they and completely unaware of the drama going on in my grandmother's house. On their return, our maternal grandfather, six foot four and in a terrible rage, literally threw my father out of the house. Four months later our astute grandmother called him back, arranging a wedding for June 1935. By this time, my mother was pregnant. It was such a disgrace in 1935. Since my grandmother did not want people to know her daughter was expecting a baby prior to her marriage, a few weeks before the baby was due she took my mother away to Clacton, where my sister Jennifer arrived on September 25, 1935 – nine months to the day after Christmas. My mother was twenty, my father twenty-three.

Grandma Takes Over

Ever determined, Grandma sorted out space for her beautiful daughter and her new husband and baby to live in her house and bought my father a large, new and splendid lorry. He had charmed her, as he had charmed her daughter. In no time at all he repaid all the money she had invested in him, bought another lorry, and established himself as a full-scale transport contractor.

Mother became pregnant again with me. After I was born, in February 1938, they moved to a sweet cottage and had a nanny and a cleaner. Their world was idyllic. Despite the wireless spewing out Nazi horrors, they were not touched in peaceful Amersham. The shock came the following year, when the Prime Minister stunned the nation by declaring that we were at war with Germany. Our parents then moved from their pretty cottage to be near my grandparents, where my grandmother took over after Doris, the nanny, went into the Land Army, helping on a farm, and Ada, the cleaner, went into a local factory.

Mother was left to cope with two small children, our home and all our father's paperwork and administration. It was hard work for her, particularly as Father had won a government contract to move essential equipment from the south of England up to Scotland. He was declared exempt from joining up as he was essential for the war effort, which required a great deal of background support. This meant our father spent the war hauling fighter-plane parts and other military equipment around the country. He took on more men and bought more lorries and, despite the huge distances, would drive up to Scotland and back in a day. He would leave in the dark and return in the dark. He saw to it that his men shared in his profits; they loved him and worked as hard as he did, and his business flourished.

By the end of the war, some six years later, our father had a whole fleet of lorries and had placed an order for one of the first Jaguar XK120s. He adored cars, and this car was the first shockingly beautiful car to be seen after the war – and a wonderment in rural Amersham. It was white with a red leather interior, and I was so proud of it. It fuelled my own love of fast sports cars.

Father also joined the Home Guard, doing drills and exercises as in *Dad's Army*, and left our mother to run the business. I remember a marvellous Christmas party the Home Guard gave. It was fancy dress, so our mother, ever inventive, decided that we should go as the Ugly Sisters. We were dressed in black and had our faces rouged, with thick ugly lipstick and had black lines applied. We certainly looked frightful, but we won first prize and our mother was delighted. Jennifer was not at all pleased; she had wanted to go as a pirate.

During the war our mother drove nurses from Amersham to Chardellows, a nearby stately home that was being used as a maternity hospital. Jennifer and I often went with her and played in the surrounding fields. In late spring when the cowslips were abundant we would pick armfuls of the sweet-smelling yellow flowers and take them home, where their scent filled the house.

Our home shrank rather quickly after the declaration of war. First, the top floor of the house was taken over by a young couple with a baby. As we were at school during the week, involved with our family circle, and away at the seaside in the holidays, we never got to know our lodgers, and I remember little about them. We had our once-a-week bath ritual in the shared bathroom upstairs – a room that was cold and smelt unpleasantly of cooking, as the young couple used it as their kitchen, placing a door over the bath to create a work surface. As it was the only bathroom in the house, cooking smells notwithstanding, we were forced to continue our weekly baths there throughout the war, having our hair washed and necks scrubbed. (Was my neck really that dirty?) We used to have to sit in the airing cupboard for at least an hour afterwards and towel-dry our hair in the winter (no hairdryers then). This was an ordeal, particularly for Jennifer, as she had long hair almost down to her waist. I spent many years plaiting her hair every morning and feeling rather proud that she wanted me to do it, while she felt impatient that it took me so long.

The ground floor was next to go. One day our mother found a scruffy, exhausted man leaning against a shop doorway. She stopped – the first person to speak to him that day. He was Jewish, and he and his young wife had just escaped from France. They had nothing but the clothes they stood up in and nowhere to go. So, of course, my compassionate mother took them home and installed them in the ground floor of our house. Actually, it was only the kitchen area really, with a huge cupboard under the stairs and an outside loo. Somehow, this young Jewish man and his wife must have slept under the stairs, and managed to live in the rest, which they did, amazingly, for a good part of the war. Not only that, in no time at all various relations had joined them – all cramming gratefully into this small, uncomfortable haven.

And so throughout much of the war our family lived on the middle floor of the house, where we had a sizeable kitchen with a range and modern gas cooker. We were the jam in the sandwich, so to speak.

Punishment

Apart from life under the care of our mother and grandmother, there were appearances of a big important man called Daddy, who was smiley and comfortable and smelt of Brylcreem and tobacco. There were sweet interludes with him when I got up early in the morning while Jennifer was still sleeping. She always had disturbed nights, as she suffered terribly from asthma, so she stayed in bed as long as possible. I found my father having breakfast alone – always eggs and bacon and fried bread – and he was pleased to be joined by this little person. He would dip soldiers of fried bread into his egg yolk and give them to me, and we talked about things I did not understand. But I understood the real warmth there was for me, and I still remember the songs he taught me to sing: 'Daisy, Daisy', and, my favourite, 'You Are My Sunshine'.

He would sit me on his lap and we would eat and sing together. I *was* his sunshine.

Although Jennifer and I had a great deal of freedom, bad behaviour was not tolerated. In those days it was not unusual to be punished with what was called 'a good hiding'. My parents were mostly sweet and loving, and some of my earliest recollections were of them admiring me: 'Isn't she sweet? Isn't she lovely? Hasn't she the most perfect smile?'

Those self-same people were equally capable of shouting, shutting Jennifer and me into our room, and beating us until our bottoms burned. It sounds appalling now, but was the norm when we were growing up.

One such occasion remains imprinted in my memory. I was about three, Jennifer five, and two of our cousins had come for lunch. We were sitting at the table, the four of us and my mother. Father wasn't there. We children were having a riot, talking and laughing at the top of our voices, and Mother tried to quieten us down.

'From now on, anyone who speaks will not get pudding,' she said.

We all fell silent. I glanced at the others and at my mother. I really didn't believe her, and decided to shout at her in what I thought was a jokey fashion.

'You wouldn't do that. You're still going to give me my pudding.'

Mother gave me a cool look. 'No, I most certainly am not.'

She passed around the pudding in large white bowls but gave me an empty one. I clambered down from my chair and faced her.

'If you don't give me my pudding I'll break my dish,' I said.

'You had better not,' she said, sternly.

I looked her directly in the eye, picked up my dish from the table and smashed it on the back of my chair. Jennifer stared at me. My cousins kept their heads down. Mother got up, swept over, picked me up and put me outside on the doorstep where I sat crying, thinking how unfair it all was. I was still there when my father came up the garden path and gathered me into his arms.

'What's wrong, Christabel?' he asked.

'Mummy has been horrible to me,' I said, tears running down my face.

He hugged me and carried me indoors.

'How could you make this little girl cry?' he asked my mother.

She told him of my appalling behaviour. Looking like thunder, my father took me up to the bedroom I shared with Jennifer and left, shutting the door behind him. I lay on the bed feeling sorry for myself. Time passed. By the time Daddy returned, he had heard the full story. My mother was very cross indeed. I had to apologize to her, he said. I refused. In my three-year-old head I felt I had done nothing terribly bad. I loved my mother. I was a good child. Wasn't I? My heart cried out for him to understand that I had NOT been rude. In my childish, clumsy way I tried to explain.

'I'm not rude,' I said. 'Mummy's just unfair.'

My father faced me, big and strong and angry. 'You will apologize to your mother,' he said.

I shook my head.

'If you won't apologize I will have to beat you.'

I said nothing. I did not want a hiding and yet for some reason could not bring myself to say sorry.

My pants were torn off, I was thrown onto my front on the bed and thoroughly smacked on the bottom. Shock, then pain as my father struck me. Tears streamed down my face. I thought, 'You can beat me and beat me as much as you like but I shan't change my mind.' Those words became seared into my brain. After my father left I lay alone in the dark, cold room, crying. I had survived. I understood with absolute certainty that while my body could be beaten my mind was my own. I could think what I liked, when I liked.

At just three years old I knew I was my own person. From that moment on I learned to listen to what others said and at the same time to think my own thoughts.

That night, by the time Jennifer came up to bed I was no longer upset and with some pride showed her the red finger-prints on my bottom. She was very impressed. It wasn't often we got a beating, but when we did, we both took pleasure in comparing the impressions our father's handprints had made on our skin. Jennifer regarded me with respect. My bottom was raw and sore, but I was unbroken. We giggled. By morning, the drama of the day before had been forgotten, but what stayed with me was the discovery I had made that my thoughts were my own. It was a powerful lesson, and one I relied upon time and again all through my life.

Amersham Shopping

In Amersham, the Bucks County Library was on the corner, with a hairdresser's upstairs. Jennifer hated it there and refused to have her hair cut, growing it almost to her waist. I acquiesced and had my hair regularly cut into a short bob. I wished for long hair, but did not feel able to assert myself. Mother wanted things her way, and this included my hair.

In town, a wet fish shop with enormous fish laid out on great blocks of white marble smothered in ice fascinated me. I watched the large cutlets of cod being cut up, and flat fish having their heads and tails removed. Jennifer always stayed outside; she hated the thought of eating flesh, as well as the smell of it. I remember watching her spitting out any fish or fowl, however it was disguised. Jennifer would not go into the butcher's, either. I would go in with our mother, kicking up the sawdust on the floor and enjoying the repartee which was always there. I certainly loved eating meat, fish or fowl.

Our favourite shop was the grocer's, with long polished wooden counters and assistants in pristine beige coats to serve us. There were wooden chairs for the customers to sit on, and mother would sit elegantly and give her order every week. I can still hear her say, 'Butter, marge, cheese, lard, sugar, tea, coffee, eggs' – then hushed whispers about what was under the counter – all very exciting. Then the detailed bill was added up and sent in a bullet-shaped container with the cash along overhead metal wires, up to the cashier seated in a glass box above us, and then the change returned down the wires, making a great whizzing noise. We then left, leaving our order to be delivered by a boy with a huge wicker basket on the front of his bicycle.

We were forbidden to go into Woolworths; we might catch something there. So Jennifer and I would take deep breaths in the fresh air immediately outside the store before rushing around inside for as long as possible without taking a further breath, thus returning to the outside world bursting. We never had time to buy anything, but as we had no pocket money it would have been impossible anyway.

Everyone we knew seemed to smoke in those days – if not cigarettes, then a pipe or cigars. I loved seeing a man with a pipe: bent ones, straight ones, large ones and small, all beautifully crafted and polished. Their owners would be very proud of them. Cigars at Christmas were a treat for everyone; we just adored the smell. We often went to the tobacconist, which was combined with the sweet shop – and how we loved the sweet shop.

Sweets were strictly rationed during the war, but as our grandmother owned the shop, the only rationing that Jennifer and I were subjected to was our mother's. Our lovely Aunty Doris would slip us a chocolate button when no one was looking.

Petticoats and knickers were never deemed necessary for our mother, who wore cami-knickers made from parachute silk – a strange yet beautiful all-in-one arrangement, done up with tiny buttons between the legs. As a young woman Mother wore corsets, peach-coloured boned contraptions, yet she had a gorgeous figure. Later, the fashion changed, and it was rubber 'roll-ons' she would slip into and haul up with extreme difficulty. We wondered why she wore them, and thought she must feel very hot in such things. Jennifer and I decided we would never wear anything like this, and indeed we never did.

Grandma Gibbs

Grandma Gibbs' house, a comfortable three-bedroom turn-of-the-century detached property with a delightful cottage garden, was warm and cosy. The sitting room had traditional, old furniture, bookshelves, a gramophone with a huge horn, and rugs. I loved it, and it was very much like my own home today. There was always lots to eat, and a warm welcome for everyone.

Eliza Gibbs was small and neat, wore her hair up in a soft bun and loved pretty clothes. She had always been very pretty, and had beautiful hands and feet. Even as an old lady she really cared for herself and never looked unkempt. She loved her family and all her children lived nearby, so every Sunday there would be a gathering, children and grandchildren around her large dining table, enjoying a massive meal. We cousins enjoyed this and played games like French and English, Oranges and Lemons and Grandma's Footsteps, a popular game then. It was wild fun but it always annoyed me that Jennifer, whose middle name was Louise, had five *E*s in her name and I only had three. *E* seemed to come up a lot, and she always won. Afterwards we would all walk down to Amersham churchyard, the grown-ups and children amicably chatting and just enjoying being together. We were a peaceful, loving family with much humour and laughter. I remember at one wedding my cousin bent over to me and said: 'Isn't it curious that our side of the family are all laughing, and the other side are not?'

It was true. Our family was blessed with love and humour, and no pain or tragedy could take this away from any of them. My Aunty Doris cheerfully coped with a war-damaged husband. Aunty Grace had shocking rheumatoid arthritis – her hands became so distorted that it was a triumph when she picked up even a small bottle – and walking became a problem for her, but she laughed at it all and the world laughed with her. She had amazing courage. Uncle Ron was forced to marry a disagreeable woman he had made pregnant and had to cope with the ramifications; nevertheless he was always cheerful, and even in his eighties would deliver Meals on Wheels from his motorbike. I particularly liked him as he would give us half a crown when he left on Sundays. Aunty Winnie opened a small shop when her husband left her, and eventually married again. All these aunts and uncles made other people's lives better for just knowing them, and our own mother was no exception.

At this time our routine fell into school during the week and family gatherings at weekends, when we would walk down to the graveyard in Old Amersham. We children would run through the woods, leap over wartime dugouts, and play around the gravestones in the churchyard. And we would always pay homage to a beautiful white marble angel on a child's grave, and Grandma would happily show us the plot where she was going to be put when she died, next to her daughter, Ivy, who had died suddenly at a young age. We thought it was a good place, under a tree and away from the hubbub of life. Now the old graveyard is dominated by a supermarket. She would not have liked that.

When we walked through Rectory Woods to Old Amersham, we visited our favourite tree, an ancient oak that we christened Jimmy Drummond after a family friend. The trunk was covered in dead ivy, and looked like this huge Scot who stayed with us from time to time: just as the ivy smothered the tree, Jimmy Drummond had a chest that was smothered in a thick mat of curly black hair. We would be mesmerized every time we saw him change his shirt. Our father had only five hairs on his chest. We knew – we had counted them.

Grandpa Gibbs was a tall quiet presence, although he could get fiercely angry. My mother told me that this huge, gentle man used to beat her brothers with his leather shaving strap and lock them in their rooms. They were only let out when my grandmother begged for their release.

I do remember very clearly, when I was still very young, his remarking on a small spot he had developed near his nose, and Eliza telling him to go to see Dr Strang. The outcome was that it needed to be removed. He went into hospital, but it was not quite as simple as they had anticipated. The spot was malignant, and the operation involved removing the entire roof of his mouth and part of the back of his throat. Today it would be horrific, but then it was even more so. It left him greatly disfigured, with drooping mouth, running nose and loud impenetrable voice. It was a miracle that he lived. Every year he was asked to go up to the Royal College of Surgeons to show off their magnificent operation. This great patient man bore it all with courage and fortitude, but as a young child I found it very frightening, and kept away from him. Jennifer did not seem to notice.

Grandpa had been a career soldier, but was left emotionally damaged by the Great War, which he served in from 1914 to 1918. He was unable to support the family financially after he returned, so Grandma was in charge and took over – first scrimping and saving money, then buying her first two cottages in Steeple Claydon, where she was born. She made a profit on the sale of these and bought other properties and shops. She was one of the first property developers, although she kept her financial dealings secret from her family, and they were all astonished when she died and left them considerably better off. We children started our first Post Office accounts with handfuls of her huge, crisp white five-pound notes. Thank you, Granny. She had been careful all her life, indeed frugal, when it came to ordinary domestic things.

'You know, Mother, you really do need a new hearth brush. This one has practically no bristles,' my mother would say.

'Definitely not, it will last quite a bit longer and I can't afford to replace it.'

Yet when she died she left each of her children a house, and her two eldest daughters two. She left nothing to Arthur, her husband, except a cottage for life. She always said that if she gave anything to him, he would just give it away. This was apparently what he had done when he found her savings while she was in hospital having her gall bladder removed. After that, she placed any money she had into Lloyds Bank. I liked going into the bank with her. The bank clerks were mostly men in dark suits, and all transactions were done in a respectful whisper. We were only allowed in if we promised to be very still and remain silent, and, of course, we did.

Although our parents were not practising Christians, my mother believed in God and my father in the Almighty; so our religious education, such as it was, was left to our grandmother and our schools. Church with Grandma on a Sunday morning was a strain – all dressed in our Sunday best, white gloves a necessity. We kept very quiet and listened to the terrifyingly powerful sermons of the Reverend Murray Page, who hovered over us like a great black eagle and seemed like God himself preaching vengeance from the pulpit. I kept myself small lest he saw me, watched him through my fingers and earnestly believed every word – I felt the fear of Hell and damnation and pestilence and famine, and the agony on the cross, and Job's torments, and I was troubled by the story of Lot's wife. I was sure I, too, would have looked back.

'Turn the other cheek,' the preacher said, and I knew what I had to do. It was not that difficult. I had disassociated my mind already, so I delighted in my ability to take physical suffering without distress, having learned to do so as a very young child, when 'good hidings' were normal. I was almost there. I would always turn the other cheek and be safe from the hell-fires. I felt deeply that I was suffering for God's blessing. It took many years, and a lot of pain, to sort this out. While I took on board 'turn the other cheek,' Jennifer as a very young girl was keen on Jesus throwing over the tables in the temple. She and I talked about this often over the years, and as I got older I certainly took on her approach of striking out for the righteous and defending the poor.

We were encouraged to go to Sunday School by our parents. Jennifer soon discovered why, when, one lovely sunny day, she bunked off. Returning home, she found our mother and father in bed enthusiastically making love. She was both shocked and fascinated, as she later informed me.

'Where did you go?' I asked her, when I got home.

'Oh, just home. It was such a nice day.'

'What did you do?' I said.

'Well, nothing really, but I just watched . . .'

'What did you watch?'

'Mummy and Daddy in bed, hugging and kissing and bouncing around. I think they were making love.'

'What did you *say*?' I asked.

'I didn't!' With that, she ran away.

I spent many years after that wondering how it was done. My imagination got no further than end-to-end; this would have been very difficult, as their bed was only six feet long! Nobody told us about the reality of the facts of life. Pregnancy was never mentioned, and when I asked my grandmother where babies came from, she told me, 'From under the gooseberry bush.' Afterwards I looked there, in her garden, and wondered for a long time. And then it was the stork, which arrived mysteriously, carrying the baby in his beak and in swaddling clothes. It wasn't until Jennifer's eleventh birthday that my mother gave her a thin blue book called *Approaching Womanhood*, with instructions to hide it from me as I was far too young. Of course, in our room late at night we shared it, trying to understand it all. It did not really address my curiosity as to how things worked.

Jennifer had been given a Lakeland Terrier puppy for her seventh birthday. She called him Bryn and adored him, trying to take him everywhere – even to Sunday School, where she hid him under her chair. When we were older there was the Free Church Youth Club in the evenings, and Bryn would come too. Jennifer and I both got rather good at table tennis. We both loved singing, and sang with our mother out in the countryside and in our bedroom at night. Jennifer's voice was certainly more powerful than mine, but I was proud that I could reach the higher notes. We were also coached to sing duets on special days: 'Flocks in Pastures Green Abiding' was a particular favourite. While Jennifer had a strong voice, a rather mean teacher with thin lips said that I was a little 'breathy'. I never quite understood *breathy*. Yet we were coached to sing duets in the church and were told that we were very, very good. We learned much of the Bible by heart. We liked the psalms, which still bring me comfort today.

We believed in God and Jesus, and periodically prayed. I do believe in a higher power, be it God or the Almighty; but I am the original doubting Thomas, covering myself by following the instructions of Jesus in my daily life, yet waiting for the unknown after death.

The Dressmaker, Her Daughter, and Betrayal

On that fateful day in the autumn of 1945 when Jennifer and I came home from Jaywick Sands to find the house empty, our lives took a dramatic turn. Initially, all that we knew was that our mother was ill. She was in hospital, although nothing was explained, and it seemed to us that she had simply disappeared. For a few days we were left to our own devices and ran back and forth to my grandmother's house, where she gave us lots to eat, returning home each evening when Father came in from work. He was just as he had always been: cheerful, loving, reassuring. We had no sense from his behaviour how ill Mother really was.

One day we were told to go to Granny's and then, later, went home. In the intervening hours our mother had returned. But when Jennifer and I went to see her, we found her propped up in bed, unable to move her left arm, her beautiful face twisted and ugly. She battled to talk, but could hardly speak. We, her daughters, one aged seven, the other only just ten, stood at the side of the bed not knowing what to do. Mother tried to put an arm around us but couldn't manage it. For us, accustomed to seeing her full of life and laughter, finding her bedridden and helpless, her lovely face nothing like it had been, was utterly shocking. We were frightened, very frightened – and worried.

For a long time we did not know what had happened to her. Slowly, over a period of years, we managed to piece events together. Some of what we learned came from our grandmother. Some was explained to us by our mother once she began to recover.

What emerged was that the day she left us at Jaywick Sands and returned home, she had suffered a stroke so severe she had almost lost her life. She had rushed into the house, up the stairs and into the bedroom, intent on springing a lovely surprise on our father – only to find him in the marital bed with his young secretary. The surprise was far from lovely. Our mother, having suffered from asthma all her life, and always delicate both physically and emotionally, was so shattered she collapsed to the floor. Much later, we found out that the secretary had left in a hurry, stepping over my mother's limp body, leaving my horrified father to call for an ambulance.

It was my mother who had unwittingly brought the young woman into my father's life in the first place. During the war, my mother did all she could to help others, while my father continued to work and earn money. My mother had a dressmaker, Mrs Galletly, a dark little woman who dressed in black and sat hunched over a sewing machine in the gloomy back room of her house. Jennifer and I only went there once, when Mother was having a fitting. The dressmaker glared at us and pushed us away from her into a corner. We were not wanted. Frightened, and really not liking the woman, we refused to go there again. Mrs Galletly was a skilled dressmaker, however, and Mother made light of our dislike, laughing at our fears. During that time many people could not find civilian work and our mother agreed to ask Father to give the dressmaker's daughter a job. She persuaded him to take the young woman on, even though neither of them had met her, arguing it would be a perfect arrangement all round and would relieve Mother of some of the office work.

Judith, the dressmaker's daughter, was twenty-two and exquisitely pretty. My father was attractive and successful. How long it took her to see him as a potential lover I cannot say but as my father adored women, it would not have been difficult for her to attract his attention, and they quickly began an affair.

Of course, Jennifer and I knew nothing of this at the time. Mummy was ill but Daddy was still there, the same as ever, always seeming cheerful. I still got out of bed early and ran downstairs to sit on his lap while he ate his breakfast, cut a soldier from his fried bread and dipped it in the yolk of his egg for me. At a time of anxiety, he was our stability.

All I remember of Christmas 1945 was that my mother was in bed, terribly unwell. Jennifer and I ran in and out of her room, two small girls anxious to make a contribution to the festivities. While Jennifer was off trying to decorate a tree and not doing very well with it, I set about making mince pies, following Mother's instructions. Jennifer hated cooking, so I was going to have to manage most of it without her help.

'It's easy,' Mother said, hesitantly, 'you just mix the fat and flour and roll it out.'

In the kitchen, I struggled with the mixture, which would not be rolled out, no matter how hard I tried. Desperate, I ran back to my mother for further instruction.

'Just roll it out,' she repeated.

I tried again, adding more and more butter to the claggy, unappealing mix until I managed a consistency that succumbed to the rolling pin. Still, I had my doubts. It did not look right to me. I filled patty tins with pastry and spooned in mincemeat, put them in the oven, and hoped for the best. At least I had done it, even if it had been an ordeal. Twenty minutes later I took the pies from the oven and discovered a grey mess. Inedible. Mother had not thought to tell me to put water in the mixture. I had done the best I could, but for this seven-year-old, mince pies had proved too much. I felt wretched, and so disappointed.

My father managed to get a bird, which he cooked and served with vegetables and his divine mashed potatoes, and we had a Christmas of sorts while my mother lay in bed.

In the months that followed our mother's stroke, we had no idea what had happened that frightful day when she had discovered Father's infidelity – that signalled the onset of the disintegration of my parents' marriage. Nor did I know that the trust and happiness that had characterized the first few years of our childhood had passed.

It had all changed.

St Francis de Sales

In January 1946, on a terrible day never to be forgotten, Jennifer and I were bundled into a small dirty car by one of my father's men, accompanied by two large trunks filled with our belongings. We had seldom seen this man before. He was in smelly dark-blue overalls, a silent, sullen individual. Neither of our parents was there to explain what was to become of us or to say goodbye, and Jennifer and I had no idea where we were being taken or what was to happen to us. Who packed our trunks? Probably our grandmother, as our mother was still in bed, but I can't remember – only the shock I felt. What had we done to be sent away?

The driver kept his eyes on the road ahead and did not speak, until, that is, I was appallingly sick in the back of his car.

'Wot d'yer wanna do dat for?' was all he said, and carried on driving.

The trunks and we two small girls, dishevelled, covered in sick and foul-smelling, eventually arrived at our unknown destination. It was a Catholic boarding school for girls, the Convent of St Francis de Sales, in Tring, about an hour's drive from Amersham. We were dumped like unwanted parcels at the bottom of the wide stone steps that led to the entrance. The driver left, taking off in a hurry without looking back.

51

I trailed along behind Jennifer as she climbed the steps and hesitantly knocked at the front door. Two nuns in black habits appeared, and my sister and I were pushed into the dark and forbidding building by these unsmiling women in their equally dark and forbidding garb. Jennifer was taken one way and I was dragged another, along a dark passage to what felt like some kind of scullery with bare walls and a flagstone floor, where I was stripped and scrubbed vigorously with ice-cold water by a frightening woman in black. I was then put into clothes that were not mine, and marched off to the sleeping quarters. I did not see my sister again for the rest of the day until I found myself alongside her in a long black building, a converted war-time Nissen hut with a corrugated-iron roof. Against its two long walls numerous narrow beds were arranged, each with its own shiny white chamber pot beneath. The only heating, which did not reach us, came from a small boiler in the centre of the room. It was cold and desolate. We looked at each other in horror but did not have the will to speak as we climbed into our allocated beds, between rough sheets on lumpy mattresses. I felt myself shrinking. What were we doing in such a dreadful place?

We were very frightened – so many rules, and so far from home. No talking. No laughing. No speaking unless addressed. Silence at all times. When seated, sit up straight, hands in lap. No fidgeting. Nothing spontaneous was allowed, only the will of the nuns, and the nuns must be obeyed. We had to attend Mass daily and, as non-Catholics, were made to sit at the back away from the other girls. On Sundays we formed crocodiles and walked to church a mile or so away, wearing insufficient clothes in the cold weather, and then spent what seemed like forever kneeling on the cold stone floor. Each day we were marched around a concrete exercise yard in the bitter cold until it was time to run in lines to sit on benches in front of bare trestle tables and be forced to eat hard brown bread and meat with slimy gristle, and other unmentionable foods. How I hated pease pudding and grey vegetables. Mealtimes were terrible. We had been used to good food, and found what was now put in front of us disgusting. At home, I was happy to eat most things, but what passed for meat at St Francis de Sales seemed to be nothing but boiled fat, and I simply could not stomach it. Jennifer had never eaten meat before and while Mother had made various attempts to persuade her, she was never successful.

'You're missing something very good,' was as much as she would say when Jennifer refused the meat or fish she had been given.

There was no such tolerance at the convent. Jennifer hid the inedible gristle and meat in her knickers, her vest, her pockets, but the nuns, patrolling the dining room, watching like birds of prey, invariably swooped.

'Deceitful girl!' they declared, and put her outside, alone, in the cold, without a jumper.

Struggling, I swallowed my allocation of gristle, choking with disgust, aware that the alternative was worse. I have a memory of one particular lunchtime, the room having emptied, only Jennifer and me still in our seats – she in one corner, me in another – both with plates of uneaten food congealing in front of us as the nuns circled and insisted we eat what we had been given. On very many occasions we were put out in the freezing cold of winter in our thin little cotton shirts and skirts, and left to shiver as punishment.

We were in different classes, where we sat in rows of double desks among silent girls with bent heads. Here we had to learn about the Rosary and the saints, as vicious nuns bearing metal-edged rulers enforced their will. We were told to forget our parents, that God was our Father now. Oh dear, oh dear. We did not understand. I can hardly bear to recall this period of our lives, dominated by the almost indescribable violence and cruelty of the nuns entrusted with our care.

I could not read well, and my writing was far from perfect. I was dyslexic, not wicked – not that anyone picked up on this at the time. My classmates had been practising copperplate handwriting for years, and I struggled to master the precise, flowing script. The nuns who taught us and prowled up and down between the rows of desks, checking our progress, would lash out without warning when any perceived sloppiness was detected, bringing down the metal-edged ruler on my hand, leaving painful red weals. Was I really the lazy, stupid girl they accused me of being?

I really was trying, but no one heard me. I sat quietly and thought my own thoughts. How Jennifer reacted when told off in class I don't know, since we were separated, but I do remember her being deeply upset at the way both of us were treated.

Jennifer and I became thin, and were always hungry and frightened and cold. So very cold. That first term, in the clutch of winter, everything was made more difficult by the freezing conditions indoors and out. I remember going to wash at sinks in the mornings and finding our flannels frozen solid. It was misery. When we asked if we could go back home there were whacks, one after another. A whack for this, a whack for that: for speaking when we were expected to stay quiet, refusing the food provided, having the temerity to admit to being unhappy. All were punished with severity. Although Jennifer suffered from asthma, her frequent attacks were disregarded. As she gasped and fought for breath, making harsh wheezing sounds that racked her body, her face filled with pain, I watched, unable to help, alarmed for her, not knowing what to do. At home we relied upon Potter's Asthma Cure, a khaki powder scooped onto a tin plate and set alight to produce a funnel of smoke that helped ease my sister's laboured breathing. At the convent, there was no one to turn to for help, no such remedy.

Jennifer decided we must write and tell our mother what was going on, how dreadful things were. We did, and poured out our hearts on paper, pleading to be allowed home, not able to understand why no one came to our rescue. What we didn't realize was that our childish pleadings were being doctored. All our correspondence went through the nuns' hands. Envelopes had to be left unsealed, presumably so that the contents could be read prior to being despatched. Our complaints were being struck out, not that we knew it. Perhaps our mother simply thought the crossings-out were our doing, or perhaps she wasn't well enough to work out what her two daughters were really saying – or to do anything about it, even if she had understood how unhappy we were.

I can only think we were sent to the convent in the first place because Mother was ill, unable to get out of bed and cope with us, and Father was running a business and too busy to deal with the needs of his small girls. I suppose it must have been his decision to send us to St Francis de Sales. It certainly can't have been my mother's, as she was quite incapable at that time. I can only surmise that someone told him about the very nice convent school not so very far away in Tring, and he seized upon it as a solution. I am certain he would not have gone there to see what the place was like; he was just too busy. In short, no one made sure we were going to a place of safety and, once we were there, no one wanted to hear what we were going through.

We were allowed home only at the half-term holiday, but with Mother unable to get out of bed and our father working most of the time, there was no one to listen to us or care for us. I spent time with my grandmother but could see that she was concerned with my mother, and I felt unable to tell her anything of our experiences at school. Jennifer escaped whenever possible with our grandfather, delighting in the great outdoors and his allotment. What was going on with Jennifer and me was not a priority, it seemed. I thought that things were about as bad as they could be.

And then they got much worse.

Father Leaves an Empty House

At that time, our father was the only source of stability in our lives. One day during half term he came down the stairs carrying a large suitcase. Running up to him, I hugged his legs.

'Daddy, where are you going?' I cried. 'Can I come too?'

He pushed me away quite roughly. My grip on him loosened.

'Not this time, Christabel.'

His voice was strained, and there were tears in his eyes. I looked for my cheerful, smiling father and could find no trace of him. He had never before told me 'No.' He had never pushed me away before. He was a loving man, full of fun, who hugged me and sat me on his lap and shared his breakfast and sang to me. I was his sunshine. Wasn't I? There was something deeply distressing to me in those few words of his, that one gesture. I sank onto the stairs, shocked. At eight years old, I was able to work out that something important and troubling was taking place. Jennifer stood on the landing at the top of the stairs, her face tight, furious. She seemed ready to explode and stared straight ahead, her gaze fixed on I don't know what, rather than on my father as he crossed the hall below. She was ten and a half by then: still very young, but perhaps wise enough to have worked out that my father was leaving us. All I knew was that he was going somewhere. I had no idea where or for how long, and did not for a moment think he wasn't coming back. We were used to him working long hours, but not to him going away. It was something he never did, so to see him with a suitcase made no sense to me. He left, dragging the case out into the street, and closed the door behind him.

Our lodgers had left some time after the end of the war, at which time Jennifer and I were given our own bedrooms.

No one played the piano or switched on the wireless any more. All was silent, only the clock ticking in the distance. Our mother, bedridden, unable to speak properly, was so shocking to us. She would lie there for hours on end trying to knit a pink silk vest. She found this extraordinarily difficult, and indeed it was never finished.

Our father no longer lived at home with us, and we were left to fend for ourselves.

I wandered into the woods alone while Jennifer left the house early on her bicycle, not returning until it got dark. No one questioned us. We would run off to Granny for comfort and food. People came and went, whispering, but no one spoke to us children. Jennifer and I seemed to be invisible to them all.

No one explained to us that Father had gone and was not coming back. We were left to work it out for ourselves. Many years later, we discovered that he had not actually wanted to leave. Our mother had not wanted him to go. It was, she told us, our grandmother who insisted he could not be allowed to stay, not after his disloyalty.

I don't think my parents ever stopped loving each other. My mother was certainly fond of saying, 'There are far worse things in life than adultery, my dear.' Even though the discovery of his affair had resulted in a stroke that almost killed her, left to her own devices, my mother would never have ended the marriage. Losing my father was something she regretted for the rest of her life. She was in such pain. When her girlfriends visited, I would sit on the stairs with Jennifer and listen to our mother weeping and talking with them about her heartache.

Once back in the convent, where no questions were allowed, I shrank even more, and Jennifer became ever more obstreperous. All joy had gone out of our lives. No running wild in the countryside, picking flowers, rolling in the grass and listening to the hum of bees and the sound of birdsong. No more the warmth of our grandmother's house to fly to, or our grandpa's allotment. Jennifer was constantly in trouble, refusing to eat, wilfully disregarding the nuns, and generally causing mayhem. Her hands and legs were bruised most of the time where she'd been whacked by the nuns, and she ached from being placed outside in the cold, facing a wall with her hands behind her back, as punishment. I saw her and wanted to cry. No other child disobeyed the nuns. Neither of us made any friends. As our mother began to recover she would come to collect us when school broke up for holidays. Always she was late, the last to arrive. We would wait, seeing all the others collected, our sense of dread growing, convinced that nobody would come for us.

Jennifer would grow furious and yell in frustration. 'Where is she? Where *is* she?'

I would keep quiet. Unspoken was the hope that we would arrive home and find our father there, and everything as it had once been.

I have a clear memory of breaking up for the long holiday

in the summer of 1946 and all the girls leaving, Jennifer and me waiting on the steps, desperate for our mother to show up. Eventually it was just the two of us, and we heard the doors to the school being closed and locked behind us. I clung to my sister's hand as she complained and grew more angry and anxious. As soon as my mother's car came up the drive, all the anger vanished and in its place was sheer joy. We had not been forgotten after all. Years later, Jennifer told me that those occasions when we waited outside the convent, fearful of having been forgotten, were absolutely heartbreaking for her. Worse for her than for me, no doubt, as she was very much the big sister, the strong one, always powerful. In the absence of my mother, Jennifer became a mother figure to me. In her, I had a champion, which was more than she had. I can see now how hard it must have been for her when, at nine years old, much of the responsibility for her little sister landed squarely on her shoulders.

After a year at the convent came the incident that led to us being expelled. It was my fault that this final eruption happened. Jennifer had been hauled to the top of the dormitory for whispering after lights-out. Sick of the deadening austerity, and with my sense of fun still just about alive, I retrieved Jennifer's large white china chamber pot from under her bed and pushed it down below her bedclothes and waited. I knew it would shock her. When she returned, somewhat subdued, got back into bed, stretched out her long legs and touched the ice-cold potty, she screamed, long and loud. Nuns came rushing down the dormitory upon us.

'You're a wicked girl. You evil child!'

I was almost as bad, they said later, in a letter sent to my mother.

Jennifer was dragged out of bed, which she resisted, kicking and punching the nun nearest to her and pulling off her skirt. Shrieks filled the dormitory, rows of frightened little girls witnessing the altercation. My sister thought she was quite right to get angry from time to time, particularly over any injustice, and would remind me that Jesus had turned over the tables in his master's house when it was misused. The incident with the nun that night was certainly righteous indignation. I watched in horror and did not know what to do when Jennifer was pushed to the floor and left wheezing her heart out. Eventually she crept quietly back to bed. Incredibly, nothing more was said, although a decision had in fact been made about our future.

We got to the end of term and our mother, late as ever, came to collect us. Once home, she announced that there had been a letter from the convent to say that we were not required to return. Apparently, we were being expelled on the basis of Jennifer's dreadful behaviour. As for me, I was almost as unruly. Since there was no suggestion that Mother was cross with us for being thrown out, you would think we would have been relieved more than anything to be rid of our hated school. In fact, we both felt rather ashamed. We had not been wanted at home and had therefore been sent away. Now we were not wanted at the convent either.

Jennifer was an extremely sensitive little girl. She was not a naughty child but a free spirit, one that had never been trampled on before. She rebelled; I withdrew. The security of our parents and extended family had gone, and our relationship was changed. Sometimes we would hug each other for comfort, sometimes Jennifer pushed me away through anger and frustration. All this at the same time. No one seemed to understand. Least of all ourselves.

Mother said we had to go and see our father at his office

every Saturday. We walked hand in hand along the cinder path that led to the yard where he ran his business. He was embarrassed and did not know what to do with two small girls and, equally, we did not know what we were meant to do. It was when watching my father and his men working on his cars that I realized I really loved cars, their lines and proportions. He always had different cars on the go; a wonderful Jaguar XK120. All Jaguars are things of beauty, and I felt this even as a child. I loved getting into the pits and looking up at their underbellies, then peering under the bonnet at the exciting shiny engines and little spark plugs with tubes and nuts and bolts. I felt so important putting on goggles to watch the welding, and loved the smell of it all. What I did not like was returning to Father's office and trying miserably to say my times tables. Jennifer spent her time clambering over forbidden equipment and sitting around disconsolately. After our visits, we dawdled back to our mother's home in silence, Jennifer striding ahead, desperately upset. Our father did his best, but what must he have felt?

After the horrors of the convent, we found ourselves returned to our old school, Belle Vue, now named Hyde House, in Hyde End. We felt embarrassed by our enforced absence. Nevertheless, it was a comfort to be back in familiar surroundings, and within a few days we were delighted. It was noticed by the lovely English teacher that I could not pronounce my Rs, so I was given extra elocution lessons. This lasted many years and I loved the lessons, learning a lot of poetry and going in for national competitions held in London. I felt very important. It certainly formed the basis of my love of poetry and acting. I was in all our school plays, and even today, I read the lesson in our church. The staff at Belle Vue were kind to us. When Jennifer trod on a wasps' nest and was left screaming and covered in wasps, Miss Plumber, the headmistress, filled a bath with water and vinegar and picked live wasps out of her hair. Jennifer was stung fifty-seven times, and Miss Plumber twelve. Although Jennifer recovered fairly quickly and said it was no worse than an asthma attack, it was a shocking episode, and I shall never forget it.

Jennifer had become angry and was often violent, protecting me one minute and the next, inexplicably grabbing me by the hair and repeatedly banging my head on the wall. I became frightened of these outbursts and did all I could to avoid any confrontation with her. One day she chased me round the house with a kitchen knife, and I escaped by locking myself in the lavatory. I could not tell you what sparked this. Nothing I had done, as far as I knew. Her fury was all to do with the collapse of our home life, and could erupt for no apparent reason.

At school one day I was in the cloakroom trying to get my coat off a hook when a girl called Susan started pushing me about. Unable to reach my coat, I ran outside with her in pursuit and there was Jennifer. When she saw I was being bullied she grabbed a riding whip and thrashed the girl. This was witnessed by dozens of little girls who, like me, looked on appalled. When Jennifer finally stopped, Susan ran away in tears. She must have been covered in awful red marks. I was sure someone would report it, but no one ever did, and nothing was said.

On the face of it, it must have seemed that things were now pretty good for us. Our mother seemed well again, though still weak on one side, with her mouth drooping somewhat. We went to a pleasant school. Yes, Jennifer was difficult and

I was quiet, but that was all. When I asked a cousin of mine what we were like as children, the answer I got was that Jennifer was wild and I was always crying. We were actually deeply unhappy as a consequence of what had happened at home. There was no house by the sea any more. It had been sold to one of my aunts, but Jennifer and I never went there again. At home, we came and went as we pleased much of the time. More than anything, we wanted our life restored to what it had been in the days when we felt carefree and happy. We wanted our father back.

I never gave up hoping this would happen, and I don't think Jennifer did either.

Miss Pears and a Royal Wedding

Once our mother's health improved she began to be very sweet again and we had a period of real happiness when she frequently took us out. Mother loved the theatre and the cinema, and every Friday evening without fail we were taken to see the latest films (not children's cinema, like other children) at the cinema in Amersham. Our mother loved all the stars: Greta Garbo, Margaret Lockwood, Clark Gable, Ginger Rogers, Fred Astaire. On Saturdays it was Amersham Repertory Theatre, with many stars in the making. A frustrated actress, Mother loved to mix during the interval and after the performances. Jennifer was left in charge of me. She would wait until Mother had gone into the foyer, then run off to mingle with I know not whom! I spent many years with only empty seats for company as I waited for the interval to be over.

In the summer of 1947 a garden party was held at the home of the actor Dirk Bogarde, who lived in a large house at the end of a drive that was almost opposite ours. The whole of the little town of Amersham seemed to be there. They had turned out, drawn by the presence of the stars – Dirk Bogarde himself, Glynis Johns and Anthony Forwood. Mother took me and Jennifer along.

A highlight of the afternoon was the staging of a Miss

Pears soap competition. As a line of eager little girls formed, Mother pushed me forward. Horrified, I shrank back.

'Go on, Chris, get into the line,' she said, giving me a determined push.

I shook my head, embarrassed. I had no wish to take part in a beauty pageant. I glanced at Jennifer, who was looking at me with undisguised disapproval. I already knew her views on such things. 'You should not be valued for the way you look,' she had said more than once.

Mother, oblivious to my awkwardness, pushed me cheerily into the line-up. 'Good luck, darling,' she said, beaming.

I cringed as the three famous judges took a long look at the contestants and, to my utter horror, declared me the winner. All I could see was my mother, thoroughly delighted, clapping and waving, while at her side Jennifer scowled.

We had to go up to London, Mother, me, and Jennifer, for a Miss Pears session at a photographic studio. Mother had dressed me in a very smart outfit for the occasion. The photographer took one look at it and decided it was not suitable. Luckily, the dress Jennifer was wearing was perfect, so we swapped clothes and I posed in my sister's hand-smocked frock with its puffed sleeves while she fumed quietly at being made to wear something of mine that was much too short for her. The slogan that went with the campaign was, 'Preparing to be a beautiful lady', and the pictures ended up in newspapers and hoardings – and even on Pathé News, which was shown at the Regent Cinema in Amersham, to the delight of various relatives. Whenever anyone mentioned Miss Pears, Jennifer glared at me and I felt thoroughly ashamed. Needless to say, Mother was thrilled.

The war was well and truly behind us and, in 1947, the impending marriage of Princess Elizabeth to Philip Mountbatten was generating huge excitement. I was nine and Jennifer was twelve, and we were caught up in the Royal Wedding fever that was sweeping through our community. A neighbour invited us to watch the day's events on a television they had bought especially for the occasion. This in itself was cause for much excitement. We did not have our own television set. In fact, we had never even seen a television at that point. The wireless was important to us for news and also entertainment, such as the popular comedy *ITMA* (It's That Man Again) with Tommy Handley, and Sunday lunchtime's *Billy Cotton Band Show* on the BBC Light Programme. Jennifer was a fan of *Dick Barton – Special Agent*, and his sidekick, Snowy. It was another year before the radio drama series *Mrs Dale's Diary*, which was about the life of a doctor's wife, started, and became a firm favourite of mine.

On the day of the wedding, November 20, we gathered in front of the much-talked-about black and white set that proved to be oh so small. Jennifer was deeply disappointed when she saw it, and said as much, then promptly disappeared. While the grown-ups partied, we children were left behind in front of the television. From time to time I wondered where my sister was, although as I was used to her going off on her own for hours on end, I was not concerned. I couldn't help thinking, however, that on this occasion she was missing something special. Even on the tiny screen, to see the elaborate royal carriage with the newlyweds process from Westminster Abbey along the Mall, crowds lining the route and cheering all the way, was really wonderful.

Jennifer finally returned several hours later, flushed with excitement.

'Where have you been?' I said. 'You've missed everything.'

She was triumphant. 'I've been to the wedding,' she said.

She had been up to London on an early train, found her way to the Mall, wriggled through the crowds to the front of the barrier, and had a marvellous view of everything. Once the procession was over, however, she realized she was trapped by thousands of people and would have to wait for the crowds to disperse before she could get away. By the look of things, she would be there for hours. Having seen the St John Ambulance team nearby, she worked out that her best chance of getting away was to feign a faint and wait for someone to pick her up, and so she happily collapsed onto the pavement. In no time at all she was hoisted over the heads of the crowds and into a waiting ambulance. Once installed she made a rapid recovery, was driven to Baker Street station, and caught the next train home.

I was amazed and full of admiration for my daring sister. Certainly, in retrospect, it was a remarkable thing for a young girl, only just twelve years old, to do, but that was Jennifer. Fearless and ingenious, always.

Although our mother was better, Grandmother remained an important person in our lives. Small and neat, with good ankles, she wore a hat with a certain panache and certainly ruled the house, although quietly.

Grandmother's chickens were her babies. She absolutely adored them and gave them names, yet she also adored eating them. I puzzled over how she could feed her 'babies' with delicious titbits as they clucked about her feet and then have another chicken cooking in the oven. There's no understanding it – I do it myself today. I even took one of mine to the Blue Cross in London when it was ill. It caused quite a stir. Anyway, it was Grandmother who ruled the house, and my grandfather idolized her. I remember one day he arrived back home late and had not seen me under the table, only his wife quietly sitting by the fire, knitting. He walked up to her, went down on his knees, cupped her face in his hands and covered her with little tiny kisses.

I watched, and wanted that for me.

Eliza, our grandmother, had to have everything her way, but no one minded as it meant a warm, pretty house with open fires and good things to eat. She was never without home-made cakes and jams and wonderful-smelling pickles, and eggs in enormous terracotta pots filled with isinglass. There was food for everyone, all this even during the war. The gramophone with its gigantic horn dominated the drawing room, with lots of records that we were allowed to play at random. Crammed onto shelves were books which we investigated and loved to feel. There was endless gossip and chatter around us. Our mother would play the latest songs. 'Coming in on a Wing and a Prayer' was my favourite, which I sang with gusto. Jennifer and I loved the Ink Spots and dancing the charleston from a very early age.

Grandmother's flower garden was a joy. We could wander around alone and pick whatever we liked. She also allowed me to brush her long, wavy hair, which had been thick, so she said, and was now like fine silver thistledown.

I loved Grandmother's house and spent a great deal of time there, certainly visiting every day. We would have tea together in exquisite china cups, and she cooked delicious food, with my enthusiastic help. I assisted her in skinning rabbits, always being given the rabbit tail for luck, and plucking birds with wonderful feathers I made into hats and crazy things for my dollies. Gutting fish was real excitement. I collected eggs from her chickens, which lived under the plum and apple trees. I grew to love chickens and would sit with them, lifting them onto my lap, chatting away to them as children do, and would climb up into the gnarled branches above them and be happy. I would stay with my grandmother overnight and we would wash each other's hair. We always collected the rainwater from a butt outside for rinsing, as she thought it conditioned the hair. It probably did.

I also remember seeing her in the morning in a pretty mob cap, which disguised the rag ends in her hair and I marvelled at the dainty breakfast tray that Arthur, her huge and ungainly husband, brought in to her every morning. How did he manage to cut the bread so thinly, and make her tea in such delicate china cups? I would sit there with her, admiring the room with its pretty curtains, rugs by the beds, and a wonderful wall clock that chimed the hour and half hour.

The visitors to Grandmother's house were mainly family, but Dr Strang, whose surgery was at Oakfield Corner, would visit her fairly frequently, as her asthma attacks were quite serious. I would watch her struggling for breath over the tin plate with its small mound of khaki powder burning away. Potter's Asthma Cure's distinctive smoke seemed to help her breathing, and permeated throughout the house. She was so courageous, this little woman, wheezing away on the bed, but still smiling, and telling me not to worry.

It was much the same in our house: mother had the occasional asthma attack, and Jennifer had them frequently too. I watched them all, not knowing what to do or what to say, but hoping that I would not have one – it looked so very horrible.

Jennifer disliked domesticity and certainly rubbed our grandmother up the wrong way, so she escaped whenever she could – mostly with my grandfather to his allotment, where he grew vegetables, pushed her around in his wheelbarrow to whoops of laughter, and told her of his life in the Scots Guards and his exploits in the Boer War. I was rather afraid of our huge grandfather, so tall and with a large booming voice when roused; but he did teach me how to grow enormous marrows by feeding them sugar water from a bottle attached to a piece of string. He also taught us how to play a mean game of draughts.

Grandma taught us to sew and knit. I loved doing long round scarves through a cotton reel for my dollies, and I loved seeing Grandma knitting socks on four needles, and gloves on more. I watched, so enchanted by her crochet work. Jennifer thought this a poor substitute for being in the great outdoors with Bryn, her dog, but she manfully struggled with the enforced teaching of a very determined lady. I became adept at anything creative.

Grandma used to say, 'Little Chrissy can make a silk purse out of a sow's ear,' while Jennifer sniffed her disapproval.

Grandma Lee

We were taken to see Grandma Lee regularly. She was a tall, severe woman who wore a long brown fur coat in summer and winter. She seldom went outside, and moved about the house carefully. Our father had moved her out of her Hawarden farm in North Wales as soon as he was able – at first to a small farm in Old Amersham, and then to her final home on Amersham Hill. It was dark, north-facing, with the Rectory Woods opposite. It was cold, not like our other grandmother's house, which was warm and sweet-smelling. Grandma Lee's house was lit by tiny gas lamps and the furniture was big and dark, as were the large pictures in heavy gilt frames. She would give us a glass of water to drink and, from a battered tin, a stale biscuit to eat. Jennifer and I hated these visits and escaped into the garden to play under the apple trees while our mother did her duty. A rather strange man, small and mean-looking, put in an appearance from time to time. I asked who he was.

'Just a gathering up of crumbs,' Grandma said, with obvious dislike.

Who was he? Apparently he was our father's older brother, Clarence, who lived with her.

On one particular occasion she said she had a treat in store for us, and to follow her. We crept through the dark hall and up the creaky stairs, and entered her bedroom for the first time. The curtains were half drawn, so we could see very little, but we managed to follow her to a huge wardrobe. She opened it. It was crammed with clothes: all black, all silk, and all seemingly unworn. What did she wear under her fur coat? Anyway, she was scrabbling in a bottom drawer, obviously worried. We waited for our present. Joyfully she found it and pulled out a small, crumpled brown paper bag, which she passed to us. It contained ancient, congealed boiled sweets.

'A gift from God,' she said.

Astonished, we quietly said, 'Thank you.'

Our mother visited her for the rest of her life, but we children would disappear if possible. She seemed to get pleasure from our mother's visits, and was never told of our parents' separation and subsequent divorce. She died in 1959 in Amersham Hospital, with gangrene taking over her body – so cruel. We last saw her with our father a few days before she died. She was lying, unrecognizable, so thin and neglected, a cage over her legs, and whispering inanities. Father held her hand, and she smiled at him.

Her son was there for her in the end.

Into the Workplace

Once our mother had recovered from her stroke, in time she found herself a job as a clerical assistant to Mr Seeley, the manager of Brentnell and Cleland, a coal merchant's in Amersham. She liked her work at the coal office and enjoyed meeting all the customers. She also liked her boss, but one day walked into her office to find his seat was empty. Mr Seeley had had a heart attack, from which he never recovered. Mother carried on holding the fort on her own for a couple of weeks, undeterred. After all, it was much less arduous than the work of setting up a business with our father when they were first married.

One day Nigel Brentnell, the owner of the coal merchant's, walked in and told her she was being promoted to manager and was to find herself a clerical assistant. She was delighted, and got an increase in salary. The assistant, Ann, became a lifelong friend. Mother started going out to lunch and dinner with Nigel in his beautiful car, and began to regain her confidence. Yet she was surprised, indeed shocked, when he asked her to marry him. How could she marry someone she did not love? There were one or two other 'hopefuls', including a chap who bragged that he was 'the sausage king'. Mother could barely contain herself when she spoke of him.

'Can you imagine it? The sausage king, indeed!' She collapsed in laughter.

All her suitors got the same answer: No. She was still very much in love with my father, and I think she hoped, as Jennifer and I did, that he might one day come back.

Gordon, however, was now living with his secretary. When did Jennifer and I first meet Judith, our father's new lady? I don't know. I do remember thinking she looked no older than Jennifer, and finding this puzzling.

My sister was a tall, lanky girl then. Judith was not much taller, and certainly very young-looking. Our father was thirty-three, but looked somewhat tired after working such long hours throughout the war. People asked if Judith was his daughter. Slim and very pretty, she wore her fair hair in a short modern style. To Jennifer and me she was very cold and ice-like. One day Daddy took Jennifer and me from his office to his new home. Judith was there. My father made an attempt at conversation and made us a cup of tea, but Judith stared at the three of us and barely said a word. Jennifer hated her on sight. After our first encounter Jennifer was so angry she went striding away, not saying anything, simply radiating rage as I ran along behind her. It was certainly extremely difficult all round, as this young woman had no idea how to cope with two stepdaughters, and faced constant battles with Jennifer.

As usual, I put my head down and kept quiet.

Our mother was determined to have no support from Gordon for herself, or, indeed, for her children.

'If a man does not want me, I do not want his money,' she said with great determination.

This was all very well, but for Jennifer and myself it was

difficult. We had been used to good food and nice things at home. The lovely steaks from the butcher became a thing of the past, and in their place were things like bacon roly-poly. While our father and his girlfriend were living in luxury, we were told there was no money, sometimes even for basics. I remember shopping for food one day with my mother and asking for an apple. The blunt response was, 'We can't afford it.'

This did not make sense to Jennifer or me. After all, our father was rich, wasn't he?

Even when the divorce was eventually finalized, Mother would claim only £1 annually for Jennifer and me, which was the minimum she could ask for at the time. She was very proud, but one day that pride was trashed as she walked up Hill Avenue towards home and saw Father's beautiful Jaguar XK120 coming towards her. He was not in the driving seat. Mother could not believe it when she saw Judith instead, laughing as she drove past.

Perhaps this was when she finally recognized that she was alone, really alone, and that our father would not be coming back. I remember more tears, and overhearing the outpouring of her feelings to her trusted circle of friends. She could barely carry on running a successful coal business. Horrible, horrible times.

In the end, the turning point came the night my mother went alone to the Station Hotel in Amersham to meet friends. They did not turn up, but at the bar was an extremely thin young man, unsmiling, looking lost. Being kindly, she broke through his obvious unhappiness and engaged him in conversation. Jock came from Glasgow, and was several years younger than my mother. He had fought in the war and told her of his experiences at the Battle of Arnhem, in 1944, and of the sleepless nights and horrific nightmares that had plagued him since. She took him home, gave him one of her sustaining meals, looked after him, and felt she was needed once more.

Our mother was a complex character. She told her friend Ann that being abandoned by our father, she felt that she had personally failed, and was deeply ashamed at finding herself in such a shocking situation. She had not only been rejected, but was also suffering the after-effects of her stroke. Still weak on one side, her face lopsided, she would say frequently, 'The girls will grow up and leave me; I cannot be left on my own.' She was terrified of being alone. Women in the 1940s were often defined as the supporting partners of men, and any man was better than none. On reflection, I can understand how this beautiful girl from a large, respectable, happy family must have felt.

The Rule of Fear

Although we had seen Mother with boyfriends before, the arrival in her life of Jock, a tall, good-looking man who resembled the film star Gregory Peck, with a rather disturbing manner, troubled us. From the very beginning, when he came to the house we were shut in Mother's bedroom. When he did see us he ignored us. We did not like him. Of course, we did not know that the war had left him damaged, and certainly had no sense of the impact he would have on our home, which proved utterly catastrophic.

I discovered only recently that shortly after Jock appeared, Mother went to our father and said she did not want her two girls living with her and that he must take us in – but, of course, Judith would have nothing of it.

In June 1948, within weeks of meeting him, Mother married Jock in Amersham.

I was ten, Jennifer twelve and a half. I don't think anyone actually told us there was to be a wedding. We were certainly not present. It was simply a case of Jock arriving in our lives, in our home. We so hated him being there, in our mother's bedroom, and hated the depressing shift this caused in the atmosphere at home. He was Mother's husband, as far as we were concerned, never our stepfather, and his being there created a perpetual sense of deep unease. Having Jock around was rather like having a grenade tossed carelessly into our midst, never knowing when someone would accidentally pull the pin and set off an explosion.

What followed was a period of years in which we sought to avoid the violence that was always present in our mother's house. Her new husband had been brought up in an impoverished working-class family, where his father drank and ruled with a rod of iron. Jock had learned well and, once he was married to our sweet mother, took over. Fear ruled within our walls.

I don't remember him ever being kind. From the start, he had nothing to say to us girls, just shouting and pushing past, storming about the place and slamming doors. We were terrified. We never ate meals with him. Mummy realized it would lead to trouble, and found ways of avoiding any likely confrontation by making sure Jennifer and I ate separately. On one occasion I was shocked and surprised when he grabbed me and started kissing me on the mouth. I was only eleven years old. When I told Jennifer, she said, 'Just keep away, it's disgusting. He tried to do it to me – I spat at him.' We never met his family. His mother and sister came to the house once, and Jennifer and I were shut in the bedroom and not allowed out until they had gone. Jock never participated in family gatherings or went to our granny's house. Mother would take us without him to visit family and friends, and never admit the truth of her shameful marriage. For her it was a horrible marriage, even in the very early days. She did all she could to keep the peace, and Jennifer and I knew to keep out of the way. If Jock was at home, Mother made it clear we had to stay out of sight. If he appeared unexpectedly, we ran and hid in a cupboard – any cupboard, whichever was nearest – until it was safe to come out and creep away. We were, quite simply, obliterated. In all this, I fell back on my usual behaviour of staying quiet and keeping my distance, while Jennifer would get on her bike and pedal away, escape for as long as she could.

What Mother soon discovered was that no matter how hard she tried, it was not possible to placate Jock. Anything not to his satisfaction would cause his temper to flare. Mother would cook a lovely meal for the two of them, set the table to create a beautiful atmosphere – and, for no reason that made any sense to her, Jock would take one look at his food and hurl his plate at the wall in absolute fury. It could have been the most innocuous thing: she had spoken out of turn, or served beef when he wanted sausages. Upstairs in our room, Jennifer and I heard the crashing of china, breaking of plates, Jock's raised voice shouting at our mother, and our mother in tears. His main weapon against her was silence. He would stop speaking – for a week, a fortnight, a month . . . three months. These debilitating silences stretched on and on. Elsie tried everything to make him happy, even finding him a job through friends at a local garage. In no time, he was sacked, as complaints poured in from customers who found him rude. After that, Mother took him on as a coal man, as he could find no other work to do.

As much as she could, Mother hid the true nature of what was going on in her marriage. She was ashamed, and pretended all was well. Of course, a few people did know. When her close friends called to see her Jock would barge through the house, ignoring them, and retreat to the study. Her assistant at the coal merchant's, her good friend Ann, begged her to leave him. Mother refused. Perhaps, at least in the early days, she thought she would be able to turn things around. She never could.

Once or twice, unable to stand the atmosphere, Jennifer lashed out at my mother.

'Get rid of him!' she yelled. 'How can you let him do this to you? He's a bully!'

It was pointless. Mother always insisted everything was fine.

Jennifer had her beloved piano to go to when things were tough. I had my sewing and painting. Mostly, I would paint pictures of woods and bluebells in spring. Before Jock came along, I had wanted to paint something really big and set my eyes on our dining-room walls. It was a very boring room, and the cream walls certainly needed a coat of paint. My mother agreed. Could I paint the walls? I wondered. Mother said I could. For weeks I laboured on, turning two adjacent walls into a woodland paradise of bluebells among beech trees, and was thrilled with the result. Indeed, everyone was thrilled – until my mother's new husband arrived in our house. I then watched him, in one short afternoon, deliberately destroy my work of art.

The effect of all this on me was that at the tender age of ten I decided I would never do as my mother had – never accept the unacceptable. Jennifer felt differently. Our parents' divorce, and all that happened subsequently, made her determined that once married she would stay with her husband no matter what, and do her duty by her children. We were not just frightened of the new man in our house, we were terrified of him, always. We also hated how Jock behaved with our mother.

'What can we do?' I asked Jennifer.

'I'm thinking about it,' she said. 'We could catch him on the stairs when he next comes in and we could force him to listen to us.'

'Are you sure?' I said.

'Yes,' she said.

We planned to form a human barricade on the staircase to stop him from going up to the sitting room. Since I was the small, sweet one – so Jennifer said – I was to tell him not to be rude to Mother. It was going to be a simple matter and then all would be well. We waited halfway up the stairs. Jock arrived and, with a face like thunder, tried to push past us. I said what we had agreed, but he did not understand and seemed to explode.

'Don't be nasty to our mother!'

He went to grab at me, and Jennifer rushed at him.

She shrieked, 'Run!'

I looked aghast at the figure now in front of me with clenched fists, turned tail and ran as fast as I could up the stairs. Behind me, Jennifer was left to deal with the aftermath. She told me later that she had flung herself at him and he lost his balance and fell down the stairs, which gave her time to escape and flee after me up to the loo where we locked ourselves in, clinging to each other, shaking. We feared he would try to beat the door down. All was silent. We did not move for a very long time, thinking he was waiting for us to come out.

Later, much later, Mother came up and took us to our bedroom. She helped us undress and get into bed. We waited for her to say something about what had happened earlier. She said nothing, and tucked us into bed.

'Good night,' was all she said, and left us.

Good night! Nothing else.

We were not going to try and tackle Jock again.

Cold Rejection

In September 1948, just a few months after our mother re-married, our father exchanged vows with Judith. Again, no one told Jennifer and me what was happening. At some point, we simply understood that there had been a wedding. Judith ruled their home. Cold rejection was to be found for Jennifer and me in her presence – never a word to us, not even a cup of tea offered, let alone any food, even though her fridge would be full – and so we mostly stayed with our mother, keeping out of the way as much as possible so as not to antagonize Jock.

Our school, a private day school for girls, was a blessed relief, where we were nurtured and taught the good manners of the day. Yet one day our good manners left us. Jennifer and I were seen walking in the field in our uniforms, eating pears. For this sin we were called to the headmistress's study to explain ourselves. It did not seem such a sin to me, and today children are seen eating in the streets all the time.

We had friends at school, and from time to time were invited to their homes for birthday parties and the like, but after the arrival of Mother's new husband no one was welcome in our house. I would have been ashamed for anyone to know what was going on behind our closed doors. Of course, this meant I felt somewhat out on a limb, different from the girls I mixed with. I watched my friends in their lovely homes with their adoring parents and was envious, for our parents had little time for us. Among my friends were Mary Goodchild, Joanna Alexander, Serena Dundas, Diane Wilkinson, Pat Fowler and Jill Thomas. I liked them all. I actually sold my first painting, a woodland scene in the style of the mural I had done at home, to Jill Thomas's mother when I was twelve. I often stayed with Jill at her home in Chorley Wood, and we shared many secrets together. Sadly, once I went to boarding school I did not see her again, and often wondered what had happened to her. I still do.

We spent a lot of time together in the woods. Camping overnight with our cousins was a great treat. Our mother gave us a basket of food – eggs, bacon, tomatoes, bread – and a frying pan, saucepan and plates. We were therefore equipped to make a splendid breakfast, having spent the night camping under the stars; no tent or sleeping bags then. I was the youngest by nearly three years, and was regarded as of little use in their games, so a fire was lit and I was then left on my own to cook for everyone on their return. Even Bryn the dog was allowed to join in their fun, but not me. I was annoyed with Jennifer about this, but what could I do? I set about cooking, and tried not to be upset. Then, one day, I dropped one of the fried eggs onto the ground. It was covered in soil and dry leaves, a terrible mess. I looked around for help and found it in the form of a stagnant pond nearby, where I took the egg and carefully washed it in the filthy water. When Jennifer and the others returned I placed the offending egg in front of my sister, and watched with satisfaction as she ate it. I confess, I hoped she would be ill. Alas, she wasn't!

We would also, Jennifer and I, go on long bike rides to

Burnham Beeches, where there was a wonderful swimming pool. Our mother came once, but she was working full-time, so Jennifer and I were left to our own devices for the long days of the holidays. We had always been independent, and were left to roam unsupervised from an early age, but Burnham Beeches was a distance of at least six miles from Amersham, with huge uphill gradients, and I had only a child's bike. I shall never forget the Christmas when I was given a new, grown-up Raleigh bike. No more struggling against impossible odds to keep up with my big, athletic sister.

Our weekly visits to our father along the cinder path to his office began to include a visit to Judith at home. She had given birth to a baby girl, Frankie, in the summer of 1949. Frankie was sweet, and I instantly wanted to hold her, but Jennifer was unsure how to respond to the new arrival, and resented her. So I followed suit and said nothing. Now, looking back, I wonder how Judith, our father's new wife, could ever have broken through such animosity, or indeed the guilt Father felt over his treatment of our mother. The answer was that she could not have.

And so we had a new half-sister. Only much later did we discover that Father and Judith had another daughter, Pat, who had been born in 1947, before they were married. For various reasons, never explained to us, her existence was kept from us, and by the time we met her she was already four years old.

Just before Christmas, on December 10, 1950, Grandma had a heart attack and died. I was twelve. It was a terrible shock, as the two of us were so close and I loved her dearly. The feeling of loss was great. Often, when things became unbearable at home, I had escaped to her – her home, just opposite ours, had come to represent a place of refuge. No more. Her body was laid out in the centre of the drawing room, and for some days friends and relatives called and filed past the coffin. The door was kept firmly closed. Nobody would let me near, yet I wanted so much to see her. I wandered around her garden, feeling bereft. I went to my mother.

'Why can't I go in?'

'Your grandmother is in her coffin,' she said.

'Yes, I know. I want to see her.'

Mother thought for a moment and nodded. 'Well, all right, if you're really sure.'

She took my hand and led me into the room and together, gingerly, we approached the coffin. It was lined in white satin and my grandmother lay there in a spectacular white gown, like an amazing wedding dress, looking beautiful – younger than I remembered, her skin white and like stone. It was as if all the lines her face had acquired over a lifetime had vanished, and the young girl she used to be had returned. I gazed at her, filled with love, grieving for her. Neither my mother nor I said a word. Finally, I turned and crept away to consider death. Death was final. There was to be no more time to share, after death.

Trouble for Jennifer

The day was sunny and bright. Jennifer and I had come home after spending the afternoon in the woods, playing hide and seek with Bryn. We were so happy. The countryside always affected us in that way, giving us joy, reminding us we were fortunate to live in such a beautiful place.

The house was empty on our return. Jennifer gravitated to the piano and I sat listening as she began playing Debussy's *Clair de Lune* and then some Chopin and Beethoven. I was enchanted and did not move. We were both unaware that time was passing.

There was only one rule in the house, and it was one we strictly obeyed; we were not allowed downstairs after five o'clock. This was to ensure we did not bump into Jock in the evenings. It also meant that we had very little contact with any adults at all during this time. We certainly saw nothing of Mother's friends who visited.

That day, as we were completely absorbed by the music, five o'clock came and went. We did not hear the door open when, at ten past five, Jock walked in. He saw Jennifer and heard her playing. Immediately, anger engulfed his whole body. Jennifer was oblivious as he strode up behind her and, with some pleasure, slammed the piano lid down onto her hands. Bizarrely, all was silent. Jennifer just stared at him and made not a sound as she removed her damaged hands and left the room. I followed her, appalled at what I had just witnessed.

I can only imagine that Jock then insisted Jennifer must go – that she was sacrificed for a possible peace. The following day, my sister had her suitcase packed by our mother and was put out on the doorstep – never to return. She was fourteen years old.

She left with her things in the small brown battered case and I watched her on the doorstep as my mother closed the door behind her. Who had made the decision to put her out? My mother had gone along with it, anyway. How foolish she was, how gullible!

We were vulnerable, all of us – Mother, Jennifer and me – to this manic man who had taken over our home. We were always watching and waiting for another eruption, or hiding from him until we hoped it would be safe to come out. Now, as I walk about the house in my mind, the long thin lavatory dominates, with its small window at the end and lock on the door. That lock saved us from much of the violence.

When Jennifer walked away from home that day she had no idea where she was going, and neither did our mother. In fact, she made her way to our cousins in Little Chalfont. They were kind, and she stayed with them for some time without mishap, apart from breaking the bed with her enthusiastic gymnastics. Jennifer and I seldom saw each other during this time, but she said she had begun to hate school, and walked out a few months later, refusing to return. I really missed her. Our mother never asked after her. Having seen what had happened to her, I felt anxious and insecure, knowing I too could be put on the doorstep at any point.

I don't know who persuaded Jennifer to do a shorthand

typing course, but Daddy paid for her to go to the Pitman's College in London, which was a great experience for her. She enjoyed the train journey from Amersham to Marylebone every day, watching the other commuters, and feeling part of the real world. And she loved being alone and away from the terrors of our mother's house. I could not wait to turn fifteen and follow her lead.

At fifteen and a half she lied about her age, claiming to be seventeen, and applied for a job as secretary to the headmaster of Dr Challoner's Grammar School, where my mother had been educated. Amazingly, given her age and inexperience, she got the job. Certainly she looked older than her years, and was remarkably confident. We both were. Our mother's attitude of 'Anything is possible,' permeated everything. So began my sister's working life: a wild, half-educated girl, alone in the world.

PART 2

Doing Away with Childish Things

Myself at Wycombe court in 1953, happy to have
escaped the atmosphere at home.

Jennifer in Devon in 1956, twenty years old
and training to be a nurse.

Jennifer in the World

Jennifer did not have any boyfriends at this time. She was much too intimidating for any young man in our milieu to approach her. She appeared taller than her height of five feet nine inches, standing very straight and always looking directly ahead with a purposeful gait as she walked. She wore clothes that showed off her immaculate figure, and she had the longest legs ever. Yet she was shy, very shy, which she disguised, showing only her intense passion for music and, later, books. She had no social graces. She could not and would not join in social conversation. She would sit and observe. Our mother's maxim of 'empty cans will rattle' we absorbed at a very early age, so we seldom rattled at all. This attitude made social intercourse very difficult. Fortunately, an old friend put me in the picture quite early. Humans are like dogs who sniff around trees to get informed about other dogs. We need to sniff, I learned – so I do, a bit. Jennifer never thought this necessary.

At Dr Challoner's, the headmaster, her boss, was a sophisticated, mature man who looked severe and imposing. Nevill Harrow was in his late fifties and had an impressive career behind him, having worked at Bletchley Park during the war, translating transcripts from the Enigma machine. He was soon to retire. Despite his sophistication, he became fascinated by the sensitive and creative girl who had become his secretary. He rapidly realized that she was remarkably intelligent, even if she could not spell and had little awareness of punctuation (this never changed), and was always asking provocative questions which delighted him. When he discovered she was younger than his sixth-formers he was horrified, and arranged for her to do his secretarial work in the mornings, giving her time off in the afternoons for reading and homework to do at night. He channelled her reading with care, realizing her great untapped potential, and they spent many hours poring over books and papers together.

Having been put out on the doorstep by our mother and her husband, Jennifer had eventually been found lodgings by our father. She was living with an old lady in a dilapidated two-up, two-down cottage next to his yard. I think Gordon felt he would be able to keep an eye on her if she was in close proximity to his business, but it didn't quite work out like that. He was extremely busy, and while Jennifer saw him come and go, beyond that she had little real contact. We neither of us had parents to talk to at a time when we needed them. Mummy was too busy suffering with Jock, and Daddy too busy with his business – and at the same time suffering with his new wife, Judith.

Meanwhile, we two girls were forgotten.

Jennifer was always hungry, as there was little for her to eat. The old lady who was meant to feed her had little realization of the appetite of a teenage girl. The house my sister was lodging in was cold, dark, damp and ugly – and where was her beloved piano? I only went to see her there once. She was terribly lonely. No one apparently visited her and, indeed, she wanted no one to see where she lived. I really don't think she even wanted me to know how she was living.

She took me into the hall, and then into a tiny, stale-smelling sitting room. The old lady whose house it was shuffled away out of view and the two of us faced one another, unable to speak. I knew from the look on my sister's face that she felt ashamed of her surroundings. I understood completely. I was ashamed of my home life too, for different reasons.

It wasn't long before I also moved house. The one we had been living in was owned by my grandmother, and when she died, my mother found that it had been left to her. Mother sold it and bought a large, pleasant bungalow with a garden a couple of miles or so away. I still had to keep out of Jock's way, hiding in cupboards to stay out of sight. The new bungalow had three bedrooms: one supposedly for mother and Jock, one for me, and a spare which was considered to be Jennifer's room when Jock was not there. Jennifer did actually move back in with Mother and me at the new place, whenever Jock was gone. Once he returned – and he always did, even though he sometimes stayed away for weeks or months – she had to go.

Jennifer was grateful for a home and good food, however fleeting her time there. She always knew it would not last and anyway we were not allowed any personal things there so it felt transient. Experience had shown both of us that we were expendable.

Jennifer lived for the time she spent with Nevill Harrow: his warmth, the books they shared, their discussions. She could talk to him about her innermost thoughts and he seemed at one with her. She confided in him about her home life and her fears for me, her sister, stifled in Mother's house, and totally obliterated by our father's new wife. The desperation she felt was palpable as she could not see a way to help me. I was still obliged to hide in cupboards or in the loo, since children were extreme irritants to Jock in what he now regarded as *his* house.

This experienced schoolmaster, Nevill Harrow, cared enough for Jennifer to arrange a meeting with our father and lay before him the nominal duties of a parent and the responsibilities expected – and, most importantly, the necessity to provide a home for us. Jennifer was delighted by the outcome of this meeting and told me all about it. Apparently, Nevill and my father got on famously and our father agreed to buy a large house for himself and Judith, with room for Jennifer and me and our two half-sisters, Pat and Frankie. Jennifer was truly and deeply grateful, and so was I. Nevill Harrow also raised the issue of my schooling. It seemed I would be escaping my mother's establishment, escaping her menacing husband, and, on the headmaster's recommendation, going to boarding school.

Nevill Harrow was the first person in a very long while, it seemed, to have valued Jennifer.

Sonamarg

Father took Jennifer and me to see the lovely old house that he had bought. It was large and Edwardian, with extensive outbuildings and many acres of land, overlooking the Misbourne Valley. It was enchanting, with no other houses nearby and birdsong overhead. Sonamarg was an earthly paradise. Father, a very busy man, left instructions with builders and decorators for the renovations. He loved the place, and had everything done to the highest specifications. Amazing central heating, thick pile carpets throughout, and an incredible modern kitchen. But Judith hated it, and did not want a house that included her husband's first wife's children. She felt that Father had disregarded her wishes, and she therefore found fault with everything in the house, including our father. She installed her mother to help out, and Father, who could not stand the woman (his words), escaped into motor racing. Much later I heard from Jennifer that he had very quickly become attached to a female architect and fellow racer, Pam, who was short, plump, and fun. I doubt Judith knew anything about this, certainly not at the beginning. Home for him was difficult, and so he escaped.

When the house was finished it was beautiful. The first time I went there it was evening, and as my father led me through the side door into the huge kitchen with its gleaming

Aga, it took my breath away – wonderful! I looked at Judith, who paid me no attention and carried on doing something or other, and I looked at my two little half-sisters, silent and unmoving, sitting at the huge kitchen table. It was like a stage set. I should have registered something, but didn't. Father helped me off with my coat and attempted to make an inroad into the pervading silence. Judith did not speak, the children did not speak. The clock in the hall struck nine. No food. Nothing. At nine-thirty, Father stood up.

'So there's no food tonight,' he said in his affable way, 'but we ate last night – so good night!'

He took my hand and moved into the hall, his usual cheerful spirits returning as he looked around, and showed me over the ground floor of my new home. We walked up the wide staircase and along the landing, opening the doors into the various rooms, all beautifully done with thick carpets and heavy interlined curtains. Not a thing out of place. Lovely. Pat's room was done out in red and white, and Frankie's in blue. My father seemed confused, however, and we returned to the kitchen, which was still silent, the unmoving children at the table.

'Where is Chris's room?' he asked.

'Next to the bathroom,' came Judith's distant reply.

Cheerfully, we mounted the stairs again, found the bathroom, and opened the door into my room. The shock was profound and I could not move. I stood there, gaping at the narrow space, taking in the bare bulb in the light fitting, bare floorboards, the small window so high up it was impossible to see through it without climbing onto a chair. Not that there was a chair. The only furniture was a narrow Army-style trestle bed with a pallet mattress – nothing else. No pillow, no bed linen or blankets, no curtains. This box room with its single make-do bed was the room allocated for Jennifer and me. Clearly, we would never be staying there together. My heart sank and my father retreated. In the kitchen I could hear him ask Judith what he could do.

'Get a blanket from the outside cupboard,' she said.

He returned with a blanket and a pillow, its ticking not covered by a pillowcase, no sheets or eiderdown. He should have got angry, but he didn't. He just said good night and left me there to weep my heart out and to feel, yet again, ashamed. I told myself that this was all I deserved. I lay down on the unmade bed.

The room was never changed. It was where the little ones were put when they were naughty. It was where Jennifer and I were put when we had nowhere else to go. Judith gave us nothing: no food, no warmth, nothing, total neglect.

I stayed at Sonamarg from time to time for short periods. I could not stand it. I used to wake up and feel sick, wander downstairs and into the kitchen. Usually, Judith was doing something at one end, my two half-sisters at the table. No one spoke. There was no radio, only the weight of an uncomfortable silence. I would rather go hungry than ask for anything to eat. Sometimes food was offered, sometimes not. I would go out into the garden and wander about – nice in the summer, hopeless in the winter months. Although the house was in a beautiful setting, it was in the middle of nowhere. Judith never took us anywhere, and I had no bicycle to escape on. The days felt long, lonely and difficult. I came and went, keeping quiet, not making any fuss. It was not unusual to go to bed hungry, just as I had on that first occasion.

The only time I remember Judith cooking, she made a spaghetti dish. It seemed to take forever. She peeled and chopped tomatoes and pulverized them and strained them through a sieve. She took the skins off mushrooms and chopped them, trimmed bacon with great care. Everything was cooked in separate pans before it all came together. I remember her seasoning it with black pepper, which wasn't something we had at Mother's. The whole dish was exotic to me. Spaghetti was not something my mother ever made. We sat round the table – Father, Pat, Frankie and me – and Judith dished up as much, or as little, as she felt we each should have. It was the most delicious thing I had ever eaten, the first time I had tasted Parmesan cheese. Even now, it's a dish I sometimes cook, and it brings back memories of that occasion, the only time I sat down to eat with my father and Judith and my two half-sisters at Sonamarg.

Jennifer and I were never at the house together. I heard – from her and also, in later years, from Frankie – of the frightful rows my sister had with Judith. As far as Jennifer was concerned, she was the eldest child and therefore the most important. I was the second most important and, in her view, Judith's children a long way behind. Jennifer felt she had every right to be there at Sonamarg; our father had told her so. On one occasion, she looked in the fridge for something to eat and found smoked salmon that was stale and rotting. She was so hungry she ate it. Judith was livid with her for daring to touch her food. Another time, Jennifer was cold and put her feet in the bottom oven of the Aga to warm up. When Judith caught her, ructions ensued. Their relationship was always abysmal and our father was never there to stand up for her. Jennifer was forever being told off and thrown out. She was constantly rejected. Nobody understood that this poor girl had lost everything.

I learned to keep my head down and say nothing.

The outside world saw the large, comfortable house we purported to live in, and the smart cars; meanwhile, we carried the secrets of our bare room and of being denied food, and felt shame.

Gordon's escape from the coldness generated by Judith was to go driving around in his new white Jaguar XK120. In fact, motor racing became his great love, and he raced his Jaguar 120 from 1951 until 1958, selling it after 125,000 miles of motoring. Guy Salmon, a Formula One racing driver from the 1960s, sold his C-type to my father in 1954 and he raced this big beast too, winning at Silverstone and at Brands Hatch. It has been said that getting close to an original C-type is like coming across a rare Turner or Rembrandt, with a price tag to match – and I agree! Sometimes – not often – he took Jennifer and me to the track with him, and pinned 'Mechanic' onto our chests. We were free to wander among the cars and into the pits at will. Jennifer hated the noise, but I loved it, and the smells; the sight of so many amazing cars, the sense of danger. I could not wait to have a sports car of my own.

Wycombe Court

In 1951 Nevill Harrow arranged for me at the age of thirteen to go to Wycombe Court, a boarding school for girls. He chose the school, and my parents were happy to accept his recommendation. Daddy would pay the fees and buy the uniform. Mother took me up to Harrods in London for my new school uniform, which comprised a tailored shirt, a silk tie, and a blazer and pleated skirt in a lovely bright blue. For Sundays there was a smart suit: a neat fitted jacket and a skirt with a slight flare in the same shade of blue. In winter we wore a little felt pill-box hat with ribbon trim, and lace-up shoes; in summer we had pretty blue and white dresses with a beautifully cut Peter Pan collar, white socks, shoes with buckle fastenings and a panama hat. For the occasions I wasn't in uniform I was given some stylish mufti clothing, including three pairs of fine lawn pyjamas with a delicate floral pattern. I loved them, really loved them, and wore them for many years. All these garments went with me to my friend Patsy Reader's house, and with her help I had to sew on more than a hundred Cash's name tapes. My mother was working, so no help from her.

Jennifer was thrilled to see me going off to school and away from the trauma of both our mother's and father's establishments. She and I were both so very pleased by this development.

Father said he would take me to the new school. On the day of departure I was rather nervous, and became increasingly so as I waited and waited in the hall alone. He had forgotten. Mother was working and so was Jennifer, so there was no one around to call and remind him. Eventually, one of his men arrived in a small scruffy car, bundled me in with my trunk, and we set off. The school was in Buckinghamshire, a few miles from High Wycombe. Unpleasant memories of being taken to the convent at Tring surfaced. I felt sick and anxious.

Wycombe Court School was set in extensive, well-tended grounds at the end of a long drive. It was an impressive building, large and rather grand-looking, with turrets at one end. My father's man stopped at the main gate and, seeing all the smart cars and high-spirited girls hanging out of the windows, backed off. He took out my trunk and left it, and me, by the side of the gate. Not at all sure what to do, I looked up and saw a tall, stooped man coming towards me. He smiled gently, picked up my trunk, and gestured for me to follow him. I felt so embarrassed walking along the grass behind him and arriving in this way. He opened the door into a huge hall, and left me standing there with my trunk. Later, I discovered that my rescuer was the gardener, and was very grateful for his kindness that day.

The hall was overflowing with chattering girls and parents – mothers and fathers – hugging and laughing and saying goodbye to each other. No one spoke to me. In time, the hall emptied and I found myself alone. I looked around at the intimidating panelling of the vast staircase. I did not know where to go or what to do, so I stood still and waited. Eventually a girl, passing through, saw me.

'Oh, you're the new girl,' she said. 'Report to Miss Boyle and Miss Robinson.'

She indicated a door, and I gave a timid knock. Two strange ladies, one large and smiling, the other thin as a stick with a forbidding air, looked up at me from behind their desks. Wycombe Court had two headmistresses, it appeared.

'Where are your parents?' the large one asked.

I could not speak. They rang a bell, and someone arrived and took me up to a dormitory with five beds, one of them for me. The four other girls already there helped me to unpack. Nervously, I looked about me – it looked all right. I soon realized that the atmosphere was nothing like the one Jennifer and I had experienced at the convent. The teachers and the girls were lovely, so kind. I was relieved to have escaped the horrors of home; the violent, intimidating atmosphere created by Jock, my mother's husband, and the coldness and rejection of Judith at Sonamarg. The lovely old house and grounds of Wycombe Court in Lane End became my only stable home for the next three and a half years, and I was happy there. I always felt somewhat lonely and a bit out of it, however, probably because I could not relate to the stories the other girls shared of their homes and their fascinating holidays – things I could only hope to experience one day.

The school had about 150 girls, mostly boarders, and was dedicated to teaching the social graces. We had our hands inspected before meals, then had to sit up straight and keep our hands folded in our laps – and no loud talking. Mealtimes were so civilized. The eight o'clock news on the radio accompanied the cooked breakfast with tea and toast that we were given on weekdays. Then on Sundays, when Cook was off, breakfast was boiled eggs, hot rolls and real coffee, which I still have to this day. We had napkins in silver napkin rings and ate good food, sitting at tables of eight where impeccable manners were a must. We rested on our beds for half an hour after lunch – no rushing about for us after meals. Lunch and supper were equally delicious. Beautiful paintings adorned the walls, and the views from the dining room extended over sweeping lawns through to the playing fields and beyond. What a relief from what I had left behind at my so-called homes.

After breakfast it was into the main hall, where we sat listening to classical music pouring forth from an enormous horn – even bigger than the one I remembered from my grandmother's – attached to an ancient gramophone. Then it was Bible reading, prayers and a hymn, before a talk by the headmistresses, who were our goddesses. Our classrooms were pleasant and the teachers were caring and considerate. I particularly loved our extremely old English teacher who, when seated on a high stool, looked like a small, brown hazelnut. I hung on her every word, and thought her wonderful.

In our sewing lessons at Wycombe Court we were instructed to make a nightie or petticoat – but as my mother had never worn either, I insisted instead on making cami-knickers, which were rather strange and very difficult. Nevertheless, at the end of the term they were displayed on the table. I felt proud, yet somehow exposed. No other parent seemed to wear cami-knickers.

We learned deportment – very important. Anything that was deemed not quite perfect had to be exercised out. I was told I had flat feet and scoliosis of the spine, and had to get up very early every morning and go into the main hall with about twenty other girls, all of us doing various exercises. I would sit, one foot stretched out at a time, rotating it at the ankle and, for my spine, I stood against the wall, pressing my back against it, standing very straight and tall. Deportment was not a new idea to me. Mother always felt it was important to stand correctly, and would have Jennifer and me walking round the house with books on our heads. At Wycombe Court I learned how to curtsey, which came in handy many years later when I was presented to the Queen at Buckingham Palace. We were also taught to rid ourselves of any vulgar pronunciations. Definitely not 'gar*idge*' but 'gar*arge*'. And certainly not 'I beg your pardon,' but 'Sorry.' I said sorry so many times.

We put on plays every term, house and school plays. I was a year older than Julie Christie, who went on to become a great actress and film star, and directed her in our first house play. She was rather mousy then, but came alive as she got into the part. We learned to sing, we learned ballroom dancing and how to play a decent game of tennis – but I cannot remember any chemistry or science lessons. Nevertheless, I achieved seven O-levels in the essentials and read the broadsheet newspapers every day as they were left in the main hall for us. So when I left school, I thought I had a good idea of what was going on in the world outside – but had I?

Swimming in the summer was not my favourite experience. The swimming pool was unheated and bitterly cold, and we were forced into it, whatever the weather, when we returned from our Easter break. The shock to our senses was great. In winter, the games were hockey and netball. Hockey was a joy to me, and I was thrilled to get my hockey colours at the end of the school year.

During one of the holidays I found, hidden at the back of some bookshelves, a copy of D. H. Lawrence's *Lady Chatterley's Lover*. This novel, which was notorious at the time, I read while locked in the lavatory, getting very hot all over. I passed it on to Jennifer before taking it back to school in my tuck box, where it went all round the school and was read by almost every girl. Such excitement. I was constantly afraid of being caught, but thankfully our teachers remained unaware. Every year group had a sitting room, and ours was up a little flight of stairs in the turret. We had a piano, comfortable chairs, and a cupboard where we kept our tuck boxes. For my fourteenth birthday I decided I would like a party, and took back to school hidden in my tuck box all sorts of things that weren't allowed, like tinned mandarin oranges, and jelly, which we planned to melt using the water from our hot-water bottles. This was something I wasn't even fond of, but it seemed like good party food. I smuggled in a birthday cake, too, and we had a wonderful time in the sitting room with our contraband and music courtesy of a chunky blue radio I had been given by my mother. Afterwards, we had a collection of empty tins and bags and didn't know what to do with them, so I slipped downstairs and secreted them into a dustbin. I thought I was safe. The following day they were found, and I was asked to go and see the headmistresses.

'It's not very honest to bring food in like this,' Miss Robinson said in a firm but mild tone.

She paused to allow this to sink in. Those few words were enough to have the desired effect. I vowed to myself that never again would I indulge in less than scrupulously honest behaviour.

'Now, we expect you to bring us some birthday cake,' she said.

Fortunately, there was still enough left for me to put two generous slices on a plate and take it as a peace offering to the headmistresses.

My holidays from school, when I returned to the familiar pattern of my home life, were unspeakable. Usually, I returned first to Mother's house – an empty shell of a place, as she was out working all day, and where I was still pushed into cupboards whenever her husband was expected. Returning home one holiday, I discovered that Mother had cleared out the bedrooms that had been mine and Jennifer's. All our valued things were gone: not so much as a book, a picture or any of the possessions that meant anything to us remained. Jennifer and I had been expunged. Her room was now a study, mine a spare. Where were Jennifer's piano and the bikes we so loved? We put on brave faces to the world, but carried within us the secrets of our diminished places.

For many years I was angry with our mother, but now I understand. She was a child of her generation and at that time you didn't easily lose a husband – particularly when you were very beautiful – so it must have been ghastly for her.

After the first few hapless days of the holidays I would be shipped off to stay with my mother's old friend Ann and her husband, or my Aunty Doris and her war-damaged husband, or my father and his acid wife. I don't suppose any of them really wanted a sensitive young girl in their midst, but my mother was very persuasive. So I was moved from place to place.

During the summer I would walk through the woods and

sit reading, alone, looking down on beautiful Old Amersham. Jennifer and I did spend some time together, although it was difficult. After all, where could we meet? She still slept in that miserable cottage, and was too ashamed for me to go there again. I was reading mostly Shakespeare or the Bible, although Jennifer introduced me to 'The Ballad of Reading Gaol', *Trilby, Dorian Gray, Dr Jekyll and Mr Hyde*, Keats, Shelley and many, many others. Her headmaster was educating us both.

During my time at Wycombe Court, I seldom considered the fate of my sister. She never complained to me about her lot and yet she was very secretive at the time, and I wondered why. She came to see me with our mother on open days, and looked around at the lovely buildings and grounds where I was spending most of my life. She looked on with satisfaction, and I am sure some envy, at the pictures, the music and the happy girls surrounding me. Jennifer, through her employer, had secured this opportunity for me. She had made me secure in our insecure world.

And yet she was still in her mean little cottage, living for much of the time on meagre rations, which she swallowed alone. What I could not understand was how she looked so radiant and happy, given her desolate living conditions.

It was her relationship with Nevill Harrow, of course, that was behind it. She was by now in love.

Rumours

For Jennifer, falling in love with her employer was really not a wise option, but nonetheless she did so. Nevill Harrow was not stupid. He had a wife and responsibilities, and had been the respected headmaster of a celebrated grammar school for nearly twenty years. Jennifer was only just sixteen, a young girl damaged by the break-up of her parents' marriage. She was alone, and she lived for the time she spent with her boss. She loved Nevill with all her heart, her soul and mind. Endless days of being in love stretched into months, and then into years. Having taken this girl on as his secretary, Nevill would do almost anything to contribute to her happiness. He took her to his favourite places, which he knew she would appreciate, and she felt exhilarated sitting alongside him in his open-top Bentley.

In Amersham, I saw them speed past me, the two of them laughing, completely unaware of anything beyond themselves, and felt puzzled. Jennifer was blossoming. What was I missing?

At this point, I had no sense of the true nature of their relationship; I was simply impressed that my sister was riding around in a fabulous car. Lucky Jennifer, I thought. As for Nevill Harrow, he seemed an old man to me – much older than our father, who was then just in his forties. Not for a moment did I consider that Jennifer and her boss were romantically involved.

When I spent time with my sister, I noticed that she was evasive. She seemed somewhat distant. Now I tend to think it was a sign that so much of what was going on in her life had to be kept secret. Our conversations tended to be about books, and we rarely strayed beyond such things.

'I'm earning my own money, having lots of lovely clothes made, and going everywhere,' she said expansively.

'Where are you going?' I asked.

'Oh theatres, concerts and things,' she said, obviously leaving out the most important bit – her relationship with Nevill. His influence coloured all her thinking. It seemed to me a good thing that she had someone who was interested enough to spend time with her and pay her attention.

'You must read the Song of Solomon. It's all about love,' she said, finding it in the Bible for me. I did, and took it in, though rather slowly.

I would look at Jennifer and somehow know there were other things on her mind; things she was not willing to share with me. She gave off a sense of superiority. At the time I could not understand it, but on reflection, I think her status as the secretary and lover of a powerful, successful man set her apart from her schoolgirl sister.

At first, Mother had been pleased to hear of Jennifer's job at Dr Challoner's Grammar School. Why would she not be? She herself had benefited from being a pupil there and greatly respected this well-known place of learning. Indeed, she enjoyed telling her friends of Jennifer's achievements. Then, later, after a year or so, she heard the gossip and insinuations about her daughter and the headmaster, and did not like it. Nevertheless, she chose to ignore it – until one day her oldest friend, Rosemary, pointed out that with the rumours persisting, Mother absolutely must talk to Jennifer. She tried, really tried – but she and Jennifer did not speak the same language.

'Jennifer, I need to have a little word with you,' Mother began. Hesitant.

'Oh, really?' Prickly.

'Yes. Aunty Rosemary thinks it would maybe be a good idea if you changed jobs . . .'

Jennifer turned on her. '*Whatever for?*'

'Well, I just wondered . . . is it really such a good idea to be spending so much time—'

Jennifer knew where this was going, and cut her off. '*No, no, no!*' she shrieked.

Mother shrank back.

'How *dare* you speak to me like this? It's no business of yours *what* I do! What sort of mother *are* you, anyway?'

Jennifer was incredibly angry, and floored Mother with a torrent of verbal abuse which she was quite incapable of dealing with. Undeterred, Jennifer stayed in her job for three years in all. It was several years before Mother told me about this difficult conversation. From that moment on, whenever she referred to her daughter's employer, she called him Nevill the Devil.

Jennifer carried on seeing Nevill Harrow. She continued to ride around Amersham with him in his Bentley. She did not care what anyone else thought. She loved him.

It seemed he loved her, too.

Wycombe Court, Work and Weevils

While Jennifer continued to fuel the rumour mill in Amersham, I was still enjoying life at Wycombe Court. I got along with everybody, although was not what I would call best friends with anyone. I always felt that the shame that shrouded my home life set me apart. I remember a remark on my final report that said something along the lines of my needing to learn to be a part of the whole, which was spot on. I was more apart than a part.

In my final year we moved up to top dormitories, and were allowed to choose who we were going to share with. Not having a close friend, I did not express a view, and ended up with a girl who told me time and again that she had an aunt who wrote for one of the newspapers. Every night, this girl would slip out of the dorm and be gone for hours. She always managed to wake me up when she came back in. I worked out that she was involved with another girl, and was sneaking off to be with her. I really couldn't have cared less, but what made me cross was that I was being disturbed night after night by their trysts. I got so angry that, for once, I behaved like my sister and decided to confront matters, locking her out one night. When she tried to get back into the room and couldn't, she made quite a scene, which woke the prefects.

'Open the door, Christine.'

'I'm sorry, I won't.'

Matron came. She couldn't persuade me to open up either. Finally, the two headmistresses were summoned. I relented, unlocked the door, and explained what had been happening and that I was fed up.

'I'm being woken up every night,' I said. 'I've had quite enough.'

Nothing more was said, but the next day all my room-mate's belongings were quietly taken to the bottom landing, and she was put in with a lot of junior girls. I had my room to myself for the rest of the year.

My school days ended in 1954, when I was sixteen and a half. I desperately wanted to go to university or to art school or, failing that, to the Royal Academy of Dramatic Art to train as an actress. I knew I had talent, and brains – but my ideas were ridiculed.

'You don't want to be an actress,' was Mother's reaction. 'It's absolutely ridiculous.'

When I went to see Daddy, he said, 'You want to get on with your life and see the real world. I can't see that so much education has helped Jimmy Drummond.'

And that was that.

Mother told me to look in the *Bucks Examiner*, the local weekly paper, and find myself a job. All my friends were staying on, or going on to finishing schools in Switzerland or the like; I felt sick and alone, thrown to the wolves. Had my sister felt like this when she left school at fifteen, a year and a half younger than I was now? I think so. Her saving miracle was getting a job at Dr Challoner's Grammar School. Was I going to be so lucky? And where was I going to live? I had little choice but to move back in with my mother.

I did as I was told, and looked in the *Bucks Examiner*. I applied for a job as a laboratory assistant – and got it. I was really excited. I had a kind and gentle boyfriend, Grenny Brightman, who had no car and, as there were no buses at night, walked miles from Chesham to Amersham to be with me. Although I was still hiding from Jock in my mother's house, life began to be fun, and I started to go around with a group of friends. Johnny Broad, with his ancient taxi, Gordon McBride, with his father's car, and the Wilmott girls, from Chesham Bois, all a bit alternative. I learned to play cards for money, so got rather good, and we all crammed into one car or another for excursions to pubs or gigs where music was played. In 1954, at sixteen and a half, I was five feet five inches tall, much shorter than my sister, but like Jennifer, I had inherited the great legs of my mother and grandmother.

I had a great love of clothes and fabrics, and always wore beautiful things. All the money I had was spent on clothes. I still remember buying my first pair of nylons, which had seams and cost 10s 6d. They laddered so easily that I was terrified putting them on and taking them off in case they snagged, many a time using soap or nail varnish to stop a ladder from running. After moving to Mother's new home in Little Chalfont and changing jobs it became more difficult for me to see Grenny, so I accepted an offer to accompany a young friend of my father's to a car club dance at the Bell in Gerrards Cross.

That night was the first time I put on eye make-up. I was wearing a long, sleeveless floral dress and thought I looked lovely. Mother took one look at me when I came out of my room, and slapped me round the face.

'Go and take that rubbish off your face – you look like a tart,' she said, disgustedly.

I was horrified. I did as I was told, washed off my eyeshadow and mascara, and went to the dance somewhat bereft. My escort was a very smart young man, who seemed rather older than me, from a lovely house up a long drive nearby. We had a wonderful night, joining Father and other friends, dancing and drinking champagne; but coming back, the car broke down, and he had to get out and mend it. That was all. He didn't even try and kiss me. Nothing happened. By the time we got home it was two or three in the morning, and my mother was waiting up. She was furious and told me I was a trollop for staying out so late, and that I couldn't see him again. She certainly ignored my protestations of innocence.

I did hate living under my mother's roof, and I did hate my job at Coopers, a research laboratory in Berkhamsted. At work, looking after the flies and weevils were my main responsibilities. The flies were kept in cages covered with fine mesh, and on the front was a fabric flap through which I had to put my hands and forearms in order to change their food. It made me feel faint with utter disgust as they crawled all over my flesh. The atmosphere was hot and humid, and the place smelt rancid. Every day for four months I had to rush out of those rooms for air, and to be sick. In another room were various creepy-crawlies which I had to sieve through, searching for weevils. It never occurred to me to leave. It was my first job, and I had in mind what my father always used to say about finishing things once you'd started, so I felt I must stick at it. Jennifer, always sensitive, came with me one weekend when I was on duty and, following me into the room full of flies, promptly fainted. It was very, very nasty.

About this time, Jennifer announced that she was to start nursing at the Royal Berkshire Hospital in Reading. She seemed quite committed, but was sorry that it was not to be in London. Apparently, with her medical history of asthma, no London hospital would have her. I remember saying that I could think of nothing worse than nursing, seeing so much suffering. Well, perhaps feeding flies was worse.

It was Nevill Harrow, so influential in every aspect of Jennifer's life, who had steered her towards a career in nursing. Aware of the depth of their feelings for one another, he recognized that Jennifer was dangerous for him; indeed, their relationship was destructive for both of them. He steeled himself, and told her that their affair had to change. The pain Jennifer experienced was terrible. She flung herself at him, crying bitterly, begging him to marry her, not able to understand why he refused. She had seen Father leave our mother, walk out on his two young daughters, and marry his young lover. Why, then, could Nevill not do the same? Appalled by what he had allowed to happen, he was decisive. A career in nursing would give Jennifer a home, and the intellectual and emotional stimulus she needed. The total impossibility of continuing their loving entanglement was paramount to him.

Of course, I knew none of this at the time. Jennifer jealously guarded her secret life with Nevill, and I was not privy to what was going on between them. I now understand why she was so private. She must have known about the gossip, the disapproval the relationship drew. Even now, I know that there are some who feel what went on between

Jennifer and Nevill was inappropriate – a word I hate. Yet it makes sense to me that Jennifer was drawn to him. Her father had left and she was crying out for love, which Nevill provided.

I am certain that in the beginning the relationship was innocent, that he was simply a mentor, a benefactor; but at some point he crossed a line and became her world. She had not experienced three wonderful years at boarding school surrounded by her peers, as I had. Jennifer was on her own, working, living in dire lodgings. No wonder she became absorbed with a man who recognized her intelligence and opened doors to learning and pleasure that had been closed to her. He was not suitable, of course. He was much older than she was, and was not free. Still, he made her happy. I cannot judge either of them. Where would Jennifer have been without him? Where would I have been? When no one else cared, he intervened and made sure that both of us were given a chance.

Only much later did she talk to me about Nevill, usually no more than a bald statement here and there, revealing enough of what had gone on for me to put the pieces together and make an almost, but not quite, complete whole.

Nursing Is the Answer

After four months of my rather creepy job, I developed a raised red rash all over my body. It seemed I was allergic to the weevils, and therefore had to leave. I was delighted, as I had become completely psychotic whenever I had to go into those hot, overpowering rooms that stank and hummed with millions of flies in hundreds of cages.

I next got a job as an assistant teacher at the Beacon House Preparatory School, a very smart little pre-prep school with very smart little children. They brought me presents, mostly flowers – wild, of course – and pears and apples, and their works of art, and were all so sweet. But the head teacher was not kind to me. In fact, she was foul, so I decided to leave. But what could I do instead? I had to get away from my mother's house. London beckoned.

I looked in the *Evening Standard* for some sort of job, any job, applied to the BBC, and was offered one. I was thrilled, and imagined getting onto the radio, at least. Not so. When I arrived I was told to go to the filing room. Policy had it that every one of the employees had to do their first three months in the filing room.

I might have achieved my seven O-levels, and I certainly appeared confident, but I was also somewhat dyslexic. The letters came in, hundreds of letters and papers, all for me to file in their appropriate boxes by the end of each day. The pressure was on. I slowly tried to sort them out, but as time passed, I resorted to stuffing the various papers into any old boxes just to get rid of them. Nobody said anything, but within a week I was promoted to my own desk, in my own office, where my job was to pay the artistes as they came in. Most of the artistes were impatient, and hungry – but I was meeting my sort of people at last.

I was eighteen, and waiting for my train on Marylebone Station, when John Denning, an ex Merchant Taylors' boy who was training to be an accountant, arrived in my life. He was six foot four, slim, beautiful, and was also a musician with the Old Merchant Taylors' jazz band. He held open the door of the train for me.

'Are you quite comfortable?' he said, once I was seated.

We kept on talking, and by the time we parted we knew we wanted to see each other again. Our relationship was all very proper and formal. I met his friends and his family, and went with him on gigs, where he played the piano. James P. Johnson was his idol, and he called his tiny sit-up-and-beg car after the great jazz pianist. I loved jiving, and Bessie Smith and Louis Armstrong were my idols. John and I played billiards and cards, and generally had fun. I loved this way of life and I loved him. We spent many a quiet evening lying on the floor in his parents' sitting room, listening to his favourite jazz records and reading poetry. We would gently caress, but going the whole way was not on my agenda. I stayed at his home in Chorley Wood most weekends, sleeping in a rather ugly room next to his grandma's, with John in his room as far away from mine as possible. I adored his handsome father, and his rather suspicious mother was kind to me. So much so that when I arrived one weekend I found that she had totally redecorated 'my' room for me. I was amazed, and said so – though unfortunately it was *so ugly*. She had painted the walls a violent mauve colour. It was truly dreadful, and although I was incredibly touched that she would do such a thing – for me! – the ghastly mauve did make me feel ill every time I entered the room.

After some months, John bought an engagement ring: Victorian, with diamonds and garnets. There was no formal marriage proposal, as such. We just became engaged, and I firmly believed that my future was secure with his family and our friends, and was delighted. I don't remember my parents being very interested. My mother met him, but I had to be careful about when I took him to see her, because of Jock. I never took him to see my father at Sonamarg because of the dreadful atmosphere Judith had created there.

I liked working at the BBC. London was so alive after Amersham; during my lunch breaks I would walk around the back streets, fascinated by the various little shops, especially the womenswear businesses. I had always loved clothes, and my Aunty Doris had given me an enormous amount of money, although she could not really afford it, to buy myself a camel-hair coat with a real fur collar. I lived in this utterly beautiful garment well into the spring. On one of my excursions I noticed that one very smart establishment had a large sign advertising for a model, and they were offering £10 a week. It seemed so much money!

I went in, enquired about it, and was given the job on the spot. I was earning only £7 a week at the BBC, so this was a great step up. But was it? Within a week, I realized that a carefully omitted part of the job description was that the model was expected to get into bed with the seedy old boss. For a week I showed off clothes to the various customers, and felt rather pleased with my £10. The following week I was told to go down to the basement, where the clothes were sorted and packed. Apparently, if I was not going to oblige the boss, this was where I was to stay; no more going into the smart shop, where there was daylight. The basement was dark and stifling, and all the staff expected me to capitulate. As spring turned into summer, it became too much. No sunny days or birdsong. Joy disappeared. £10 a week was not enough! So I left, after four months in the basement, with no other job in mind and nowhere to go.

It was at this point that Jennifer arrived at Mother's house wearing a beautifully cut suit. She looked amazing, and was loving nursing.

'It's wonderful. Just what I should have been doing all my life,' she told us.

We talked over my problems. The main one was having no permanent roof over my head. I could stay only briefly at my mother's house, if I agreed to hide if anyone came to the door; and the hateful room in my father's house was so, so traumatic.

'What are you going to do?' Jennifer said.

'I really don't know.'

'You must come and nurse. Nursing is the answer. You're so kind, so sweet – the patients will love you, and you will have a place of your own.'

Certainly it was tempting. I went to my father for advice.

'Well, on consideration,' he said, 'it's nursing or the Army.'

'No other choices?' I asked.

'It will be good for you to have the corners rubbed off. I don't like useless women,' he said.

And that was it. The Army, with its marching and discipline, sounded too awful, so I plumped for nursing. At least

I would be close to my sister. In 1957, I applied to join Jennifer at the Royal Berkshire Hospital in Reading. After a rather terrifying interview with a very formidable lady called Miss Aldwinkle, OBE, Matron, and in complete charge of the entire hospital, I was accepted. I don't remember much about the interview; I was completely intimidated. What did I say? Why did I want to be a nurse? Actually, I didn't: I just wanted a home, and to be with my sister. Jennifer had told me I was sweet and kind and that the patients would love me. I repeated her words, and added that I loved old people too. Father had driven me over to Reading, and seemed very pleased with the result. As for me, I just felt bewildered. Was this really what I wanted? I was just going along with the tide.

My first three months were at the Preliminary Training School in Reading. There were about a dozen of us new girls, and I found I was quite shocked by some of my colleagues. I had been used to the atmosphere at Wycombe Court, and was now in with girls who were noisy and shrieked and yelled. There was bad language, bad table manners. There was nothing wrong with the girls themselves, but it just wasn't what I was accustomed to, and it took some time to adjust. I found it difficult to wake up in the morning but was lucky enough to become friends with a girl called Maureen, who would come and knock for me every day.

Much of our training seemed to be concerned with what appeared to be trivial matters. We had to learn the correct way to fill a hot-water bottle, for instance. A tray had to be set up with a kettle, the bottle and its cover. The bottle had to be laid flat and only the neck tilted up while it was filled, to avoid air getting in or hot water leaking out. There were strict protocols for everything. After three months, and still with no real idea about what the nursing side of our job entailed, we were considered ready to go onto the wards, and to move into the nurses' home.

The nurses' home was a pleasant enough sanctuary. The rooms were cell-like, just big enough for a single bed, a fitted wardrobe and a chair. There were so many rooms along the main corridor, with two bathrooms in the middle. At each end were two rooms at least twice the size of the others, one of which was occupied by Home Sister, Sister Burrell – small, efficient, and very much in charge – while the other was allocated to Jennifer. Having been in lodgings for so long, Jennifer arrived at the nurses' home with all her possessions, including a collection of books that far outnumbered anything anyone else had. Apparently, Sister Burrell told her that she was giving her the big room not because she was an untidy or a dirty nurse, but because she had so many things and needed the extra space. Jennifer was, of course, delighted. She had been living in a room half the size for years.

We had maids to clean our rooms, our uniforms were laundered for us, and our beds were changed. There was also plenty of good food to eat, something that had not been the case for Jennifer for a long time. She was in her element. She was being cared for, and had enough time off for her beloved books. She sailed through her nursing exams with top marks all the way, and was set for higher things. Jennifer loved the challenge of it all, the nitty-gritty; even dentures, sputum and bedpans. She and I were so different.

Her best friend at the Royal Berkshire, Wendy, was also an inspired nurse, and they spent a great deal of time together talking about their experiences and the longing they felt for their lovers – who, in both their cases, were many miles away. They wrote love letters together, Jennifer editing and embellishing Wendy's missives with heartfelt declarations of love.

There was only one public telephone on the landing of the nurses' home, available for all of us to use. Communication therefore typically meant a note under the door, or catching up with each other when passing to or from the wards. Jennifer needed me to sew on buttons or to fix her hems, even though she could sew perfectly well. We had been taught by our grandmother, Eliza, and by Mrs Mather, the 100-year-old aunt of the headmistress at Belle Vue School.

When Jennifer and I began nursing we were paid less than £10 a month, and we had to do three months' night duty a year, working from 8 p.m. to 8 a.m. It was hard work and the discipline was harsh, but I loved the peaceful atmosphere at night, when we could give the very sick our attention and be of comfort to the dying. We had time to listen and talk with them, which was wonderful. But it was so difficult to keep awake from two until five in the morning!

Day duty was from 8 a.m. until 2 p.m., or 2 p.m. to 8 p.m. Jennifer and I worked different months on night duty, during which we scarcely saw each other, perhaps just passing on the stairs of the nurses' home while rushing on or off duty; this meant that for months of the year we could barely speak. Day duty was not much better, as we never worked on the same wards and never seemed to have the same off-duty periods. The off-duty times were given to us in advance by Sister, and to ask for anything different caused a major crisis. There were also study blocks of two weeks at a time, and various lectures after coming off duty. We were always tired and, indeed, I saw more than one nurse asleep at her desk. So when did I see my sister? Rarely. We never had time to share anything important, and we each had to deal with our own problems when they arose. I was aware, however, that she was still seeing Nevill, who would call for her in the Bentley and take her out.

Jennifer had been made to face the impossibility of her relationship developing in the way she had hoped with Nevill, but despite this, she still dreamed of marrying her great love. She could not accept that he would not leave his wife for her one day. Why would he not, when he loved her? She clung to the fact that her father had left her mother, and hoped and believed that Nevill would one day do the same.

Parties and Music

Jennifer and I both loved music, having had it around us from an early age. I gravitated to big band music and traditional jazz while Jennifer was faithful to her first love, classical music, and went to concerts whenever she could fit them in. I had learned the charleston and quickly picked up jiving, but the nurses' home dances were formal, and we were asked to wear long dresses. Our social lives were very different. Only once did I see Jennifer at a nurses' dance. I was in my first year of training, and the venue was the hall underneath the nurses' home. There was a band, and invitations had gone out to the university. I took John, my fiancé, and Jennifer went without a partner.

Jennifer was in a beautiful blue dress, rather refined. My dress was white, strapless and very up-to-date, and I thought it wonderful. The band, an ancient lot, played interminable music for ballroom dancing. John and I danced together well and were enjoying ourselves, but I did think it rather dull compared to jazz and jiving. So we enlivened the dance floor. For the moment I forgot I was in a long, strapless dress and noticed people were looking at me. I did not mind until I looked down and saw my small, pert breasts completely exposed.

Jennifer, meanwhile, appeared aloof and apart from it all.

I didn't see her on the dance floor, although she could have been. She looked very pretty, but created an atmosphere around herself that said she was not interested in any of the young men there. After all, she was in love with someone older and far more sophisticated; but I feel sure she must have felt very lonely inside.

The doctors' parties were more exciting. Much later, I heard that the innocuous-looking punch was laced with neat alcohol, so no wonder. The nurses' home was locked up at ten o'clock when the dances were still in full swing. We knew that a small side door was left for Night Sister to close at midnight. My friend Nancy and I went to these parties whenever we could, but one day we left it too late, and found ourselves locked out. We tried every window and door. All were locked. We looked about in desperation, and then I spied an upstairs loo window open. We climbed up the adjacent fire escape, Nancy panicking and repeatedly saying she could not do it. Ignoring her, I took a deep breath, heaved myself up, and squeezed through the top window, falling onto the floor beneath.

'Come on, Nancy, it's fine – I'll catch you,' I whispered.

She looked down and stayed down, but staying out on her own all night was not an option. Eventually I helped to get her top half through the window, but I had forgotten she was quite a bit plumper than me. I pulled and pulled at her in desperation, until she could hardly breathe and had tears running down her face. Suddenly she gave a big cough and, head first, shot right down into the lavatory pan.

We were safe at last.

My first ward was Benyon, male surgical, with Sister Rutter, a terrifying woman who shouted at me on my first day. She was at one end of the ward, me the other, with thirty beds between us.

'Nurse Lee, what do you think you are doing? Talking to the patients when you should be working!' she bellowed.

My face turned scarlet, and I began fiercely cleaning the locker tops, in humiliated silence. As a first-year nurse, particularly a first-month nurse, one was there to be abused and to endlessly clean the sluice – the room where we washed up items used on the ward, and bagged up soiled laundry. There were dirty bedpans, sterilizers, kidney bowls with noxious things in them, and mountains of dentures and sputum mugs. How I hated it all! But what could I do? My only place of security was here with my sister, so I struggled on.

The denture round was bad; all the men on the surgical ward dropping their filthy dentures onto my tray, except for Mr Green, who said he could not manage, and when I helped him up he got his teeth out and dumped them onto my bare hands. I was so disgusted I scurried off to scrub and scrub my hands until they became quite sore. I still had to scrub and scrub all the dentures, and then return them to their rightful owners. But I had mixed them up! Chaos ensued! The sputum mug round was definitely the worst. All the patients seemed to have sputum mugs then, particularly after an op. The men coughed and spluttered, and frequently missed the inside of the mugs altogether, leaving coagulated sputum hanging down in fronds on the outside. I heaved at the very sight of it all, let alone having to deal with it.

Sterilizers were a problem. These contraptions were the size of large catering microwaves, and powered by electricity. To operate them you opened the top and fed water in via a mains pipe, which emptied through a drain outlet. As with a kettle, you had to take care not to overfill, and to allow enough headroom for the boiling water. No one had taught us about them at Preliminary Training School, where more emphasis was given to how to lay up a tray to fill a hot-water bottle correctly. What a useless thing to learn, I thought! Anyway, one day I filled my sterilizer to the very brim, knowing no better. It boiled and boiled – and the first moment I realized there was a problem, and that it was my fault, was when boiling water was seen coming under the sluice door and into the ward. All hell was let loose, and somehow I had to mop it all up.

In those days the domestic cleaners were gods. *Never upset the cleaner* was the rule. They shouted and fumed at us nurses when the men's urinary bottles, attached under their beds, overflowed, or when someone was sick on *their* floor, or blood leaked from a drip. *They* did not want to see it, or touch it. Nor must we place any glass or cup on the sink in *their* kitchen. I avoided them, with care.

Jennifer was always at odds with the cleaners, apparently. She told me that on one occasion she was trying to help an elderly lady eat some breakfast, and was in the kitchen making up a tray for her.

'What are you doing in my kitchen?' demanded the cleaner, when she came in.

'I'm boiling an egg,' Jennifer said.

'You're not boiling an egg in *my* kitchen,' was the cleaner's response.

'Then where do you expect me to do it?'

'Not here.' She looked defiant and ominous. Jennifer picked up the egg in its saucepan of boiling water and threw it into the sink, stalking off and shouting behind her, 'Have it, then, and eat it – I hope it chokes you.'

*

Seniority on the wards made such a difference. You had to stand back and let any senior nurse pass, even if she was only six months ahead of you in her training. In fact, at the beginning, just in case, the norm was standing back for everyone!

Visiting times on the wards were in the afternoon from two to four, and in the evening from six to eight. We hated visiting times: the extra work and tidying up afterwards, stuffing beautiful flowers that had been brought in into empty jam jars.

Nursing was painful to me. I loved the patients, but not the suffering that I saw every day. I felt for them all, felt it every time I gave an injection, particularly when I had to inject the emaciated or the elderly. I felt it when I had to change dressings, treat bedsores, and watch the dying die. Life was so cruel then, with only limited painkillers available.

Grandpa Dies

The year I began nursing, 1956, our grandfather died at the age of eight-six. Jennifer had loved him deeply. She felt so sad, and went to the funeral, but I was on duty and unable to be there. We saw very little of our father during the war and in the years after, and our grandfather was certainly the man who most influenced Jennifer as a child. He gave her a Bible for her twenty-first birthday, and me a white prayer book for my eighteenth, and in mine in the front he wrote 'PP'. When I asked him what it meant, he said, 'Patience and perseverance – you will need them both in abundance to get through life.'

At eighteen I did not appreciate this, and hated this reminder every time I looked in this very beautiful prayer book. I realize now that Jennifer and I both had these qualities in abundance. I too now value my grandfather's quiet simplicity and wisdom.

Jennifer would go off for long walks with him in the countryside, and he would name all the birds and trees and flowers, and when we went off together she would show off her knowledge, and so I too learned them all. We would also go to his allotment, where we would help with picking beans, digging potatoes and growing the most enormous marrows. And as our grandmother loved flowers, he grew dahlias in many different colours and sizes in the autumn, and in the summer presented her with many bunches of sweet peas. She always loved to have flowers around her.

When Eliza died in 1950, Grandpa was desolate. His reason for living was gone. Both he and Mother were with her and my mother told us of Grandpa holding his dear wife in his arms, tenderly kissing her and stroking her face throughout the hour before she passed away. For the next several years he lived alone in their original cottage on Amersham Hill, where they had lived early in their marriage, and was happy enough there with his memories.

I remember he still had the chocolate in a small tin that he had saved for his darling wife so many years before, when it had been given out to the troops during the Boer War. He had refused the offer to become a Chelsea Pensioner, as he wanted to be close to his children while he grew old. As he became more infirm with the years, our saintly Aunty Doris would come down to Amersham every day on the train from Harrow, where she lived, to look after him.

Grandpa had more sorrow to face when my uncle Cyril, his eldest son, took his life in 1954 at the age of only forty. Uncle Cyril was always cheerful, but the builders' business he had created went downhill, and when bankruptcy loomed he saw no alternative but to take his own life. I was very fond of my uncle, and of his son Michael. How dreadful for him to be without a father at sixteen – and on top of that loss, to have the further upheaval of being forced to leave Berkhamsted, the public school he loved. Jennifer was at the funeral, and heard Grandpa say, 'Why could it not have been me? My life is over. My only wish is to join my dear wife in her grave, but he, my son, had everything to live for.' The pain must have been nearly unbearable. He had to live with the burden of these two deaths as he withdrew from life and waited for the end.

I had been nursing for about a year when John, my fiancé, decided to end our relationship. It had become difficult for us to see one another. He was in Chorley Wood, just too far from Reading, and my allocated time off never seemed to fit in with his. Since it was practically a sin to ask to change your hours, I never did. On the occasions when John did manage to come to see me, he had a three-hour round trip in James P., his sit-up-and-beg car, and I rarely made it to any of his gigs. It was not easy for either of us.

One night he drove over to Reading to take me out and I dashed out of the nurses' home and jumped into the car, ready to go. I knew at once something was wrong.

'I can't keep doing this, Chris,' he said. 'It's just impossible. I never see you.'

He asked for his ring back. I took it off and gave it to him, too devastated to speak. I got out of the car and went back inside and up to my room, where I sat on the edge of my bed, feeling sick. Losing him left me bereft and in total shock, as I loved him, and the time I spent at his home when I was away from the hospital. I loved the stability of his family life.

In the weeks that followed I was so upset I let my uniform get dirty. My cap, which was meant to be crisp and fresh on each week, was neglected and crumpled. I didn't wash my hair as much as I should have done, and began really to hate nursing even more. Jennifer did not seem to care about this. She had not been that enamoured with my tall, good-looking ex-fiancé, and thought me faintly ridiculous. She told me as much.

'He's far too good-looking, and anyway, you're far too creative to settle for an accountant,' she said.

Her behaviour hurt me almost as much as losing John. I felt I was reaching out to her and that she was beyond my grasp. I so wanted to leave nursing. I now hated the discipline, the horrors I had to deal with every day on the wards, and the long, unsociable hours. I wrote out my notice, but the letter stayed in my pocket as I pondered my future. What brought me to my senses was being stopped by one of the Sisters one day.

'Do you realize what you look like?' she said. 'You should *not* walk around the hospital with your uniform in that state. Do something about it, Nurse.'

I was so ashamed to be on the end of this reprimand that I thought, my God, I really have to pull myself together.

The writing out of my notice was repeated with regularity throughout my three-year nursing training. Nursing, for me, was an emotional rollercoaster. For Jennifer it was a challenge to be overcome. But each time I thought about handing in my notice, at the moment of delivery my father's words would come back to me: 'Never walk out on anything without being able to return, and always finish a project, no matter how difficult.'

His words were imprinted on my mind, for better or for worse. And so, each time I felt like giving up, my notice was never actually delivered.

A little while after breaking off our engagement, John asked if he could see me, and I met him at my mother's house.

'I want you to have the ring,' he said.

I shook my head. 'I don't want it.'

In the end, he left it on the mantelpiece, and Mother wore it for years.

Night Duty

A nurse alone in the middle of the night, seated in the centre of a ward of thirty or so under a small lamp, the only sounds the coughing and snoring and crying out of people in pain and the gasps of people dying; this was her lot. When a patient died the eyes had to be closed, the jaw tied up, the body washed all over, the orifices stuffed. Can anyone be immune from the effects of these traumatic events? I think not. Then, when all this was done, it was washing down the bedstead with carbolic, and rubbing down the mattress, both sides: and then the side table, inside and out, with disinfectant. That done thoroughly, the bed had to be made up afresh, and only then were the curtains drawn back. We nurses had to do it all. The cleaners would not touch any part of it.

But by night, as by day, romances flourished, mainly with the junior doctors, and mainly in the linen cupboard, where the fear of being caught certainly added a certain frisson. There were the occasional clandestine arrangements that we did not speak of; certainly not about the particularly gorgeous female Anglo-Indian staff nurse, who crept into a certain side ward at about two in the morning and, a couple of hours later, left behind a very happy young man.

Some patients played chess, and became very close to

their chess partners. When we drew back the curtains one morning on a deceased patient's empty bed, his neighbour looked very distraught.

'Wot's 'e got'n dun dat for? Game's not arfway fru.'

One day a strong and healthy young man of about twenty came into the ward, laughing and chatting to the nurses. He must be special, I thought, as he was being admitted into a side ward. Was he a doctor's son, or something? He did not seem ill and was tanned, an outdoor type, and I wondered what on earth was wrong with him. He seemed to be having cramps, and mild spasms. I was puzzled. Day by day the spasms got worse, and affected his neck and abdomen. It was horrible to see his increasing pain. Then side bars were erected around his bed, as the spasms affected his back, which arched, and his limbs flayed about out of control. We had to hold him down. He was having seizures, and could not breathe. We gave him oxygen, and injected sedatives, but nothing gave him relief, as his terrified eyes testified. What more could we do? The medical staff just shook their heads and walked away. Mercifully, his heart gave way in the end. This traumatic period of his life lasted about three weeks. It was so very gruelling for all the nurses attending him, and I went off the ward with huge relief when he died. It turned out that such a small incident had caused this living hell. He was a farmer's son, loved riding, and on leading his horse through a gateway had scratched his ankle on a protruding nail. It was of no consequence to this spirited young man, who had no idea that at that moment he had injected himself with the deadly spores of tetanus.

The very nature of nursing meant that so much was horrifying to both Jennifer and me. But there were occasional good surprises. I don't know how he arranged it, but our father rang up the Home Sister and said he wanted to take his two daughters out for the evening. Nobody disagreed with our father, and Sister Burrell respected all men, so I was whisked off the ward and told to hurry up and change as my father was waiting. The same happened to Jennifer. The two of us met in the hall, concerned and expectant. Outside, Father was sitting in his new Raleigh Pathfinder. He was rather pleased with himself, and we drove off to the Compleat Angler at Marlow, very grand after the nurses' dining room. A really wonderful evening followed. Amazing things to eat, and we talked and talked – so much that our father let three coffees get cold, and had to keep asking the waiter for a fresh cup. We walked through the lovely gardens to the river. It was so beautiful, and such a peaceful change from Reading, with the ever-present unpleasant smell that emanated from the Huntley and Palmer's biscuit factory, and the stench of glue that always pervaded the air in the town.

Jennifer thought nothing of hitching a lift whenever she wanted to go anywhere. 'No one would ever dare touch me,' she said.

I agreed. She looked so powerful. But when I decided to follow suit I made the mistake of telling my father, who was appalled, forbidding me ever to do so again. Within a week he had bought both Jennifer and me a small motorbike each, to put a stop to our hitchhiking forever. The motorbikes were great and gave us a real sense of independence, but that was in the summer months. Motorbikes were not so good in the winter, when it rained. Our waterproofs were not really waterproof, and Jennifer and I would arrive at our destinations very cold and bedraggled. It was going up a hill on my machine from Bourne End to Amersham that I experienced my first orgasm. I became heated and excited by the vibrations of the motorbike and, with difficulty, saved myself from flying into a ditch. So this was all it was about!

We also bought a kayak, a two-seater, from a junior doctor on the move. It was rather ancient, and cost very little, but on our very first outing we discovered it went very fast with the wind behind it and a strong current beneath. Jennifer and I were thrilled, but we had to get back to the hospital, and it was with regret that we turned the boat around. Despite our efforts we were going backwards. We rowed like mad, but our lovely little boat did not respond. Time was passing, and Jennifer was due on duty. The Thames was strong, stronger than two young ladies in a hurry – and then it started to rain.

Somehow we got our lightweight craft onto the riverbank. Jennifer was wheezing, yet determined to get back on duty. We climbed through overgrown weeds and a private garden, completely unaware that we were being watched. Our observer, an elegant man, came across the vast area of lawn towards us, and we struggled, out of breath, to tell him that we just had to be back on duty in twenty-five minutes' time. The observer, Jennifer and I, all ran across the lawn and fell into his gleaming white car. He drove like the devil, weaving in and out of traffic, arriving at the nurses' home with just minutes to spare. We barely thanked him in our rush to get changed out of our dripping wet, muddy clothes. What must this man's pale leather seats have looked like after we left? Would a man today approach two young girls in that way, and would the girls jump into the car of an unknown stranger? And would he have left them with a grin all over his face? I think not – definitely not, knowing the state of the interior of his car!

Certainly our boat, after the initial inauguration, gave Jennifer and me so much pleasure. We could take it out on a calm day and just relax on the water with a book or a friend. I know that Jennifer used the boat more than I did and loved quietly tying up near the French Horn in Sonning, a very smart hotel and restaurant, to remember the utter joy of being there with the man she adored. But the motorbikes were not an unqualified success. In the winter I developed bronchitis, and Jennifer had frequent asthma attacks, so my father bought me my first car – a small black Ford, not very stylish, but enormously practical. He had taught me to drive in his Raleigh Pathfinder but I'd never taken my test, so I organized three lessons with the British School of Motoring and took the test in the centre of Reading, which was one of the most frightening moments of my life to date. Nevertheless I passed first time, and had the freedom of four wheels.

Nancy's Twenty-First Birthday Party

My social life picked up again and I started going out a lot. I had several boyfriends; one I went ballroom dancing with, one who took me jiving, and several who took me out for dinner. I was so busy going out that I had to set aside one night a week to wash my hair. Jennifer took a dim view of my frenetic social life, always feeling the need to care for me, while I felt at the time that she was very judgemental.

'Have you been studying?' Her tone was invariably sniffy.

'Oh, I'm having much too good a time,' was my standard reply. She would look at me and shake her head.

Jennifer was always somewhat disapproving of my extra-curricular activities: the parties, the boyfriends, the dances, the drinking and so on. I also wore the latest fashions, coloured tights, mascara, and a lot of the time used a long cigarette holder with Balkan Sobranie cigarettes. She would roll her eyes at what she perceived to be my lack of moral virtues. Yes, I was enjoying myself, but in the 1950s there was no reliable contraception, and there was no way I was going to go 'the whole way'. I remember being mortified when one of the doctors told me I was a prick teaser. What was a prick teaser? I knew it was meant as an insult, and didn't like it at all.

Then I fell in love with a doctor who was about to return

to South Africa. He had been diagnosed with bone cancer and was going home to be with his family. Although I had only been out with him a few times, I was heartbroken, and for some months stayed in until my friend Nancy insisted I go with her to a doctors' dance. I really didn't want to go.

Once there, I saw one of the doctors looking at me. He was dark and good-looking, but I thought, oh no, he's not my type at all. I went for the tall, slim variety, and he was short and square. He did have a wonderful face, however, with a beautiful resonant voice and a profile to die for. In fact he looked rather Latin, more Spanish than English. I found him very attractive. He asked me to dance, and despite my initial reservations, I discovered he was great fun, with a warm, explosive character. Mike took me out to dinner, often to the White Hart at Nettlebed, which became a favourite of ours. I liked him and had a very good time in his company; we bounced off one another. He played a great clarinet, and had run the St Thomas's Jazz Band in his younger days at St Thomas's Hospital. He was much admired at the hospital as he was a natural in the operating theatre, and I was certainly flattered by his attention.

Mike arranged to take me to Nancy's twenty-first birthday party, a rather special affair her parents were giving. He came off duty late and we got into his new car, a Wolseley, and drove like mad to what we thought was the Old Mill at Arborfield, only to find a dilapidated old place and certainly not a party venue. On checking the invitation we saw that we had come in the wrong direction. Mike turned the car round, put his foot down on the accelerator and we were off again in a hurry. It was a sit-down do, and we knew it was important to get there on time. The road was wet and we were going fast – too fast. As we rounded a bend we left the road and went over a hedge, landing upside down in a ploughed field.

Mike got out, a farmer came running, and somehow I clambered free – cars had no seatbelts then. How either of us were on our feet, apparently unscathed, I have no idea. Between them, Mike and the farmer turned the car over and got it back onto the road. It wouldn't start, and I was helped into the driving seat while they began to push. The car rolled down the slight incline in the road while they tried to bump-start it. I was shaking so much, I could hardly hold the steering wheel. Finally the engine caught, and shouts from behind told me to turn the car round and head back to where Mike was waiting.

'Whatever you do, don't stop,' he yelled. 'Don't let the engine cut out.'

The car lurched along as I revved the accelerator. I slowed down as I got close to Mike, and he jumped in beside me. Somehow, in a state of shock, I managed to drive us the rest of the way, and we arrived at the party only an hour late. I had rather a lot to drink and arrived back at the nurses' home well after the ten o'clock deadline. This time the door was unlocked, and I got to my room without being caught, sinking thankfully into my bed. The next morning the alarm clock shrieked into my fuzzy head, but I found I was unable to move. The pain in my back was excruciating. It was only then that I realized I had injured myself in the car crash. All I could think was that the pain had been numbed by alcohol the night before. Somehow, I don't remember how, I got to the sanatorium, where I stayed in a great deal of pain for a week. Jennifer visited and brought me a plant – a gloxinia – to cheer me up, but was not at all sympathetic.

'No wonder, Chris,' she said, 'going to all these parties, out till all hours. And with a doctor . . .'

Jennifer had never had much respect for doctors, who were usually treated as demigods by all the nursing staff. If she did not agree with them, she said so. As I lay there, I started to feel that the accident was all my fault. We were running late, and I had given Mike the wrong address, after all, which was why we went the wrong way in the first place. I felt awful about it.

Nursing Alone

After the car crash I was put onto light duties. No more heavy lifting for me. I found myself on Outpatients at the Royal Berkshire, where the atmosphere was very different from the wards, with their strict discipline and little to smile about. It was really quite a relief. All the staff on Outpatients, a mixed bunch, seemed to laugh a lot and play jokes, perhaps as most of the seriously ill patients went down to the Battle Hospital.

I was in Outpatients when a huge young man, with the most enormous penis I have ever seen – before or since – exposed and pointing to the sky, was wheeled in on a trolley. I was told to take him into the side ward, and stay with him. I was also told that it was very important to watch his 'thing' and note any changes. So I watched, and waited, and waited . . . flushing with embarrassment, and trying to appear normal. It was not normal, however, trying to hold a sympathetic conversation with a distraught young man in such a state in a solitary side ward. Time passed. I heard the door squeak and looked up. Through the gap I saw several heads, their owners hugging themselves with laughter. It was one of their jokes, and I had fallen for it! The poor man had a condition known as phimosis, where the foreskin is too tight to be pulled over the head of the penis, and needed urgent attention.

Next I was put on the Special Clinic – the clinic for venereal diseases, where the embarrassed patients crept in through a side door. There was no real cure for syphilis then, and gonorrhoea was rampant in Reading. After every clinic, I was convinced I had caught 'IT'. Then it was nights on the gynae ward, which I loved. The women were so stoic, and so gentle.

One night I was taken off to go to an emergency with the ambulance crew. We went at speed through the seedier parts of Reading, eventually reaching a derelict caravan park. A man waited outside one of the caravans with a torch, and the two crew and I piled in. Inside it was filthy, and smelt noxious. Under some rough blankets on the floor in the corner, a woman lay moaning. A huge television set took up most of the space at the far end, and the man proceeded to watch it. I had never seen such conditions. Could human beings really live like this? I went up to the woman and asked her a few relevant questions. The surprise came when she answered in a clear, cultivated upper-crust voice.

'I expect you are wondering how I got like this?'

'Of course not,' I lied, with no time to waste on speculation.

The poor woman was suffering an ectopic pregnancy, and needed emergency treatment. She was bleeding heavily and in great pain, and needed to get to hospital quickly. We somehow got her into the ambulance and into hospital where the operating theatre staff were waiting, and our lady of the night was saved. Yet for what? I could not help reflecting on the vicissitudes of life. How did this personable young woman come to this?

Jennifer in Big Trouble

Jennifer was in the last few months of training. She was impatient, and longing to get on with her life. She had passed all her State Registered Nurse exams with top marks, but still had to work for another three months in order to get her hospital accreditation and hospital badge, which she would need when working in other hospitals as a staff nurse or midwife.

Unfortunately she was put on the children's ward for these final few months, and found it very hard. The ward sister did not like Jennifer, and she did not like the ward sister. She also found very young children boring. She was concerned with what she was to do after finishing her training. She had not yet given up on her dream of marrying Nevill, even though he remained resolutely with his wife. The pain this caused her must have been immense. She needed to talk this over with him, something she spoke about with me and her friend Wendy.

After another distressing phone call from him, she arrived onto the ward late to find a particularly difficult child throwing her faeces around. Jennifer had cleaned up after this child many times before. It was a frequent occurrence, but this time she snapped. Furious, she gave the child a smack on the bottom, and was seen doing so by the appalled mother.

The child screamed, the mother screamed, and nurses came running to see what was causing all the commotion. Jennifer, utterly devastated, was frogmarched to Matron's office. Matron had no option other than to dismiss her on the spot.

I was in the nurses' home, on my way downstairs to go on duty, when I bumped into two girls I didn't much like coming towards me.

'You know your sister's been chucked out,' one of them said. They both dissolved into laughter. I stopped in my tracks.

'For smacking a baby,' the other one added.

Heart thumping, I turned and ran back up the stairs to Jennifer's room. The door was unlocked, the room cleared of belongings. She had gone. I raced along the corridor to my room to see if there was a note under the door from her. Nothing. I felt utterly helpless. Where was she? Had she really left without saying goodbye?

I could only imagine how difficult it was for Jennifer to be forced out in this way. She was an excellent nurse, top in everything she did. The consultants would pin up on the noticeboard her near-perfect exam papers as an example to the rest of us. To have to leave in such circumstances must have been dreadful. Without her hospital badge, it was unlikely she would be able to nurse again.

Once she had left the hospital I heard nothing from my sister, and had no idea where she was or what she was doing. There were no calls or letters, not even the briefest of messages scribbled on a postcard. It was as if she had vanished off the face of the earth. Weeks turned into months as I hoped for word from her.

I felt her absence with every passing day, and missed her terribly.

No News of Jennifer

The last three months of my training at the Royal Berkshire were spent in theatre, where I heard of Jennifer's notorious reaction to a particularly rude surgeon. In those days the consultants were always rude to everybody, and nurses in general did not dare to answer back. Jennifer was different. She apparently thanked this particular man not to speak to her in such a derogatory manner, dropped the surgical instruments back into their tray, and stalked out of the operating theatre, leaving him unable to complete his job. Chaos ensued, and another nurse had to step in. Everyone was stunned and it was still a talking point when I came to theatre. I had to admire her spirit and, although it wasn't my way, Jennifer's outspoken behaviour did get results. I doubt the surgeon she walked out on ever spoke to another nurse so rudely. He certainly never reported my sister. I couldn't say I wanted to be more like her, but I did admire her spirit, and understood why she found it impossible to keep her temper in check at times. My feeling was that at least some of her outbursts were a consequence of the frustrations surrounding her relationship with Nevill, which was never what she wanted it to be. Wanting someone she could not have must have been an enormous pressure.

As I approached the end of my training, a decision had

to be made – whether I would stay on working in Reading as a staff nurse, or do my midwifery training in London. As I thought about both, I knew in my heart that neither really appealed. I had hoped that over the years of training I would come to feel that nursing was right for me, but it didn't happen. Meanwhile Mike had asked me many times to marry him, and the chance to create a stable, loving family of my own was impossible to resist. I loved this man but was not in love with him; at the time I believed sincerely that this would be enough. We were comfortable with each other, sharing our thoughts and ideas and hospital repartee. So, the next time the subject came up, I said yes.

PART 3

Knowing in Part

Jennifer with my mother at my wedding to Mike.

Aston Tirrold Manor, 1968.

Wedding Day

Mike took me to the most expensive jewellery shop in Reading and bought me an enormous emerald and diamond engagement ring. It was too large to wear on my hand, so at work I had to put it on a chain around my neck. My father was pleased about my impending nuptials. He liked Mike a lot, and thought he was going places. Mike was ambitious, an extremely capable doctor, with an enormous sense of fun.

Jennifer was constantly on my mind. I wanted to talk to her, share my thoughts and ask her advice. If such big changes were taking place in my life, what was going on in hers? I had no idea, no way of finding out. I supposed she would be in touch when she was ready. I hoped so, anyway.

I had six months to plan the wedding, and I set about making arrangements. We were to be married in a Catholic service at Douai Abbey in Berkshire, where Mike had gone to school. My father had agreed to give me away, saying that I could leave from his house and he would pay for the reception. My mother was too involved with her husband to be interested, so I had to make all the arrangements myself while still working forty-four hours a week. The build-up to the wedding was awful: there was no one to help me do anything, and I'd never had to organize anything like this before. I was really sick of my mother, who offered no support. I did everything – went into Newbury, found the smartest hotel and booked the reception and organized invitations, which read: 'Mr Gordon Lee requests the pleasure of your company at the wedding of his daughter, Christine . . .' I did not see why Mother's name should appear. She was livid.

'I am your mother. I must be on the invitations.'

I had to get them all re-done, at considerable expense.

I was exhausted, and had no dress to wear only two weeks before the wedding. I felt rather frightened about trying on wedding dresses by myself, and the loneliness I experienced was crushing. Anyway, Mike took over and together we went to London, found our way to Liberty's where he chose my dress, a three-quarter-length white silk over a layer of pale blue, with a full skirt. I didn't much like it, to be honest, although I very much liked the shoes that went with it; elegant heels with a T-bar. I had asked Nancy to be my bridesmaid, and we also found a dress for her.

The evening before the wedding, Mike dropped me off and I crept into my father's house with my suitcase, my wedding dress over my arm. Judith did not speak, and my two little half-sisters sat in silence as usual. I was offered nothing to eat. I went up to the hated attic room, still unchanged and still without bed linen. I looked about me, feeling sick, and wept. My overwhelming feelings were of pain and loneliness. I felt I deserved better. It hurt dreadfully to be leaving for my wedding from THIS. I suddenly became aware of what weddings were meant to be about, the happiness that should have been in the air. I sat on the bed in the bare little room, and it struck me that I needed my mother. I needed my sister, too. Nobody was there for me. When my father arrived at around nine o'clock, I went down to greet him.

'All ready for the great day?' he said, his usual cheerful self, full of warmth.

I was far from ready, but muttered something half-hearted to indicate I was. Judith looked on, stony-faced.

It was not a very auspicious start, for when I awoke on the morning of February 14, 1959 I had developed flu, feeling utterly ghastly. I insisted that my father find a thermometer. I had a temperature of 104 degrees. I managed to get up and get dressed, but I felt like death. On the way to Douai Abbey I fought back the urge to be sick. My head was thumping.

'I can't do this,' I said. 'I'm just too ill.'

'It's too late now, dear,' was my father's response.

We continued on our journey. At the abbey, as I walked down the aisle on my father's arm, I could see the pleasure on his face. In front of me was Mike, grinning broadly. He had come off duty, changed into a smart City suit and dashed to the abbey. All around were the smiling faces of my friends and family.

Then I saw Jennifer, tall and elegant, smiling above the rest.

It was the first time I had set eyes on her in more than a year, and the shock was so great that had I not been holding on to my father, I might have toppled over.

I have no memory of the ceremony. I must have said my vows, but the whole thing was a blank. I was so ill that all I could think about was not collapsing or, worse, being sick. Throughout, I was aware that in the pew next to my mother, a few yards away from where I stood at the altar, was my sister. I could not make sense of this. How did she know where I was, and where to come to for my wedding? Who had told her? Who had been in contact with her while I was left to wonder what had become of her?

At the reception, we barely spoke. And while I did what I could to hide the fact I was so ill, it must have been pretty obvious, as I had to keep disappearing to be sick. As the guests mingled I saw my sister, still seeming somehow set apart from everyone around her. It was such a shock seeing her like this after so long an absence, and mixed with my happiness that she had come was sadness that she had known about my wedding, and yet had not got in touch beforehand.

Jennifer had always favoured tailored suits that were elegant and at the same time quirky. She was twenty-three and pretty, with a wonderful figure and fantastic legs. A photograph from that day shows Jennifer, conservatively turned out in a fitted suit, towering in her heels over Mother, who wore a smart coat with a little mink collar and, for once, a restrained hat.

It was my mother Jennifer had been in touch with, of course, and she had kept news of my sister's whereabouts secret from me. Why she did this, I have no idea. Jennifer later told me that she assumed our mother had put me in the picture. I could not shake the feeling that for years, aside from rare, fleeting moments, my sister had been lost to me – ever since she had become involved with Nevill.

From the scraps of information I gleaned, I worked out that Jennifer had been too traumatized on the day she departed the Royal Berkshire to say goodbye to Wendy or to me. She had packed her things and left as quickly as she could. Nevill came to collect her and took her for dinner that night to discuss what she might do. It was agreed that a spell in Paris would be suitable, and an advert was placed in *Le Figaro* for nurse/au pair work. Nevill, a fluent French speaker, must have taken charge of this, as Jennifer certainly had no command of the French language then.

While arrangements were being made she went to Blackpool and took a waitressing job, and then departed for Paris. She loved the city, the lively cafes, the people, the buildings, and the art – all so different from the subdued atmosphere of Amersham or Reading – and she wanted to stay there forever. But Nevill, the man she loved, was not there, and so she was eventually drawn back to England. Paris proved an enchanting interlude.

It transpired that Jennifer had returned from Paris to England some time before my wedding, applied to train in midwifery in London, and been accepted. Her only problem was that she had no hospital badge. The absence of this would undoubtedly have been noticed, and questions asked. The answer lay with Wendy, who no longer needed her badge, and was only too willing to lend it to her friend. Jennifer could then start her training as a midwife. For the last six months she had been only a few miles from where I was in Reading, doing the first part of her midwifery training at a London hospital, and had not come near. On reflection, I have to consider that she had always been the most important person in my life and when she left Reading she knew she had let me down, so probably felt ashamed.

A Doctor's Wife

After our wedding, Mike and I drove to Devon on honeymoon. Halfway there he had to stop the car so that I could
be sick. We arrived in Salcombe at the Marine Hotel, and
went in to dinner. I had not eaten a thing all day but, wanting to please him, tried to get something down, and ended
up having to run from the restaurant. I did not quite make it
back to the room, and was sick again in the corridor. Mike
was furious with me for making a scene. Inside our room, he
rounded on me.

'How dare you let me down like this?'

My stomach churned again. I waited for him to reassure
me, but he kept quiet. I looked at him and thought, I don't
like you, Mike. It was not the best of beginnings.

Mike was twenty-eight, and vastly experienced. I was
twenty-one and pretty innocent, particularly as far as sex
was concerned, and rather dreaded that side of the arrangement. Mike thought that he would remedy this by giving me
a book called *Ideal Marriage: Its Physiology and Technique*,
by Theodoor Hendrik Van de Velde, as an early twenty-
first birthday present. I read it avidly during the two weeks
before our wedding.

I hated it, especially the diagrams and the vivid descrip-
tions. I hated the very thought of it all, but still I thought we

would be very happy together. We had a sweet flat opposite the hospital, and I marvelled at having my own home for the first time in my life. But for me, sex was hell. The car crash had left me with excruciating lower back pain a great deal of the time. My new husband must have been very disillusioned with me. He was convinced the pain I complained of was all in my mind.

After a while, I began to believe him.

Jennifer was still in London in 1959, and had chosen to spend the next six months in what she thought was a small private hospital in the East End to undertake the second part of her midwifery training. Arriving in Poplar on her first day, she had no idea she was in fact knocking on the door of a convent, not a hospital – nor that the Anglican Nursing Sisters of St John the Divine would have such a profound and lasting impact on her life. She told me later she was shocked to find she was entering a religious establishment. At that point she thought of herself as agnostic, and was not convinced she would fit in. She had no choice, however, but to proceed as planned since, having no home to fall back on, she needed a roof over her head, and the convent had very comfortable quarters for the nurses.

Jennifer was as surprised as anyone when she fell so completely under the influence of the Sisters of St John the Divine that she gave serious consideration to joining the Order. While working with the nuns, she learned to respect the power of prayer and was drawn by the tranquillity that seemed to emanate from the sisters. In the end, though, the life of a nun was not for her.

'I could do poverty and chastity, Chris, but never, *ever* obedience!' she said.

She could not join the order, but she found she could not forget all it stood for, either.

Not long after our wedding, Mike had to begin studying for his Fellowship at the Royal College of Surgeons in London. It was a full-time course with no salary. My father came up with the answer. He was now living at Sonamarg alone. In the summer of 1959, Judith had left with her two young daughters for a new life in Scotland, to be near to her mother. I suspect that what prompted this was the realization that Daddy was having an affair with his racing friend Pam.

The beautiful place was now more or less empty, yet my father seemed completely happy. We could live in one of his derelict barns rent-free, he said, and Mike could commute to London. I was a bit doubtful. The barn was filthy dirty, with broken windows and covered in cobwebs, but needs must. We borrowed a van and took our few possessions over to this place of dereliction, with me quite prepared to do a massive cleaning job.

Father was not there to greet us, but undaunted, we opened the stable door to our new home. What greeted us was not the filthy barn we had previously seen, but a freshly painted, completely transformed space with white walls and sugar-pink ceilings. My father had done this for us! In the main sitting room he had even cleaned up the ancient stove, which was gleaming and black. Amazing!

We lived there happily for many months. How we used that stove: Mike bringing in wood, me cooking delicious meals on it. Mike studied and commuted, and I took on a staff nurse post at Amersham Hospital. It felt good to be supporting my husband in this way, and the fact that we had little money was of no consequence. In the evening we would compare our days over dinner and I would test Mike on all he had learned that day.

I remember little about Amersham Hospital then, apart from one day when I was on theatre. There was a storm brewing, and we had a woman on the operating table undergoing a hysterectomy. Suddenly there was a crash of thunder, followed by sheets of lightning, and all the lights went out. Panic ensued. The surgeon was barely halfway through the operation. The anaesthetist raced to his car, placing it so that it beamed directly into the operating theatre windows with full headlights blazing, but the surgeon was still unable to see into the cavity and yelled for us to collect any lights we could find – and fast. The bicycle park was nearby. So it was, I found myself pointing a bicycle lamp into the abdominal hole while the surgeon calmly finished the operation. There was no emergency lighting then, yet our patient fully recovered, totally unaware of the drama involved in her operation.

Mike passed his FRCS and was taken on as a surgical registrar in Plymouth towards the end of 1959 – so we had to leave our lovely sanctuary, my father and friends, and move to a hospital flat that was situated near the main hospital entrance. It was noisy and ugly.

I was having a difficult time, as I had become pregnant and was experiencing severe back pain. Mike was running out of patience with me. He gave me another book, *Childbirth without Fear*. Jennifer was by now a qualified midwife and must have attended numerous births. By contrast, my knowledge was poor. I had seen pictures in textbooks, and that was about the extent of it. I had not even been to antenatal classes, which were not then universally available. Perhaps Jennifer felt it was better not to interfere – certainly there was nothing forthcoming from her on giving birth, or how I might prepare, and it was difficult to reach her as she was working all hours.

On July 23, 1960, Joanna was born in Freedom Fields Hospital, Plymouth. The state of my back made the actual delivery excruciating, but once my baby arrived the pain I had experienced was pushed aside. Mike was operating and I was on my own. I remember waking up in a side ward, a privilege then for doctors' wives, with the smell of flowers permeating through the room. The sun was shining and all was peaceful. I held the baby in my arms and wondered at this new little life; what was in store for her? I could see so much of her father in her. She even had his double crown. I cradled her, not knowing that the problems with my back were going to make it almost impossible to pick her up.

Mike came in to see us, as jovial as ever, with absolutely no comprehension of the ordeal I had been through. I wanted to show him our baby, I wanted to share it all with him – but he had other more important things to deal with, and left, scarcely looking at his new daughter. I felt so alone, lying in bed with a strange little creature in my arms. I longed for my mother. And where was my sister? No one seemed to care about me or my baby.

Then, amazingly, my sister was walking through the door towards me. She had made the journey from the other side of London to Plymouth to see me. I was so very touched. I had not seen her since my wedding the previous year, and although we had kept in contact through phone calls, there was still so much to say. But what was that under her coat? Laughing, she pulled out my dog, Bertie, and dropped him

Grandma Lee,
my father's mother.

My other grandma, Eliza Gibbs,
as a pretty young woman.

Grandma and Grandpa Gibbs in their garden.
I took this photograph when I was nine.

Our mother, Elsie Louise Gibbs.   Our father, Gordon Lee.

With my big sister Jennifer in 1939.

LEFT: At Clacton-on-Sea, where Jennifer and I spent so many happy times, in 1943.

BELOW: Jennifer in 1947.

LEFT: Myself in an advert for Pears soap in 1947 – wearing Jennifer's dress.

RIGHT: With Jennifer and her beloved dog Bryn in 1951.

LEFT: This was taken in 1957 when I was a trainee nurse in Reading.

ABOVE: Myself and Jennifer at a hospital dance in 1959, drinking tea!

LEFT: Mike and me on our wedding day, 1959.

My father Gordon at Silverstone in a C-Type Jaguar, 1962.

Jennifer and Philip's wedding in 1962.
My parents are on the right and Joanna is her bridesmaid.

ABOVE LEFT: Jennifer
with her daughters
Suzannah and Juliette in
West Bexington, 1965.

ABOVE: Simon and
I married in 1966.

LEFT: My mother
with Joanna and
baby Louise, 1967.

With Dan and Louise at Aston Tirrold in 1971.

Frankie, Pat, myself and Jennifer in 1994. The portrait on the wall is Nevill Harrow.

Being presented
to HM the Queen in
Stratford-upon-Avon
in 1996.

The Swans
of Avon.

on the bed, where he squirmed with happiness at seeing me, yapping loudly.

Almost at once, the door to my lovely side ward was thrown open and the consultant gynaecologist appeared, red-faced and furious. He must have followed Jennifer, curious to see what she was smuggling in with her. How Jennifer thought she was going to get away with sneaking a squirming poodle onto a ward full of hawk-eyed staff was beyond me.

'Get that dog out of my hospital!' the consultant shouted, and turned on his heel.

Jennifer grabbed Bertie and ran. Open-mouthed, I watched her hurry away, the little dog still yapping with excitement. Sadly, she had not managed to see my baby, and we had not exchanged a single word. Oh, Jennifer, I thought. Later, I found out that Jennifer had been in touch with Mike to arrange her surprise visit, that he had left keys out for her so she could let herself into our flat before coming in to see me. She had obviously thought that I would love to see my sweet little dog.

Within half an hour of her coming in, I was on a trolley and ignominiously transferred to the centre of a huge and noisy maternity ward!

A few weeks after the birth, Father arrived unheralded in Plymouth. It was wonderful to see him, but I felt a mess and was up to my elbows in soap suds, struggling to deal with buckets of dirty nappies – one hell of a job. We had no such thing as disposables then. Father helped me hang the nappies on the washing line and sat with me, having a cup of tea, his new granddaughter happy on his lap. I ached when he left. I really wanted to spend more time with him. A week later, a new Hoover twin tub washing machine arrived. I felt overwhelmed that my father would think of sending this to me. Nappy washing thereafter became a joy.

My mother had not been to see us and it was not until Christmas 1960, five months later, that Mike and I travelled up to Amersham to show off our new addition. Mother adored her for about five minutes and then we had to leave, as her husband was expected home.

Mike's next job was as an orthopaedic registrar in Kingston-upon-Thames. We packed up and left Plymouth in 1961, exchanging our rather sedate doctor's car for a wonderful new red MGA sports car. At this point my father helped us to buy our first house in East Molesey, in Surrey, about a mile from Hampton Court Palace. It was a pleasant 1930s detached property, with gardens front and back. Mike constructed an amazing kitchen, and we bought our first fridge. All so exciting. As Mike worked on the kitchen, I painted walls, while music enveloped the house.

While living in East Molesey, I became Night Sister at Weybridge Hospital. I was the only trained staff on duty all night, with no resident doctors. There were, of course, assistant nurses, but all the responsibility of the hospital for twelve hours a night rested with me. On reflection, it was a mammoth task. Doctors on call did not like to be called – as often as not they said, 'Deal with it, Sister,' so I did.

I had a men's ward, a women's ward and a children's ward with weekly tonsillectomies. Then there was a private wing where serious surgical procedures had been carried out – and, of course, there was Outpatients to deal with. I became rather good at sewing up cuts after the occasional brawl or minor accident. But the night of the tonsil operations was horrendous, as bleeding was a real concern and the children needed so much attention. This added to the general settling of the other wards, and doing a medicine round to be checked and double-checked by another nurse. It was all a bit of a nightmare, but I always came off duty elated by doing this mammoth job well. I really began to understand Jennifer's joy in nursing.

But one night, six months into the job, was not so joyful.

The hospital was as busy as usual – no tonsillectomies, thank God, and we seemed to be getting on rather well. I moved into the private patients' corridor to deal with any problems there and settle them for the night. There had been two major operations that day, so there were two blood drips to watch, injections to give, wounds to examine and catheters to watch. The minor operations having been made comfortable and given sedatives for the night, all seemed well.

Then one of the major operations from the private wing began ringing his bell frantically. He was in real pain, and needed sedation. At the same time, the Outpatient door was ringing and I needed to go there. Added to this, half the men's ward suddenly seemed to be awake and needing help. I simply raced through the private wing, looking for the patient who had rung. When I got to the last ward, I saw that the blood drip had congealed. I was horrified. I knew that this poor man had lost a great deal of blood during the operation, and the blood from the drip was essential for him.

I rushed to the medicine cupboard, took down the anti-coagulating agent and injected it directly into the tube where the blood was congealed. I watched with relief as it cleared and the blood began to flow freely again. I returned to the medicine cupboard to put the anti-coagulant away only to see that in my rush I had picked up the wrong container. I was horrified. What had I done? It may have cleared the blood clots, but what effect would it have on my patient? I sat down, feeling sick, saliva engorging my mouth. What was I to do? It dawned on me. Of course, Jennifer was an experienced ward sister, she would know. I rang her up. Jennifer was not at all nonplussed.

'Well, he'll either die or he won't,' she said matter-of-factly.

'This is all?' I said.

'Yes,' she said, adding, 'And say nothing.' And she put the phone down.

I crept back to my patient. I spent most of the night with the man, who experienced severe rigors, shaking and perspiring at intervals. All my previous nursing experience came into play as I gave him fluids and by turn, ice packs and warm blankets, encouraging him through this ghastly night. He seemed peaceful when I left, so I omitted to tell the full story in my report and I limped home, almost certain that I had killed him. The next night I dragged myself into the hospital, having barely slept, and took over from the day staff. My patient was not mentioned. Was he dead? I immediately went to his room. I had to know what had happened. There he was, sitting up in bed, surrounded by visitors telling them about his ordeal the previous night. When he saw me, he introduced me as the best nurse ever – the wonderful person who had saved him in the night. They looked at me with admiration. I felt a worm! We were always chronically understaffed at night, but guilt persisted for a long, long time.

Father also helped Jennifer to buy her first house, in Hampstead Garden Suburb in north London. In 1961 she was working as a ward sister at the Queen Mary maternity home, near Hampstead, and, as she was not terribly well off, to help make ends meet, she took in a lodger. Philip Worth was an academic in an unchallenging job in an insurance office, which he hated.

We didn't see much of Jennifer, since Mike was busy at the hospital, and the episode with the poodle on the maternity ward had definitely coloured his perception of her. 'Nutty as a fruit cake' was how he rather bluntly summed her up. Once she had settled into her new home, though, she invited us over – and for the first and the only time that I can remember, Jennifer, who hated cooking, actually made a meal for us. I remember it well, as it was so very delicious: veal, with cream and mushrooms and spinach, followed by an elaborate pudding. I had never known my sister eat meat, and yet that night she had exactly the same as we did, and seemed to thoroughly enjoy it.

Philip was invited to join us. As soon as he spoke, his Scottish accent brought back memories of Jock, which I found difficult; but unlike Jock, he had a gentle humour and a keen interest in the economy. Philip was sandy-haired, a pipe-smoker, dressed in an old Fair Isle tank top and a tweed jacket.

Jennifer took great pleasure in showing us her house, a charming period cottage in lovely surroundings. It was a delightful evening, and I felt as if it represented something of a breakthrough. For the first time, Mike had seen the lovely side of my sister, and he softened in his attitude towards her. I was thrilled and Jennifer was very, very happy to have a home of her own at last.

Back in his new job, Mike was growing in stature as an orthopaedic registrar, a middle-ranking surgeon. Meanwhile, I was walking around in constant pain from my back and, as a consequence, was struggling to bond with my daughter.

I could not even pick up a teapot, let alone my little girl, and was deeply sad and frustrated about my limitations. I longed to show my little girl all the love I felt, but there was so much I was unable to do; small, everyday things most mothers would take for granted, like scooping up their child for a cuddle when she was distressed. My little girl had to climb up onto my knee by herself. We had to have an au pair, lovely Gratzilla.

Mike – poor Mike – had to forget any expectations of sex, but since he was incredibly busy at the hospital and exhausted most of the time, he was not at home much. I felt pretty lonely, but East Molesey was a lovely place to live, and the house and garden were a delight. And, of course, living near Hampton Court and walking through the magnificent grounds was a real privilege.

A Surgical Solution

Although I was in and out of hospital with my chronic back pain, nothing showed up, not on X-ray, so they tried traction – agony! They tried manipulation – more agony! There were horrific corsets with metal strips, and plaster of Paris supports. In one contraption my torso was encased in a plaster cast that became so loose, I could turn it round completely. Nothing helped.

I lost a great deal of weight. I was living on pills, trying to disguise my pain from my very busy and now irritable husband, who was fed up and repeatedly told me it was all in my mind. I believed him. After all, he was a much respected surgeon. I prayed to God, but no relief came. In the evening, just before Mike was due home, I would take a triple dose of codeine so he didn't see how bad I was. At work, he was surrounded by people who thought him wonderful. At home, he had a damaged wife. It can't have been much fun for him.

Then a new state-of-the-art piece of equipment arrived at Kingston Hospital: a tomograph, an X-ray machine that took photographs on an arc throughout the body. I went for a scan, and the results shocked everyone. I was walking around with my fifth lumbar vertebrae floating, the two side bones completely severed. I was so relieved by this diagnosis.

At last I knew that my constant back pain was not all in my mind. Suddenly I was taken seriously, but still I had no idea just how serious it was. Immediately I was transferred to Surbiton Hospital, where a complete plaster bed was made. The following day, Douglas Freebody, the consultant surgeon, performed an elaborate new operation. He opened up my abdomen and attacked the anterior part of my spine from in front. The crest of the hip was then fashioned to fit onto the fractured vertebrae. The operation took many hours, and many pints (units) of blood.

I was returned to the ward, placed in the plaster bed, a blood drip continued, suction put in place, and a junior special nurse left to look after me all night. I was told before the op that I would have to spend at least two months in this plaster contraption and must not move at all during this time, or the fusion would break down.

I came to in the middle of the night, feeling horribly sick. The young, untrained special nurse looked at me, terrified. I knew that I must *not* be sick. I had in situ a gastric tube, which ran from my stomach into a container nearby. I saw that it was clamped off, so no wonder I was feeling sick. Somehow I attracted the girl's attention, and indicated the tube. Thank God I had trained as a nurse. This young 'special' had no idea what to do, so without moving, I had to show her how to unclamp it. The next time I woke the nurse was half dozing in a chair nearby. Poor girl, I thought. Then, looking up at my blood drip, I saw that it was empty! This could cause an aneurysm, and death. I knew it, and again I somehow got the nurse to wake up.

'Look for Sister,' I whispered. 'The bottle needs changing.'

She ran. Sister arrived, reconnecting more blood, and I went to sleep, thanking God once again for my training.

The months I spent in hospital were both a blessing and a curse. The plaster cast encased my entire body and was hung up onto an overhead beam. It was cut in half, lengthways, so I was always lying in half a shell of my own body, unable to move at all. The really nasty bit was when the nurses had to fix the top half to the bottom, and flip me over. This had to happen every three hours, day and night, to prevent bedsores, and every three hours I held my breath and prayed that I would not fall through the gap in the middle. But the nursing was brilliant and I soon became 'hospitalized', enjoying the attention and a side ward full of flowers. I read copiously, starting with Boris Pasternak's *Doctor Zhivago*, and then on to the work of other Russian authors. My big achievement was learning to eat boiled eggs while lying flat on my back! My big 'nasty' was having to use an adapted bedpan, which always seemed to leak into my plaster.

My father arrived with a new girlfriend one day, but I just wanted him to myself for half an hour, and afterwards I felt bad that I was rather off with him. What happened to my little daughter during all this? The two grandmothers took it in turns to look after her, two weeks in Bexhill followed by two weeks in Amersham. I did worry in the beginning about her being in the house with Jock, but Mike reassured me she was fine. Joanna loved spending time with her grandmother, and Jock was uninterested in her, as she was very young and usually in bed before he got home. Mike's only time off duty was spent travelling to or from Bexhill to Amersham, with no time in which to relax. This lasted for about three months.

When I was told that I could go home, I was horrified to find that even moving from the plaster bed to a chair was impossible without a great deal of help. I had lost weight and was so terribly weak that I could not stand. The pain from the bone graft in my left hip was excruciating. I was not going to be paralysed (hurrah!), but felt that a shadow was cast over me. I could not pick up my daughter for months yet, and she still had to climb up onto my knees by herself for a cuddle. We were both exhausted by it all.

Mike was seldom around, and when he was, the last thing he wanted was his sick wife. He was working back at St Thomas's Hospital, where he had trained as a senior house surgeon, as a senior registrar, the last stepping stone before becoming a consultant. He was admired and respected by all the hospital staff, who were only too glad to do his bidding. But when Mike returned home to his sickly wife it was a different matter – no fun for him at all. I understood his frustration, and yet my ill health was not my fault. My problems with my back all stemmed from the car crash some four years earlier.

It was when I made a huge effort to dress and prepare for the first doctors' party in months that I realized something was seriously wrong with our relationship. I had been so looking forward to going out, our first party together for so long. I dosed up on codeine, put on a smart cocktail dress, did my hair, and risked a pair of heels. I got out of the car, pulled myself upright, and painfully followed Mike towards the hospital steps. Words, violent and disgusted, spewed from his lips.

'For God's sake, stop limping – what will people think I've got with me!'

Shocked and humiliated, I followed him. Once inside, he placed me on a stool near the bar and left me alone nursing a gin and 'It' while he spent the rest of the evening dancing and canoodling with one of the more attractive nurses.

I could not move without help and sat, transfixed, as the whole charade was played out before me. I absorbed the fact I was redundant. What to do? I could stay and suffer the humiliation, or leave Mike. In the 1960s, however, it was not an easy thing to contemplate divorce, and I had a small child to consider. Inside, I was churned up and sad, but I couldn't talk to Mike about it. He was working so hard, typically more than a hundred hours a week, and on his days off, much of the time he slept.

At Christmas 1961, my father came to visit and brought a gigantic panda for Joanna. We named him Peter Porter Panda, and she adored him for many years. I was so pleased to see my father. Regardless of what had happened during our childhood, I felt no antagonism towards him – only a huge amount of love, always. It had been an easy matter for me to forgive him for breaking things apart. Not so for Jennifer, though, whose anger towards him never abated.

Six months after that dreadful party I had been to with Mike, I was at a crossroads. I prayed for help – guidance of any kind – but none came. I was on my own. Finally, I left him, driving off with my young, vulnerable daughter beside me, my dog, Bertie, and a small suitcase in the back. I took nothing else, leaving Mike a note to find on his return.

I had no plan, no idea where to go. Somehow the car headed to Amersham. It was three in the afternoon when we reached my mother's house. It had been a long drive, and Joanna and I were both exhausted. Mother was not pleased to see us.

'No, you can't stay here, it's not possible,' she said.

I was staggered. Could my mother really turn us away like this? Yes, she could, and did. Her husband was due back home, and that was all that mattered to her. In less than five minutes, without having had so much as a cup of tea or a chance to use the loo, Joanna and I were packed off back into the car. It took us to my father's place. Having sold the main house, he was now living in the converted stables at Sonamarg, surrounded by the gardens he loved, and was surprised yet happy to see us.

He had only the one bedroom, with another room which had been untouched since the builders had left. It was turned four o'clock. He gave us tea, and agreed to look after Joanna as I raced into Amersham, where I bought two deckchair loungers. Gordon had spare blankets and so, on returning, I made up our beds in the derelict room, put Joanna to bed, and sat down with my father to recover. My father never probed about why I had left Mike, and all I said was that things had been difficult and I had been unable to stay.

Mike arrived during our second week there, to collect his car. He had brought with him a few of my most treasured possessions, including a clock that had been a wedding present, and I was grateful.

'Chris, come back,' he said.

I shook my head. Nothing he could say would make me return. We sat on the step, the two of us, and he wept. It was a shock to see my strong husband in tears, and I felt for him. It was too late for me, though. He knew I would never go back. He had hurt me too much. We did not have to go into the painful details.

'I can't. I'm sorry,' I said.

I had no idea what I was going to do, and was shocked by the enormity of my own actions. Leaving my ambitious husband for the unknown had not been in my plan. I had been brought up on *Mrs Dale's Diary*, where life was comfortable and middle class and scandal free; then again, I had witnessed the misery bad marriages had brought to both of my parents. Nothing would persuade me to do as my mother had and stay in an unhappy union.

My father left me alone with my thoughts, which was exactly what I needed, and I began to recover. He did not make things easy for me, however – in the hope, I suspect, that I would eventually go back to Mike.

At Sonamarg we were about two miles from the nearest shops, which were down the hill in Little Missenden. Once Mike had collected his car I had no means of transport, and Daddy refused to loan me his. I had to walk down the hill with Joanna in the pushchair, do the shopping, and heave everything back up. On more than one occasion my father drove past, gave a toot and a wave, and kept going. I was so cross.

'Why didn't you stop?' I said when I finally made it home, exhausted. 'You could see me struggling with the shopping.'

He laughed. 'Oh, sorry, darling, I thought you wanted the exercise.'

I knew what his motives were, and they weren't going to work. I would not return to Mike.

Joanna and I stayed with my father for three months. I was grateful for his company, always loving and generous, forever seeing the humorous side of life. He never, ever criticized or lectured, and wanted everyone around him to enjoy life. As a consequence, our life with him was comfortable and peaceful.

Ronnie

Early one evening in the late spring of 1962, as I was sitting with Joanna playing on the floor, there was a knock on the door. My father answered, returning to the room with an unexpected guest. To my absolute amazement, the guest was a man I had seen only once before. His name was Ronnie Seddon.

Months earlier at a party, while living in East Molesey, I had looked across a crowded room and seen Ronnie. I did not even know his name then, and yet felt a stab of instant recognition. What I noticed was his wide, open smile, the warmth in his brown eyes. I judged he was older than my father but it didn't matter in the least. My heart lurched.

We were not introduced, which was just as well, as simply being in the same room as him rendered me quite incapable of speech. He seemed similarly afflicted. We stared at one another. If it was possible to fall in love at first sight then this had to be how it felt. I was overwhelmed by the strength of my feelings, utterly knocked sideways, but I was a married woman with a baby and had responsibilities. I turned away, swallowed hard, and left the party, cursing my fate.

I had not seen him since. How had he found his way to Sonamarg, and why? Breathless, we exchanged a few awkward words. I could not compose myself and, shaking, left the room to put Joanna to bed, while he chatted amiably to my father. This man, whom I had instantly loved but then obliterated from my mind, had found me. He left, to return the next day.

'We must find you a flat,' Ronnie said, as if it was the most natural thing in the world, and we went looking for one in Bourne End, leaving Joanna happily playing with my father.

We went to see a place in The Riversdale and it was lovely, just right – part of a very large old house that had been converted, with views facing onto a lawn that swept down to the river. I moved in with Joanna almost immediately. Ronnie had left his wife, Lucia, some months before, and was living in London. Thus began a time of extreme happiness. Ronnie and I were so utterly attuned to each other. Sex was really wonderful and I delighted in not being frigid any more. Amazingly, my back improved.

Ronnie was perfect; sensitive, good-looking, and caring. He was also creative and the owner of a successful business, making toys. We went to all the smart places around, driving in his rather lovely Bentley, and I became a kept woman and loved it. I was back on good terms with my mother, since I was never able to stay angry with her for long, and she or my father would babysit so that Ronnie and I could spend time together. We had idyllic weekends at the sumptuous Lygon Arms in the Cotswolds; he took me shopping and delighted in buying me beautiful clothes, and was utterly sweet with my little daughter. I had found the person I would spend the rest of my life with. For six months, life was the best it had ever been. I told myself that nothing could put an end to our happiness.

Cruelly, something did.

Ronnie had a son with autism, whom he loved dearly, and every day he would leave early to take him to school, an arrangement that was very special to both of them. One day when he arrived to take his son to school he found him distraught. Although Ronnie had not left his marriage for me, and had been separated for many months before coming to find me, once Lucia found out about us she became very upset. Each time Ronnie went home there were scenes, awful things said in front of his son. After we returned from a weekend away, he turned to me for help.

'I just don't know what to do,' he said.

For a moment neither of us spoke. Then I found myself uttering the words, 'You have to go back, you have to stay with her. I cannot be responsible for all this.'

It was agony. I loved this man. I wanted him more than life itself. How could I say this? Perhaps if I had been more mature, I would have said it seemed to me that Lucia was using emotional blackmail and that it would be wrong to give in; but it simply did not occur to me. Moments later, Ronnie turned and left, got into his car and drove away.

That was the last time I saw him.

I don't know how I survived. I wanted to die. I went to see a doctor friend and told him how distressed I was and he prescribed me the sleeping pill Soneryl. I came away with 100 tablets, enough to kill myself two or three times over. At home, I put Joanna to bed, went into the bathroom with the pills and started to take them. I have no idea what brought me to my senses, but I was suddenly aware of my beautiful daughter in the room next door. Tears ran down my cheeks. I tipped the pills into the lavatory and went into my child's bedroom. She was asleep, utterly peaceful. I could not believe I had considered leaving her.

For the next several months I acted a part, going through the motions, being a good mother, spending time with Joanna, and only at the end of the day, once I had put her to bed, allowing myself to feel the pain and the emptiness of being without Ronnie. I wrote down memories not to be forgotten, and wept, and looked into the distance to a future of I knew not what.

Later, much later, a letter arrived from Ronnie describing his loneliness within his family. I could not reply. The loneliness I felt could not be put down on paper. I simply could not find the words.

With great clarity, I understood my sister as never before. She had also had to accept the loss of the love of her life, and now I was doing the same. It was agonizing, and it seemed fitting that Jennifer came to my rescue.

She phoned to ask me to stay with her and I jumped at the chance, thinking it would be good for both Joanna and me to be somewhere else. I arrived at my sister's pretty cottage in Hampstead Garden Suburb with my little daughter in a pushchair and a small suitcase. Jennifer was happy and working in one of the London hospitals full-time. Philip was still there, although whether he and Jennifer were involved or it was still purely a lodger arrangement, I really could not say. Jennifer was incredibly kind. She was always wonderful when it came to caring for people in distress and had only to look at me, pale and thin and raw, to know how much I needed her. I had lost the man I loved more than life, and Jennifer, of all people, could identify with that.

I had missed my sister dreadfully, and now it seemed I had her back. The pleasure this gave me was indescribable. If I think back and try to put my finger on what exactly she did that was so restorative, it's a struggle to explain. She made no fuss of me. There was no mollycoddling, no smothering with sympathy. No cups of tea in bed. That was most definitely not her style. Her gift to me was simply to be there and allow me the time and space to heal.

Jennifer had never bothered much about cleaning, so while she was out working I would sort out her home and fill it with flowers. There was little to eat in the house, so I found my way to some shops around the corner and enjoyed the repartee of the shopkeepers – and Jennifer and Philip's appreciation of my cooking. I stayed for weeks, and she and I managed to fill in some of the gaps in our relationship – and there were big gaps.

Never one to pull her punches, Jennifer told me she thought that by marrying Mike I had behaved ridiculously. 'You were far too young. It was just so foolish,' she said, in her customary blunt fashion.

I could not argue with her; but in my defence, I had not been able to ask her opinion prior to the marriage, as she had vanished from my life. Whatever happened, I did not want to lose her again.

'You have a little girl now, and you must look after her,' she said. 'You have to decide what you're going to do.'

'Once the house in East Molesey is sold I'll have some money.'

Jennifer had an idea. 'Give it some thought. Start a business. Something creative.'

It was so good for me to be in a place where painful memories could begin to recede. My sister and I shared at least some of our secrets during this precious time. I learned a little about Nevill, the depth of her feelings for him. The ring he had given her, an opal, was one of her most treasured possessions. She continued to wear it throughout her life.

When autumn came and I felt ready to leave, I decided to make a really splendid casserole and apple pie as a farewell dinner. In the shops, everyone was happy and gay and when I entered the butcher's the staff and customers were all kissing each other. In no time at all, I too was included. It was lovely, but I could not work it out. Over the meal, which was very much appreciated, I told my sister of the experiences of my day and what had happened in the butcher's.

'Everybody was so lovely,' I said. 'It was almost as if I had walked into a great party.'

'Where did you shop?' she asked. When I told her, she hooted with laughter.

'Darling, how can you be so naïve? It's the Jewish New Year and you have been shopping in kosher shops.'

I felt so ignorant. I had never even heard of a kosher shop, and I was supposed to be a sophisticated, not-yet-divorced woman of twenty-four. I had no idea that the Jewish people prepared their meat differently from Christians.

Jennifer had said I should start a business of my own, and it was something I thought about. I had enough capital to do something; but what? I returned to Bourne End pondering my future. I had a little daughter. It was not just myself I had to consider – what was best for her came into the equation. I needed to be there for her, and I wanted her to live in the countryside where I felt at peace, so I rented a shop in Maidenhead.

The shop, with workroom above, was quite small, wedge-shaped, like a cheese, and the rent was not too exorbitant. I went to Harrods and Liberty's and bought up swathes of beautiful materials, and I hired Ros, a Dior-trained dressmaker. We set to work designing unique pieces – cocktail dresses, suits and evening wear – the kind of clothes I would have liked to wear myself, but could never find in shops in Buckinghamshire or Berkshire.

Ros and I worked feverishly for six weeks and in that time the shop was transformed, and many exquisite pieces were ready on the rails. It felt good. The garments flew out of the shop, and we could not keep up with demand, so Julie put in an appearance – tall, slim, good-looking, an exceptional salesperson – leaving me time to buy in more clothes and help Ros finish off the unique handmade garments. It was hectic, but I have always enjoyed a challenge, and this was certainly one.

Jennifer and our mother came over to see me and the shop, and had great fun trying on numerous garments. Mother left with two two-piece suits in jersey, and Jennifer was carrying a bag with a lovely dress that our mother had bought for her. It was a rare and happy occasion involving all three of us.

Jennifer

At the age of twenty-seven, Jennifer very much wanted a husband and children. This was something she had spoken to me about. In some respects Philip was similar to Nevill. Philip was learned, intellectually able. He had studied the classics and seemed a supportive addition to her life. She found that she had grown very fond of him, although not in the way she had loved before.

She was able to pinpoint the precise moment when she first considered that she might marry Philip. Having bought tickets to the opera, she invited him to go with her. Dressed for the occasion in a long evening gown and jewellery, she waited for Philip on the landing of the staircase at the Royal Opera House in Covent Garden. When he came rushing in, late, and saw her at the top of the stairs, she knew at once from the look on his face that he considered her to be quite marvellous. It was just what she wanted. Although not in love with Philip, she cared about him, and was practical enough to recognize that this was a good reason to consider him a possible husband.

During the months when I had stayed with Jennifer at her home in Hampstead Garden Suburb, it was clear she was still deeply in love with Nevill and believed they would one day be married. Before very much longer, however, she was forced to accept that he would never leave his wife for her. She saw the man she loved and adored for their final meeting, and the pain was intolerable. I learned of this from my mother, to whom Jennifer had gone afterwards, utterly inconsolable.

'Nevill the Devil has broken your sister's heart,' Mother told me.

Jennifer returned home to Philip, and later that same night she agreed to be his wife. I only found this out months later, when I asked what had made her decide to marry Philip. She admitted she would never love anyone as she loved Nevill, but had come to accept her life as it was then, with the help of her relationship with God.

They were married on April 4, 1963, at St Jude-on-the-Hill, Hampstead. Our father gave her away, and Joanna was her only bridesmaid. Mother was wearing a hat like a huge meringue, and I was there very much on my own. The reception was in Jennifer's sweet cottage, and there was lots of champagne to drink.

Jennifer looked very beautiful in a full-length, straight satin dress that she had designed herself, with a bright pink panel at the front and a full lace mantilla. It was very unusual at the time, she made a striking and modern bride. She was surrounded by friends that day, and seemed almost deliriously happy. She had married a really good friend, and was looking forward to being a wife and mother.

At that time she sent me the copy of 'Ode to a Nightingale' that Nevill had given her. It was a poem she completely related to and a gift from the man she would never forget, and who most influenced her life. I'm not sure why she wanted me to have it, or why it was not subjected to the same fate as his letters, which she mostly destroyed. Perhaps she no longer wanted to keep it but was unable to let go of it altogether, and so consigned it to what she knew would be a safe pair of hands. I still have it.

In 1964 Jennifer had a daughter, Suzannah. Jennifer took pregnancy and childbirth in her stride; after all, she was an experienced midwife, and giving birth held no mystery for her. She loved Suzannah deeply and was determined to give her own children the stability that she had lacked. Sadly, she had to move from her adored cottage in Hampstead Garden Suburb when Philip, who had been working in an insurance office, applied for a job as a schoolmaster. Jennifer so wanted him to emulate Nevill Harrow. She told me rather proudly that he had been offered two positions, one at a rather smart public school and the other as a junior master at a large comprehensive near Hemel Hempstead. Jennifer, always more interested in helping people who had the least, decided the comprehensive school was to be the one. With Philip's degrees in Classics and Law, the school was lucky – but not so Jennifer.

They moved to a house near the school at Bennetts End, an estate that had been built in the 1950s as part of the new town and comprised mostly council housing. I sensed that Jennifer did not want me to see the new house, and when I visited, I found her on an estate with houses jammed together and gardens with no flowers. It was difficult for her as it was such a big change from her home in Hampstead Garden Suburb.

Jennifer had experienced real poverty before, of course, when she was working in Poplar; but her job there as a mid-wife had conferred a certain status and respect. In Poplar she was not dwelling in the tenements but in the comparative comfort of the convent, and so she remained to some extent apart. It was different at Bennetts End. She was not the midwife. She wore outlandish clothes: see-through kaftans, full-length velvet coats, long gloves, theatrical gowns and jackets – at a time when miniskirts and hot pants were popular. She had a splendid grand piano filling the living room on the ground floor and sang, loudly and long, playing the piano at every opportunity. Classical music, her favourite – certainly not pop music or jazz. The neighbours complained.

It was clear to me that life on the estate was less than ideal.

'I'm lonely, you know,' she said, when I went to see her. 'They're not like me here. There's nothing wrong with Bennetts End; I just don't fit in.'

It was during this stay that I became aware of the significance of the time she had spent at the convent in Poplar. Although she had only been there a few months, the impact on her had been profound: she had, it seemed, experienced a kind of religious epiphany and emerged with an unshakeable faith in God. To my great shock, she told me that the nuns were now her family, and God her father. The sisters now came first, before me and our parents.

I was completely taken aback. I think I said something about this being ridiculous – that you can't just decide to replace your family. Jennifer was determined, however, and from then on it was as if she became withdrawn and kept her real family at a distance. It was so painful.

Whenever I tried to get her to say more, she clammed up. As was always the case, she had said as much as she was prepared to and the subject was then closed.

Deeply influenced by the nuns of Poplar, my sister began to dissociate herself in many ways from the real world. Not for her the ambitions and excitement of others her own age. She read the Bible daily and went on long religious retreats. She would be obedient to God's word only. The rules of man, any man, were of no significance to her.

Although I can relate to this way of thinking, I myself am not as extreme. I do believe in God the Almighty, the Higher Power, and I do believe in forgiveness for all, whatever our faith. We are all products of our family background and up-bringing and the people we meet on our journey through life. Jennifer and I were similar in many ways, having shared a hateful childhood, but our lives were by now going in very different directions. We were both escaping from our past traumas and trying to find meaning in life.

In 1966 Jennifer had a second daughter, Juliette, to whom I became godmother. Jennifer remained very much in her own world, without friends in the neighbourhood. She was working part-time as a night sister in a local hospital and could seldom afford to go to the opera or the theatre, which was her love. As the children got older, they played happily underneath the piano while she practised. She was completely unaware of the neighbours, nothing was going to stop her music or singing. Meanwhile, Philip was content to work in his study upstairs.

A New Start

For many months after Ronnie left I had felt numb, a broken reed. I managed as best I could and somehow took care of my daughter, but I was acting the whole time. Few people knew what had been going on, or how I really felt.

At around that time my neighbours, who were renting for the summer the main house in Bourne End where I had my flat, were extremely kind to me. Joanna and I were invited to join them on boat trips and picnics. I remember going with them and feeling set apart from everyone else, so ravaged by the loss of Ronnie that I was almost unable to breathe.

Time passed. In the evenings, once I had put Joanna to bed, I would sit at the table looking out over the lawn towards the river – sometimes weeping, sometimes not. One night I was vaguely aware of a figure meandering across the open space in front of me. The door to the house was open and the first I knew of the presence of someone inside was when I felt an arm across my shoulders. It was one of my neighbour's sons, Simon, who I had met on the various family outings I had been on. His presence was comforting, and my weeping abated. Only then did I turn and look at him.

'You look as if you need a change of scene,' he said. 'Let me take you out for a meal, or something.'

'I can't. I have no babysitter,' I said.

He left, returning within minutes. 'My stepmother will babysit, so come on.'

Against my will, I allowed myself to be led to a tiny Morris 1000 by a man who seemed to me to be so very young, I was almost embarrassed to go out with him. Ronnie had been two years older than my father, and I was accustomed to being with older men.

Simon and I arrived at the Old Bell in Hurley, a wonderful, stylish hotel, and I was surprised at how accomplished he was at dealing with waiters, ordering drinks, and generally giving me a really enjoyable evening. He was *so* young, or so I thought. Later, I discovered he was twenty-six, a week older than me. He had an interesting-sounding job with the Copper Development Council, and he loved horses.

He came down from London night after night, and his stepmother continued to babysit, and slowly I recovered from the appalling trauma of losing Ronnie. I began to enjoy this new person in my life. He was tall, graceful and very good-looking, in a Dirk Bogarde sort of way. He was also sensitive and kind; everything I needed at that time. He took me horse racing, a new experience for me. He took me out in London to nightclubs, and we mingled with his interesting and elegant friends. He took me to Spain to stay with his equally elegant mother, and I loved it.

Eventually he asked me to marry him, and I agreed – but with some misgivings, as he was so different from my father and from other men I'd previously known. Simon was more European and debonair in his outlook. He once described me as parochial. His Aunty Mabel – the first lady Master of the Surrey Union Hunt, and an extremely astute woman when it came to both horseflesh and people – told me she thought I would be very good for Simon, but was not at all sure he was right for me. Anyway, we got engaged and were thrilled. Sim (my pet name for him) bought me a magnificent engagement ring of sapphires, rubies and diamonds. I loved it. My mother said it looked like a bowl of fruit salad.

Two years passed, and a deep friendship developed. Simon and I moved into a rambling cottage in Cookham Dean. Joanna began nursery school, and loved coming to the shop in Maidenhead. As time went on, family and friends began asking, 'When is the wedding?' With some hesitation, I agreed to the date of October 14, 1966.

A week beforehand, our two mothers met. Simon's well-travelled Mama was staying with us and as she dressed to meet my mother, arriving from Amersham in rural England, her thinking turned out to be somewhat misguided. She changed out of her elegant clothes into tweed trousers and an olive green twin-set, which did not suit her at all. My mother arrived straight from the hairdresser's, looking immaculate in a fine silk suit that showed off her amazing figure and legs to die for. The two matriarchs eyed one another with suspicion. We had a difficult tea.

On walking back to her car my mother said, 'What an extremely silly woman!' Nothing more.

On walking back to the cottage, Simon's mother was very angry. 'Why did you not tell me that your mother was so beautiful?'

With that, she stalked away.

The wedding took place in London, at the registry office in Old Marylebone Town Hall, with a reception at the United Hunts Club. Joan, my future mother-in-law, had arranged it all, and of course it was elegant and charming; how different from my first wedding. Simon's brother, Jeremy, was his best man, and there were many of our friends there. However, my father did not come. I was so unhappy about this, concerned something had happened to him on the journey up to London, and phoned at the first opportunity to ask what had made him miss the ceremony.

'Oh, the cat got stuck up a tree,' he said.

I was baffled. 'What do you mean?'

He laughed. 'Just that, dear.'

I could not get any more out of him, and was so disappointed. Later he confessed that he thought my leaving Mike had been, as he put it, a tragedy. He had liked Mike enormously, and I suppose he did not appreciate why I had ended the marriage. I had never gone into any detail about what went wrong between us. When it came to my second marriage, my father simply found it impossible to celebrate with me. Jennifer probably felt the same, for she did not come either. At the time she made an excuse, but she told my mother – who then told me – that she disapproved of my being divorced and marrying for a second time. As for my mother, she was too put out by Joan's arrangements to put in an appearance. At least we were spared another of her hats, and it was a good day, nevertheless.

The honeymoon was in Paris, where we stayed in the Place Vendôme at the Hotel Vendôme, an old and truly beautiful hotel. We wandered around Paris by day and went to the Crazy Horse Saloon until the early hours every night, becoming exhausted by too much pink champagne and extensive nightlife. It was not my idea of a romantic honeymoon, but I loved Simon, and went along with it all. Eight and a half months later, on June 25, 1967, my daughter Louise was born at The Shrubbery, a maternity hospital in High Wycombe. This time my husband was with me for the birth. It was really important to me – although on seeing the afterbirth he fainted outright, and had to be carried away to recover from his ordeal.

It was so good to be with Simon in our new home with our new baby and Joanna, who was by now seven years old. Simon loved pushing Louise in her coach-built pram throughout the countryside, lifting pram with baby and himself over five-bar gates, while I cooked. We developed the garden together and I also made a Wendy House for Joanna which was very special. We'd moved to an old cottage in Aston Rowant, which reminded me of my roots in Old Amersham. I'd given up the shop just before I married Simon, so now I had time to enjoy the whole business of making a silk purse out of a sow's ear. I loved the plastering and painting of walls. I put up shelves and designed the garden, chose carpets and made curtains. It was a revelation. In no time at all this sorry-looking cottage appeared twice the size, and very beautiful.

The cottage had four very small bedrooms, the spare being not much bigger than a box. Nevertheless, Simon's elderly cousin Dorothy was determined to come down to stay with us. Simon collected her from her mansion in Walton Street, Knightsbridge, London, while I looked doubtfully at the spare room with its small double bed pushed against the wall in the corner. I was rather horrified when I saw her unpacking her beautiful clothes from an equally beautiful suitcase, and later saw her walk along the landing in pale pink silk slippers with a housecoat to match. She looked so out of place in our cramped cottage with minimal furniture.

Simon's mother was from a wealthy old English family, and as she had lived abroad most of her life she had sent

Simon to board at Lancing, a public school. She saw him only in the summer holidays, and it was up to her relations to care for him during the rest of the year. Cousin Dorothy was one of them, Aunty Mabel another. Dorothy loved Simon, and we had a delightful weekend.

While she had enjoyed her stay with us, she said that the house was too small and that we should buy somewhere bigger – and soon. As she left in a taxi, having told Simon to go to her house and choose some decent furniture – anything he liked, a present, of course – I walked into the dining room, where, on the table, Dorothy had left an envelope with my name on it. How polite of her, I thought, to leave a thank-you note. On opening the envelope, I was completely astounded. She had left a cheque for £5,000 with instructions to buy a bigger house.

In 1967, we put our home on the market. We had been there for less than a year, yet it had doubled in value. All our hard work had paid off. So with Dorothy's present, we now had £13,500 in the bank to buy something big, as she had instructed. I set about looking for suitable – in other words, big – houses. There were many on the market at that time, and I became friendly with an estate agent who kept me informed about what was available. Simon was working in London all week and riding out with his friend, the race-horse trainer Toby Balding, on Saturdays, and sometimes going racing in the afternoons, so Sunday was his only free day. He therefore left it to me to find our new home.

One week, my friendly agent, Tom Linacre of Nicholls in Reading, tried to put me off our usual viewings as he had to go to an auction of one of the great houses in the area.

'Can I come with you?' I said.

'Yes, of course,' was his reply.

He sent me a brochure for the property in the post. Simon and I looked at the details for Aston Tirrold Manor and were overwhelmed by its magnificence: a tennis court, swimming pool, ten acres (four of them cultivated), nine main bedrooms, five bathrooms, stables, outhouses, all in excellent order. It was a perfect Georgian manor house, and certainly out of our league, but I just had to go.

On the day of the auction I wore my utterly lovely red French jersey coat (a present from Ronnie), added the ruby and diamond earrings that Simon had given me that Christmas, and put on a pair of high heels. On setting out to meet Tom in my old Ford car, I wondered why I was wearing such opulence. We went to the auction, which had attracted hundreds of people, and sat at the back. Amazingly, the stunning manor house did not reach its reserve. Tom, ever hopeful, scuttled off to find out why.

'Would you like that house?' he said when he returned.

'Of course,' I replied, blithely.

'What would you pay for it?' he asked.

I was blunt. 'I've only £13,500.'

Tom returned to his friends at the front of the room. At length, he came back.

'It's yours!' he announced. 'Follow me. All you have to do is to sign and write out a cheque for the deposit.'

Overwhelmed, yet somewhat concerned that the unbelievable was happening, I followed Tom, passing through the throng of people, who all seemed to be looking in my direction. At the front, I found myself signing the auctioneer's particulars and giving him a cheque for the deposit to seal the deal. I was really in a state of shock.

There had been no time to talk to Simon. What would he say?

I left Tom, who was delighted at the outcome, and staggered back to my car. I was shaking so much I could hardly drive home, and the car was going all over the place. I had no food in for dinner, it was late, and Simon was due home in half an hour. I fed the girls, put them to bed, saw the babysitter, booked a table for dinner at our favourite restaurant, and waited. What had I done?

Simon arrived, happily asking about my day. 'Did you go to the auction, then?'

'Yes,' I said meekly.

'How much did it go for?'

'£13,500.'

'What a shame, what a bloody damn shame! Do you know who it went to?'

'Yes,' I said.

'Who?' Simon waited.

I took a deep breath. 'You.'

He looked at me, aghast, as my news sank in.

'You fool! You crazy bloody fool! What are we to do?'

'I've booked a table for dinner,' I replied.

From the look on his face, he was beginning to suspect I had gone utterly insane.

Silently, and both somewhat shocked, we drove to the restaurant. As we ate and drank, the reality of what I had done sank in, and we began to laugh . . . and laughed some more. We began to really like the idea of moving into this utterly beautiful manor house. Cousin Dorothy had said that we needed a big house, and this was certainly big. We had taken her at her word, and Aston Tirrold Manor, a perfect Georgian gem in Berkshire, was ours.

Four days later, Tom Linacre rang to say we had been offered £10,000 more to sell the house on. This time, Simon and I made the joint decision to turn the offer down. We had both grown rather pleased to be moving into such a beautiful place – and to hell with all the doubters in this world!

Aston Tirrold

We drove away from our sweet cottage with Domie, our au pair, in the back of the car with the children, and the cat on her lap. The rather small furniture van followed. Simon and I were in a serious mood. We were certainly moving into the unknown. Joanna looked pensive, Louise was crying, and the cat peed on Domie's lap.

Tom was waiting for us at the front door with the keys. It was good to see an encouraging, familiar face. We opened up and stepped into the hallway of our new home. The house echoed and felt so, so big – but it was also so, so beautiful. I was overwhelmed by the beauty and proportions of the place. There were lovely old wooden floors, a wide oak staircase that curved around to the rooms above. The sitting room had not one but two Adam fireplaces, with enchanting Delft tiles. There were windows at either end and, along the far wall, three more, all with views out over the gardens.

The grounds were exquisite. The swimming pool had espaliered limes all the way round; there were vast greenhouses, a huge kitchen garden and a tennis court. Any doubts Simon or I may have had about my impulsive purchase melted away. I gazed at our new surroundings and I felt as if I had properly come home. It was about the same size as my old school, Wycombe Court.

All our furniture fitted into the hall alone. Then Dorothy's furniture arrived, and later, some amazing Persian rugs. An old friend, Micky, wanted somewhere to store his period furniture while away for an indefinite period, so we fitted that in too, and I set to making thirty full-length fully-lined silk curtains. Joan, my mother-in-law, paid for all the materials. Within a month, the house was furnished and really ours.

I was twenty-nine when we moved to Aston Tirrold Manor in 1967. There I had to learn, and quickly, how to run a very large house (I could never decide quite how many rooms there were). My mother was still under the influence of her controlling husband, and was of little help, but my father came over a great deal. He produced a particularly huge tyre from a lorry and made a sandpit for the children, and found an equally huge old tricycle and painted it sky blue. Both became firm favourites. Father soon got into the habit of paying unscheduled visits, and I would arrive back from somewhere or other to find him sitting in his car waiting for me. It was always a delight to see him, and the children adored him. I was truly happy.

Father was always an enterprising man, and had built up a considerable transport business during the war, but after the war had ended the company was taken over and nationalized by the government. He was not too pleased, but being the character he was, quickly moved on and purchased a run-down timber mill. He had been transporting huge quantities of timber during the war and after, so he knew a bit about it. Hyde End Timber became his new project, along with motor racing – he loved them both. With his enormous energy he, and they, flourished. But it was not too long before he received an offer he could not refuse, and sold the now large and successful business. He was only forty-seven.

One day he arrived unexpectedly, bringing my half-sister Frankie with him. I had not seen her for many years, not since Judith had left and moved to Scotland with both girls in 1959. Father had no need to explain who this young girl was; she was a carbon copy of her mother. The same sparse frame, the same voice and tinkling laugh. Very pretty. Seeing her brought back into sharp focus the horrors of being at Sonamarg as a child. Frankie had failed her exams and refused to go back to her mother, and so Daddy had arranged for her to stay with him and go to a crammer nearby before retaking her exams. I came to love Frankie, but each time I saw her I had the same reaction, remembering her mother. She had the same effect on Jennifer, who struggled to overcome the sense of antipathy Frankie's appearance invariably triggered in her. However, Frankie did visit Jennifer in Bennetts End, and she babysat a lot so that Jennifer was free to go out. Our other half-sister, Pat, also came back into our lives a little later when she was in her twenties, and over time, Jennifer became very close to her.

At Aston Tirrold we found we had inherited an aged gardener, Mr Wheeler, who had worked there all his life. He looked after the majority of the garden, coming in every day without fail – and, without fail, delivering a huge basket of vegetables every Friday. He told me that there had formerly been seven gardeners at the Manor – and how he missed those days. He was certainly a bit lonely, so I made time for him, and taught the children to respect *his* garden. He had been in the habit of growing new potatoes in the greenhouse and ensuring they were ready for the house at Easter, and he continued to do so for us. We found, too, that we had inherited a hard-working 'daily' – or rather, a three-times-a-weekly. And of course Domie was there, to help out with the children.

The Manor was particularly beautiful, and I loved the gardens, the stream and ponds with their fantastic plants. Who could see a giant gunnera and not be impressed? The artist in me sang.

I was aware, however, that it was difficult for Jennifer to come to terms with Aston Tirrold Manor. The contrast between our circumstances had never been more pronounced. I knew how she felt about living at Bennetts End, and chose my words carefully when I spoke to her about the new house, tempering the excitement I felt. I also knew her views on wealth and possessions. She did not feel that anyone should have so much, and found the very idea of Aston Tirrold excessive. When she came to visit, we walked around the gardens and I picked flowers for her. She would not take them.

'What would I want with flowers?' she said, definitely sounding sniffy. 'If I take them home I'll only have to find pots for them, and worse, once they're dead I'll have to take them out again.'

We remained in touch by phone, both, I suspect, aware that something of a chasm had opened up between us. Knowing she was unhappy at Bennetts End, I felt unable to share the good fortune I felt. We tiptoed around one another, and made small talk. At a time in my life when I was at my happiest, our conversations were about the weather, gardening and polite enquiries about each other's families. Jennifer's concerns lay with the lot of the poor and underprivileged. She was focused on the tragedies of life to the exclusion of all else.

Yet she desperately wanted a 'substantial' home of her

own. She needed somewhere she could play her music without antagonizing the neighbours; she needed space in which to breathe. I understood. It was exactly how I had felt. Both of us had grown up being made to feel unwelcome at home, and Jennifer had certainly been abandoned by our parents. We each of us needed a good foundation to call home, almost as proof that nothing we had been through mattered. We wanted to show we had survived, that we were as good as anyone. I think that was also why we both had a taste for large, ostentatious rings. Jennifer had two or three, including a huge opal with diamonds that was a real rock.

A Privileged Life

Simon and I enjoyed our lives in Aston Tirrold. We were very good friends and loved each other. But he worked all week in London, leaving at five in the morning to avoid the traffic, and not returning until about seven in the evening, which meant he got pretty tired. Still, we enjoyed the evenings together once the children were in bed. Simon also left at five on Saturdays to ride out for Toby Balding, and then went off with him racing, arriving home about eight in the evening or later. I sometimes joined him, but always felt sidelined at both the Baldings' and on the racetrack. All these friends were totally involved with the intricacies of horse racing, breeding and betting. I loved the visual aspects, but had little or no knowledge of the sport. I could talk about motor racing forever, but no one was interested. I am sure they thought me very tedious, and I could not keep up with the hard drinkers.

One night at the Baldings' the celebrated chef Clement Freud was cooking about five courses, finishing the meal with a wonderful cheese soufflé. Each course had its accompanying wine, and I attempted to keep up with the others, but when I tried to stand up at the end of the meal I found I could only stagger. Feeling unwell, I lurched through the open French doors into the garden.

'It's all right, just be sick,' came a firm command.

I felt so ashamed, bringing up all the delicious food and wine I had consumed. 'That's better,' the voice said. I felt an arm around my shoulder, and looked up to see Clement Freud smiling at me. His wonderful, half-digested food lay on the grass, but he couldn't have cared less, and he walked me round the garden until I felt better.

We had a great number of guests then. People loved to come down from London for weekends in the country, and my father would come over to offer good advice and generally join in the fun. Financially, everything was fine, as Simon had left the Copper Development Council and become a stockbroker earning a great deal of money. The one horror was when we got our first electricity bill, after our first winter. It was for more than £2,000, an enormous sum in 1968! Surely it had to be a mistake? I arranged for a heating engineer to investigate. Two of them spent an entire morning on the job, before reporting back to me that everything was in order but perhaps I should consider turning off the heating to the swimming pool in the winter. I was appalled. It had been my decision to take over the running of the swimming pool, since I was the practical one. I felt very ashamed, and waited uncomfortably to admit my inadequacy to my husband. After dinner, I admitted the painful truth. Dear Simon just looked at pathetic me and laughed, and then we both laughed and laughed. I had wondered why the swimming pool had not frozen over in the winter months.

My old Ford had become impossibly unreliable, and one great joy was when I was given a new Ford Capri when they first came out. It was a gift from Nick Bolton, a good friend from London and the son of George Bolton, the then Governor of the Bank of England. A comparable joy for Simon was when he bought a racehorse, and had it in training with Toby Balding. It was fun to own a racehorse, but I am a doer, not a watcher, and this was brought home to me as I led our horse into the winner's enclosure at Ascot and felt nothing despite friends jostling about, congratulating me. I remember thinking how much I would prefer to be at home, doing something with the children or taking the dogs out. Sadly, the horse broke down after only moderate success. It was always ridden by Bob Champion, later a Grand National winning jockey, whom I liked a lot. He was one of the few in the racing fraternity to talk to me as a person. At that time, the racing fraternity did not much value him either.

Aston Tirrold was a remarkable village, with many fine houses. Frank Cundell was training racehorses; William Piggot-Brown was entertaining his many lovelies. Dave Dick, a Grand National-winning jockey, was married to Caroline, an inspired eventer. Then there were Michael Tain, a talented painter; Alison, his wife; David and Tessa Penny; and many more. I was particularly pleased when I was asked to join the Parish Council. Simon and I were wonderfully happy, and our life seemed idyllic in many ways.

Two years in, I became pregnant again. My back absolutely hated the added burden of a growing baby inside me, giving me hell once more, but Simon helped me as much as possible. He was always kind if I was suffering and in pain, and I was grateful. This time I had to have a Caesarean section. Having done his bit with the birth of Louise, Simon felt he was not needed, and went racing.

Daniel was born on March 21, 1970, at two in the afternoon at the John Radcliffe Hospital in Oxford. Simon arrived after it was all over with the children, Joanna and Louise, a huge bunch of flowers, and champagne. They all took turns holding the baby, and I wept with happiness. But a Caesarean was a significant operation, and it took several weeks before I felt back to normal. I was told what to expect, so I had organized the house and the children beforehand, with a monthly nurse arriving for the new baby when I returned home.

On my return, I found that the nurse had gone, having fallen out with the au pair. I was still bleeding quite heavily, and had been told that I must have complete bed rest until it stopped. My back, which always caused me pain to some degree, was also bad, and yet again I was unable to lift my new baby; there really was a problem. My friend Alison Tain stepped in and quickly organized another nurse, who duly arrived the next day. She was old and severe, and had no intention of helping out with the other children or indeed me. She took over the baby and forbade Joanna or Louise admittance to the nursery. I remained in bed, comforting two very unhappy children. A knock at my bedroom door a little later, and the nurse entered.

'When do we dine?' she said.

'We don't,' I replied. 'There is plenty of food in the kitchen, and you are welcome to any of it.'

She left, slamming the door behind her. Domie, the au pair, put the children to bed, and I think I got a glass of milk for supper.

The next morning all was quiet, and I wanted to see my baby, so I crept along the landing and opened the nursery door. I was met by the vision of the nurse leaning over the Moses basket, smoking a cigarette. The air was overladen with smoke, and ash had fallen onto my newborn baby. I was furious. The nurse was insolent. She left in haste. I picked up my baby and struggled with him back to bed, shaking. There was no one to help me, as Simon was away working. The situation was bad. I never thought of phoning my mother, since Jock was still on the scene – or indeed Jennifer, who was working and had her own small children to take care of.

I realized that I did not want a monthly nurse – I needed someone to help me with all my children, so I rang up Norland Nannies. Liz arrived in perfect Norland Nanny uniform, complete with badge. She was fantastic, organizing all the children and me, and I was able to recover from my Caesarean in peace. Our home became a delight. Liz stayed for two years, until she left to get married. A trained Norland Nanny is second to none. She was a wonderful addition to our family.

Daniel was the first grandson to be born to either side of our families, and everyone was overjoyed. I arranged a splendid christening party, which lasted for two days. There were sixty friends and relations, most staying in the house. Daniel wore an ancient family christening gown from Simon's family. Simon's mother, Joan, was there, as was my mother, in one of her ghastly hats, a crocheted confection the colour and texture of a large sponge cake. They were never going to be friends, but Joan did adore my father, flirting with him outrageously, and of course he loved it.

The sun shone, and all was perfect. Dan's godfathers were Nick Bolton and Toby Balding, and an old nursing friend of mine, Jean Crawford, was godmother. Later, everyone changed into evening dress and a four-piece band played. The huge central hall became alive with dancing, and the champagne flowed. Looking at my friends and family, eating and having such a wonderful time, I felt deeply happy.

Jennifer did not come to the christening, feeling, as ever, that my lifestyle was too opulent. She had various ways of expressing her displeasure; she might simply raise herself to her full height and give me an imperious look, or deliver a withering, 'Really?' when I told her what I was doing. That single word spoke volumes.

Any kind of friction between us always bothered me. I wanted her approval. If I was happy, I wanted her to share in my delight. It was not to be. I was working hard at being a good wife and mother, but all Jennifer saw was privilege and wealth – too much of it. Our lives were so different that we had difficulty relating to one another, which made me sad. I'm sure she felt the same.

Her life was a struggle, and she was under stress. She was living in Bennetts End, only fifty miles away but a world apart, working terribly hard. She had two little girls to look after, and in contrast to her spoilt sister, had no help. Philip was absorbed in his job and while Jennifer, still nursing, enjoyed her job too, she was constantly worried about money. Always full of energy, she decided to set up a knitting business with outworkers, and even bought a knitting machine. She had to make more money somehow, but my poor impractical sister never came to grips with it and eventually had to close it all down, not having made a penny.

Jennifer was always fond of Joanna, and invited her to stay. The first night she was there Joanna, who must have been nine or ten at the time, phoned me in tears, terribly homesick. I did my best to cheer her up and hoped she would feel better after a night's sleep. The next morning, she was in the same tearful state, adamant she wanted to come home.

Jennifer had to put her on the train. Apparently my sister, who never cooked much and survived mainly on bread and cheese, had produced chipolata sausages for tea and, much to Joanna's dismay, asked: 'Would you like one, or half of one?' Joanna loved her food and was not used to such frugal provisions, and had no wish to stay.

From a very young age Jennifer's children, Suzannah and Juliette, also came to visit us. Suzannah suffered from asthma and was very shy, finding it difficult to join in. Juliette was bright and bubbly, and fell into our household as if it was the most natural thing in the world. Each time Jennifer brought them or came to collect them in her battered minivan, the two of us would spend time in the garden and talk about things of no importance. I kept my concerns from my sister, taking care not to say anything likely to bring forth a sniffy, 'Really?'

All this time, I was surrounded by so much beauty in my life that I did not consider doing much artwork. I was simply grateful for everything that was given to me – all so very different from the rigours of my childhood. I loved Simon, I loved my children, and I loved the world I lived in. I felt so secure.

Change

In 1972, my life changed suddenly and shockingly. Simon, who specialized in mines and metals, had been away in Australia for three months, inspecting the mines in which he was investing our money as well as my father's. Our main investment was in Poseidon shares, and on paper we were worth millions. It was so exciting to watch them going up every day – until, without warning, the bubble burst. Poor Simon, stuck in Australia, found it impossible to contact the stock market to sell our holdings. It took him three days to get home, and in that time our investments became worthless.

We had to sell our beautiful home to raise capital, and I found myself on the road looking for somewhere new to live – this time, something much smaller. It was painful. I loved Aston Tirrold Manor. I knew, however, that we had been excessively fortunate to live there at all. So I pulled myself together and looked around the villages nearby to see what they were like, and whether we would like to live there. One had a beautiful village green and church with an exquisite Queen Anne house beside it. It was utterly charming, and I must have been looking at it for some time when a tall elderly man came up to me.

'It's so lovely,' I said. 'I'm having to sell the beautiful house I love – it's so hard.'

'Come in, my dear, and meet my wife. Have a cup of tea with us,' he said.

The sun was shining, and we sat in the garden listening to the birds and smelling the scents of summer.

'We are getting old now, and have decided that we must sell our house too.'

I empathized.

'Would you like it?' he asked.

I was flabbergasted. Of course I would – but we had only a limited amount of money, and I thought it unlikely we could afford it. I left my number with them (sadly I can't remember their names), as I liked them enormously, but I expected to hear no more. That evening, the phone rang.

'My wife would like you to have our house,' he said. 'What can you afford?'

I told him, and we agreed there and then. Six weeks later we were moving into our new house, with enough money in the bank for Simon to start his own business.

This lovely house in Stanford-in-the-Vale was ours, and we all loved it – a perfect Queen Anne house with gardens, outbuildings and stable block. There were nine bedrooms, a wonderful staircase with barley-sugar uprights and an oak-panelled dining room.

At around this time I fell ill with flu and had what I thought of as a 'leaving life' experience. Simon was out, and I was in bed feeling dreadful. The doctor came and prescribed anti-biotics, but I could not get to the chemist for them. Simon was late home and by then I was in a terrible state, quite delirious. I could not even speak.

I watched myself from above the bed and became aware

of being drawn along a passage with a bright golden light at the end and wonderful music surrounding me. I did not want to come back, but was suddenly dragged by our doctor and my husband from my bed and lowered into a tepid bath. It was excruciatingly painful, as if I was being thrown into broken glass, but it worked, and I am still here. This more than anything convinced me that on our death we return to a better place.

Jennifer, with her frequent appalling asthma attacks, was always interested in the next world. As a child, she had spoken about something of what she went through during a bad attack, saying she felt so bad she thought she would die, but I had not quite been able to grasp her meaning. Now I understood.

I was concerned that Simon and I were living very separate lives. His life was work in London during the week, and horse racing at weekends; mine was my home, my children, and my friends. I had met a Dutch girl, Wilhemien, on the school run. She was creative and fun, and I liked her a lot. As I returned her children one day, I watched her attempting to make a portrait head in modelling clay of her daughter, and I was fascinated. She said she would make one for me of Dan when she got back from her holiday, but I could not wait. Impatient and intrigued, I bought some Newclay and proceeded to try my hand at it. The result was a really delightful portrait of my son. I was thrilled, and could not stop. I made the dogs, the horses and crib figures, and the children joined in too.

Soon, all I wanted to do in my spare time was create three-dimensional figures. I later made a sculpture of long dogs for the Lambourne Lurcher Show, and was asked to present the Championship Trophy. This was followed by a local horse trainer, John Bosely, asking me to make a model of his favourite racehorse. I spent many hours at his stables, protected only by straw bales, working on drawings and all the time expecting to be kicked or trampled upon by this huge and excitable beast. I was making sculpture for the first time in my life, but needed more. I had heard about Hydie Seton Lloyd, a respected sculptor from the nearby village of Uffington, and went to her studio unannounced one day on the off chance she would see me. She was not welcoming.

'Go home and bring back some of your work for me to look at,' she said fiercely.

The next day, with my small offerings, I arrived. I tentatively placed them on a table and waited. I waited a long time.

'You are a sculptor,' she said, imperiously. 'Come tomorrow and we'll set up a work bench for you.'

So I started working with this fascinating woman in her beautiful studio and was greatly influenced by her talent and her ethics. I left only when offered a place at St Martin's.

'You have a gift – you don't need to go there,' was her reaction to my news, but I did go. I wanted to be recognized as a proper sculptor, and felt I needed proper training.

In 1973, I sadly concluded that my husband had been seeing other women. I was utterly traumatized. I felt numb. Our perfect idyll was broken. I felt redundant again.

Dan was three, Louise six and Joanna thirteen. I was in a quandary. I had left one husband, and did not want to leave another, but I felt cold and empty inside. I confronted Simon. His feelings for me had not changed, he said. He loved me – I was his wife. I think he hoped that our marriage could continue on the same basis but I was deeply hurt, allowing myself to feel the pain and weep in the garden alone. I stayed with him, as I did not want my children to suffer.

After several months, hurt and heartsick, I succumbed to the kindness of a friend and embarked on an affair. Allan Miller was powerfully built and hugely charismatic, with a wife and two children. His huge support made life possible. Simon seemed pleased; I think it relieved him in some way – I was not happy at his reaction.

In time, Allan and I became lovers; he had a beautiful custom-built racing yacht, which was moored at the marina on the Hamble. We spent many days roaring up and down on the A34 from Oxfordshire in his Aston Martin. We also spent a week at Cowes every year. Racing in a fast yacht is hugely exciting whatever the weather, and going back to Cowes Castle, the base of the Royal Yacht Squadron (where you would often glimpse Prince Philip), and reliving the races over drinks with convivial friends was very enjoyable. But there were risks: late one evening, when returning from the Cherbourg race, we went aground onto rocks. Panic ensued, the anchor was lowered and the sails brought down. Allan was shouting orders, and the storm that was brewing arrived fiercely. The boat was battered from side to side – we were lost. It seemed that the depth gauge was not functioning. No one had checked the batteries before leaving France. We had to stay where we were until dawn.

Lying on the floor of the boat, being flung from side to side in the storm, being sick, soaking wet and clinging onto something or other, I thought of my children and prayed. The wind howled and the waves raged. It was deafening, and the cracking of the boat on the rocks sounded extremely nasty. But with the arrival of dawn, the storm abated, and as the tide came in the boat was lifted in the water. At last we could see where we were; the anchor was raised, and somehow we sailed back to the Hamble, exhausted, shaking and very hungry.

The situation with Simon spending a great deal of time in London and me living in the country continued for many years, and I found myself falling in love with Allan – not something I wanted, or indeed had looked for. I felt torn in half; there was a certain frisson of excitement about all this, yet I hated the deception, and I hated the fact that Simon did not mind. I began to hate my husband and love him at the same time. I wanted to confide in Jennifer, to have her tell me what she thought in that blunt way of hers, and I tried to find an opportunity during one of her visits.

'How's Philip?' I said, as we strolled in the garden.

'Oh, wonderful.' She gave a beatific smile.

I wondered. I thought about the unhappy state of my own marriage. I stole a look at Jennifer. She seemed enveloped in thoughts of her own. I took a deep breath.

'We shall miss having our new potatoes at Easter,' I said, losing my nerve.

Jennifer gave me a curious look.

'At Aston Tirrold, wonderful Mr Wheeler took such pride in supplying the house with new potatoes every year, in time for Easter.' It came out sounding all wrong, as if I was showing off.

'Really?' Jennifer said, frowning.

'I'm sure he will do the same for the new owners . . .'

I juddered to a halt. Why was I talking about my old gardener when there were more important matters to discuss, when my life was unravelling? Jennifer seemed many miles from me, unreachable, and yet she was right there, so close I could have put a hand on her arm. It was as if an invisible force field of sorts shrouded her. In my heart, I knew I would tell her nothing of the reality of my circumstances and that she would say nothing, in turn, of hers. It was simply how things were between us. A moment or two passed, and then I asked if she would like some tea, and we went indoors.

Simon's business venture was not a success, and was eating up all our capital. It was obvious that drastic action was necessary. We had to sell our second lovely manor house to cover the debts, as well as the horses – all except Lou's pony. It was so painful. We had less money to buy another new home than we had started out with ten years before.

Thankfully, I found an unfinished barn with several acres, near Bampton, at a knock-down price. Again, I painted walls, made curtains and sorted out furniture, Simon worked on the garden at weekends, and we tried to rebuild our life. We still had the dogs and had inherited a feral cat, which lived in the barn before we arrived. As we were not too far from Stanford-in-the-Vale, we kept most of our friends and the children could continue to go to the same schools.

The house was in a beautiful position at the top of a hill, with far-reaching views, and we could see Lou's pony from the windows that overlooked the field. One day, on returning home from shopping, I found the pony settled in our newly decorated sitting room. I had left the French doors open, and that clever little pony was lonely and curious, and came looking for us. I smiled and hugged him as I led him back to his rather solitary splat. He was a sociable little animal who did not like being alone after his friends had gone, so we decided he would have to move on to somewhere he had company.

The huge open spaces around the house were healing,

and I tried to adjust to our new circumstances and made desperate efforts to retrieve our marriage, but I found it almost impossible. I did not trust my husband any more.

Elsie Louise

In 1973, my mother finally left her abusive husband. It was hugely brave of her. He had dominated her for so many years, had taken over her house, got rid of her friends and obliterated her daughters. He had spent weeks and months refusing to speak to her or indeed look at her, yet it took her twenty-five years to make up her mind to leave.

'If he does not speak to me for another three months, I will go,' she said, having finally come to a decision. No matter that it meant that she would have to leave her home and everything that was in it.

She was too frightened of Jock to say anything to him, so she stole away in the dark with only a small suitcase. Some years before, she had bought a bungalow at West Bexington, on the Dorset coast, with spectacular views across to the Golden Cap. She used to go there in the summer and let it out during winter. When she left Jock there were tenants in the house in Dorset, so she moved temporarily into a small caravan in a field of cows. At the beginning she was terrified that Jock would haul her back, but he didn't. He probably enjoyed being master of his house alone. As for Mother, she loved her new home, renewing contact with her friends and family. From that moment on she declared she was to be known by her middle name, Louise. She had always hated the name Elsie.

She was always immensely hospitable, and even in a small space she could produce delicious meals. She was adamant she wanted her grandchildren around her. They had at times stayed with her and were very happy at her house – except when they were forced to hide in cupboards to avoid Jock, just as Jennifer and I had done.

She repeatedly said: 'I have been such a dreadful mother; I want to be a wonderful grandmother.'

For the most part, she was. All her grandchildren delighted in her company, the fun, the generosity and the joy she found in little things. But it was not quite the same for Jennifer and me. She had rejected us for too long, and although we could forgive her, we could never forget.

Over time, she and Jock divorced. I went with her to see the solicitor when it looked as if she might lose her house, which had been completely financed by my grandmother's legacy. It was clear she had not spoken up nearly strongly enough about where the money for the property had come from in the first place. In the end, she was given only half the house. It was so unjust – yet she was happy, incredibly happy, and decided to renovate the dilapidated bungalow and move to West Bexington. She flourished in her new surroundings by the sea. She wrote books of unpublished poetry, as well as a hymn for Swyre Church, which we played at her funeral.

After leaving Jock, our mother would always spend Christmas Day either with me or with Jennifer and then go on to the other for Boxing Day with her home-made Christmas cake, mince pies and sacks of presents. Mother loved Christmas, but said she found my Christmases too perfect, and at Jennifer's house she never got enough to eat.

While both Mother and I loved to cook and were interested in food, Jennifer's priorities lay more with music and singing than cooking. Jennifer also invariably gave our mother a hard time over the dreadful childhood we had endured. As children, we had suffered for so many years, and it was difficult for Jennifer to put this to one side. Mother, finding herself under attack for past wrongs and never willing to apologize, would repeatedly say, 'I'm trying not to be hurt,' and take herself off for a walk. The children picked up on her words and copied her, so that 'I'm trying not to be hurt,' rang out constantly in my sister's household over the years.

Jennifer, deeply wounded from Mother's appalling treatment of her, was no doubt trying not to be hurt too. If only our mother had said she was sorry, things might well have been different. We will never know.

On one occasion – a birthday celebration, I seem to remember – Mother had come to stay with us, and the children were full of excitement, insisting they were going to prepare all the food and get everything ready for a little party. Mother came down from her room to find Joanna, Louise and Daniel lined up, expectant, almost bursting with pride at the spread they had arranged. Mother said nothing.

'Look what the children have done,' I said, indicating the food.

She remained silent.

'They've done really well,' I said. 'See what an effort they've made.'

Silence.

'Mother, they've gone to all this effort for you . . .'

She glared at me. 'And *I* have dressed up, and *nobody* has noticed.' Without another word she turned, flounced back upstairs, changed, packed her suitcase and left.

In spite of occasional outbursts like this, Joanna always loved staying with her grandmother. She was a bit older than the others, and would go to Dorset on her own so that the two of them could spend time together. They had a lovely time and Mother made a great fuss of her; Joanna was always special, being the first grandchild.

On one occasion my mother asked for Louise and Dan to go and stay. They were very young at the time, seven and five respectively. I said they could, but not when Jennifer's children were staying, as they did not get along together at that time. Without telling me, Mother arranged for them all to be there at the same time and after a few days I got a call out of the blue instructing me to go to Dorset to collect Louise and Dan. I was bewildered.

'But why – aren't they having a nice time?'

'You must come and get them,' Mother said.

'But I wasn't expecting to come until—'

'They'll be waiting for you.' She would say nothing more.

It took me five hours to drive from Oxfordshire to Dorset. When I drew up in front of my mother's house I saw the children sitting on the step, in tears, with their bags. The place was locked up. My mother had gone off with Suzannah and Juliette and left them.

They were hungry and distressed. I put them in the car, stopped off at a garage for something to eat, and spent another five hours on the road heading home. Once they had calmed down I found out what had happened. Mother had told them that Suzannah was in the bathroom and they mustn't go in. Dan, full of fun, found a stepladder in the garden, climbed up to the bathroom window, which was open, and shouted, 'Coo-ee.' Suzannah screamed the place down. It was a child's prank, no more – but Mother was not amused, and threw Daniel and Louise out.

I was furious. How could she have turned out two small children? Then again, hadn't she turned Jennifer out? After I left Mike, hadn't she turned me and Joanna away when we needed a roof over our heads? I knew from bitter experience what she was capable of, but would never understand it.

Gordon

After our father sold his business he was able to live off investments and put his energy into his great passion, motor racing. He had bought his D-type (an ex-Le Mans car, like all his Jaguars) in the mid-1950s, and raced it on ten occasions during the following year.

I watched my father before and after the races, and saw the nerves he experienced. Racing these hot cars in those days was extremely dangerous, and there were catastrophic accidents in which drivers and, on occasion, spectators lost their lives. He knew the danger. 'I don't mind dying,' he said, 'but being maimed for life is another matter.' In fact, he sold his D-type in the early sixties, giving up racing for a few years after one of his friends had a fatal accident. In 1966, he bought the car back and raced it again.

In the early sixties my father bought another big beast, this time a Lister Jaguar, a remarkably difficult car to drive, and in one year he raced it six times at Brands Hatch and Silverstone, coming first, second and third. By now in his late forties, he was affectionately known as 'the granddad of the track'. He was still racing in 1970, aged fifty-nine, and when I took the children to watch Granddad do his bit, he drove Dan, aged two, around the track. He retired shortly after this but remained a judge for both Formula 1 and 2, and on occasion drove his car ahead of all the Formula 1 cars on the track.

Eventually, fed up with getting bronchitis in the winter and paying so much tax, he decided to move to the Isle of Man. There were many things to consider – one being that his youngest daughter, Frankie, was living with him, and he felt he could not leave until she left to get married. He wanted to be there for at least one of his daughters. Frankie did leave in 1969, but in the end my father did not get to the Isle of Man until 1973.

Appalled at the estimate he was given by a removals firm, he remedied this by buying a lorry. He and Frankie's new husband, Malcolm, packed everything onto it – a gigantic undertaking – and Father was ready to leave. He got into the lorry, waved goodbye to his past life and happily drove the big beast up to Liverpool, onto the ferry, and off the other end to his new home. He found someone to help him unload and promptly sold the lorry, making a large profit. He then returned to England, his new base left behind, and went to see my mother in Dorset. Over the years they had always been in touch, and she was wonderful to my half-sisters. Pat, in particular, used to stay with Mother a lot. When I asked my mother how she was able to do this, she said, 'Well, she's Gordon's daughter. I love him, and I can love his daughter.'

When Father asked her to go and live with him on the Isle of Man she was somewhat surprised and, on consideration, thought not; she had her family and friends in England, and would miss them. Our father understood, but would return to see her, spending as much time as possible with her. Despite all that had happened between them, they enjoyed again the fun and laughter of their youth. I didn't know how close they had become until after his death a few years later. According to friends, they still loved each other, and radiated happiness in each other's company. The circle had been completed.

I loved to visit my father on the Isle of Man. He went out of his way to make things special: laying on delicious food, getting people round, creating a little party. He had bought a bungalow just north of Douglas, and while he constantly talked about looking for a bigger house – and he and I did go to see one or two – he never did anything about it. I think if my mother had agreed to join him there, it would have been a different story.

He was happy, nonetheless, and every time anybody phoned, he extolled the virtues of his new home.

'It's glorious – the sun is shining,' was his stock reply to enquiries about the weather. Occasionally, when he came off the phone, I would say, 'It's not sunny.'

He would smile. 'No, Christabel, but *they* don't know that!'

He and I always had a lovely time. I learned to appreciate the love he gave me, and let go of what had gone on in the past.

In June 1977, when the phone rang at home in Oxfordshire, I was told that our father had suffered a heart attack but was in hospital recovering. No need to fly to the Isle of Man, as he was being sent home the next day. The sun shone down on me as I walked along the lane feeling pensive. I went to see Sue Fisher-Hock, a doctor friend of mine, told her what had happened, and waited for her response. She was tough, was Sue.

'You know as well as I do that your father could have another one at any minute,' she said.

Why was I trying to avoid the truth? I left her, went home, organized the children, and bought a ticket to Douglas airport.

Within a few hours of receiving the call, I was by my father's side in Ramsey Hospital. It was morning, another wonderful sunny day, and as I walked – almost ran – towards his bed, he saw me and his eyes lit up, his face suffused with smiles. He stretched out his arms to me. We hugged and kissed, and he could not stop staying, 'How wonderful!'

The nurses passed, the doctors came.

'You must meet my favourite daughter,' he said to them, again and again (he referred to all of his daughters this way), and the whole ward was happy for him. He was getting better, and would be sent home the next day.

Ramsey Hospital was a small cottage establishment with none of the high-tech equipment found in most hospitals today. It was cosy, and the staff seemed to have time for the patients. My father was happy, and so was I for him. I went back to his bungalow, where Frankie and her small son Colin were waiting. We spent a delightful evening together, laughing and talking, confident that Father was OK.

The next morning my father was sitting up in bed, waiting for me, all smiles. We talked about him coming home, the new jacket and trousers I must look out that were hanging in his wardrobe. This man, my father, and I were always easy with each other, and we laughed and chatted, waiting for the doctor to come round and discharge him. He didn't.

'Just one more day,' the doctor said.

I went to see Sister, in her office.

'He's doing really well,' she said, 'and there's an eighty per cent chance we'll let him out tomorrow.'

I relayed Sister's message. My father nodded with understanding and some seriousness as he absorbed Sister's words. I left several hours later, without him, to return to his home, to Frankie plus baby. Did she want to visit? I would look after her little one. She thought not; she hated hospitals. It would be best for her to look after Colin since Father would be coming home the following day, anyway. We went down to the empty beach, where seals were frolicking in the shallow water and seagulls swooping and diving. We sat together quietly, absorbing the peaceful and beautiful scene of which we were a part.

After a good night's sleep in my father's bed, and having checked out his new jacket and trousers, I spoke to Jennifer on the phone.

'I want to come over,' she said. 'Is it all right?'

I knew that she had come to stay with him with her two girls a few months previously, and that they had had yet another ghastly row. My father told me some of what had happened. It was stormy and threatening, and Jennifer decided to stride out along the beach with the children for a five-mile walk.

'I really don't think it's wise to go out in this,' he had said.

Jennifer was determined. 'We'll be absolutely fine,' she retorted.

She told him where they would end up, and asked him to collect them. They were setting off without waterproofs, and Father was adamant they should not go. Jennifer disregarded his advice and went anyway. While they were out, the rain came down with a vengeance. He went out in the car to look for them and found them soaking wet, thoroughly bedraggled.

'Jennifer, you're a bloody fool,' he said.

She turned on him, letting loose a torrent of abuse. He was ridiculous. Foolish, a cackling old man. And more, besides. When my father told me what had transpired during that last visit, I knew he had toned down what Jennifer had actually said to him. It was too painful for him to repeat. The trouble was, she had never got over him leaving us, and she certainly never forgave him. Her whole life, she wanted a loving relationship with him, but whenever they were together the hurts of the past rose up. She was desperate that he understand her pain and his part in it, whereas I was able to let go of the past.

I told her I would ask him if it was all right for her to come.

I arrived at the hospital that morning, again through the stunning scenery of the island, and walked joyfully into the ward. My father looked tired; he had not had a great night, and was not being allowed out yet. Nevertheless, he cheered up very quickly when I told him I thought his new clothes were beautiful. He chuckled, and said that Reg, his neighbour, had seen them and envied them. Then Father sent me out with a shopping list of all his favourite foods – smoked salmon, sliced rare beef, tomatoes, lemons, lots of fruit, and good bread from his favourite bakery – a vast picnic which we consumed together in total happiness. Much better than hospital stuff!

We chatted, and he teased me about the time when, while Joanna and I were staying with him at Sonamarg after leaving Mike, I had thrown away a Yorkshire pudding he had considered his.

'Perfectly good Yorkshire pudding,' he said.

'Not by the time you ate it,' I countered.

I had cooked a roast dinner, but my father was late coming

home, and I had already eaten mine and cleared everything away. The Yorkshire pudding I had set aside for him was cold, and looking rather flat and sorry for itself. I opened the kitchen window and hurled it out for the birds. It landed on top of a tree. When Father came home, he could see it, but not reach it. He loved eating Yorkshire pudding, hot or cold, so he quickly devised a long pole with a scoop on top, and successfully retrieved it. The pudding fell into his waiting hands. My father was a very creative man and allowed nothing to defeat him.

Just before I left the hospital, I told him that Jennifer had phoned and wanted to come over.

'Tell her not to bother,' he said firmly.

There was to be no arguing: he had spoken. Jennifer rang again that night, and the following night.

'Ask him if it's all right for me to come,' she said, again. And every day, when I told him of her request, the reply was the same.

'Tell her not to bother.' And then, in the end, 'Tell her not to bother – she's killed me. She said I was nothing but a ridiculous, cackling old man. I don't need her.'

I was shocked, but never repeated the full extent of his words to her. However, she must have realized the trauma she had caused on her last visit, because every day she asked and every day I had to repeat my father's words: she was not to come.

The five days I spent alone with my father were some of the most important of my life. Every day we laughed and joked. Every day he would ask me what I had seen on the journey to hospital: the weather, the people, the sea, the sky and the flowers. And every day he asked me, with interest: 'What do you give for my chances today, love?'

It began with a seventy-five per cent chance, and he agreed. The next day it was sixty-six and two-thirds per cent. Again, he agreed. And so on. He was not improving. He told me about his Sundays, when he chose to be alone and, whatever the weather, he would cycle down the long country lanes to the beach. He would often pass an old woman on her way down her cottage garden to the hut that served as a lavatory. Always, she had a newspaper under her arm, and they both knew that it was not for reading. They waved to each other in understanding.

'I love Sundays,' he said. 'No people or drinks parties, just peace. I come to be with the Almighty.'

My father was magnificent.

'What do you give for my chances today, love?' he said.

I could not lie to him. 'Thirty-three and a third per cent,' I said.

'Umm,' came his response. We carried on as before, laughing and joking about the world.

I went to see Sister again.

'I am afraid he is not responding to treatment,' she said. She had nothing more to tell me. I went back to his home with a heavy heart.

When I returned to the hospital the next day, he really did look bad. He was not eating or drinking, and his poor mouth was dry, but he smiled and took my hand. I asked the nurse for a bowl of water and swabs, and cleaned out his mouth. I tried to give him sips of water, but he took very little. We spent the day together, holding hands, with only occasional words, but many smiles. At eight o'clock that evening, I did not want to leave.

'You must go, love, you're tired,' he said. 'I'll be here in the morning.'

There was no arguing. The evening passed, I know not how. But I did know the real dread in my heart as I drove to the hospital the next day. I slowly walked towards his bed. He was still there, and smiled at me. He had said he would be there in the morning, and he was. I was overwhelmed with love for this man, and felt that keeping his promise to me must have taken phenomenal effort and courage. We looked at each other in recognition. A small smile, a sigh, and he was gone. All that was left on the bed was my father's body, the empty clothes he did not need any more. I called Frankie, who came quickly, and we got away from the hospital as quickly as we could.

We left in the car, Father's car, and headed for the beach, the same empty beach he had always headed to on a Sunday. We did not speak, but lay in the sand with our own thoughts, surrounded by the presence of our father. He was there for us, and always would be.

I felt privileged to have those days with him, and to have had a nurse's training, which never leaves. I was there to be calm, honest and caring in his last moments. My beloved father. He was only sixty-five.

Jennifer came over for the funeral. My mother wanted to come, but I said I didn't think it was a good idea. I knew that Pam, his girlfriend of many years, was coming, and that a lady friend from the Isle of Man would also be there. Also, Judith intended to come. What I didn't know at that stage was how much my parents had been seeing of each other, or that they had rekindled their love. If only I had, I would not have stopped my mother from coming.

We had a service in the large church nearest to Father's home, then had his body cremated so that it could be returned in a box to be buried with his mother in the Wirral. Jennifer organized a family gathering for the interment of his ashes at Burton churchyard. I decided not to be there. I had said my goodbyes, and felt Jennifer needed to do this alone. She sent me photos of his final resting place and wrote that she was shocked when his brother Clarence came through the gate, as in old age he looked so like our father. For all her challenging behaviour with our father, my sister was heartbroken when he died.

Father had left an equal share of his estate to each of his four daughters: Jennifer, myself, and Pat and Frankie, our half-sisters. I considered what to do.

One of the last things my father had said to me was, 'Don't let Simon get his hands on my money; money to him is like pee in the sea,' and it had stuck.

I knew I needed help. Sitting in a country pub with horsey friends, I blurted out, 'I need a really good, tough solicitor.'

A chorus came back: 'Philip Druce.'

The next day I was in his office, in Witney. I liked this blunt Yorkshireman, and immediately trusted him. He remained my solicitor and friend until he died. I do miss him.

'Put your money in trust with this firm so that when your husband asks you for it you will have to apply to us, which will relieve you of pressure,' was his advice. And so I did.

Duly, Simon did ask me to help fund another of his projects, and I had to tell him what I had done. He was furious. On reflection, I decided that once was a habit, and I needed to keep my money, as my father had advised me, for myself and my children. I separated my affairs from Simon's, found a delightful cottage opposite the church in the Oxfordshire village of Ascott-under-Wychwood, and bought it on the spot. It took a great deal of courage to leave my husband for the unknown after ten years, but somehow I found the strength to do so. My father's strength seemed to have spilled over into my very being. 'All things are possible,' he had always said. 'You have two arms, two legs and a perfectly good head, so use it.' So I did, and have realized that this is a gift beyond measure. I remember saying to my son not so long ago, 'I know I may not have been the most perfect mother, but I must have been really good at something.'

'Oh, yes,' he replied in an instant. 'You made me know that all things are possible.' So our family philosophy lives on.

I told Simon what I had done and why, and moved out of the marital home, taking the children and only a few possessions.

Vine House was in terrible order, old and very run-down. The builders came in to my new wreck, and I sorted out the garden and did my usual painting and decorating. I felt certain that I had done the right thing, and protected my father's money. The children seemed happy, and I was involved in creating a new home. Simon came from time to time to see me, but I would not relent. At the same time I made the decision to give up my affair with Allan. I had had enough of deceit in my life.

When my mother came to visit, the builders were in, and I took her to the pub for something to eat. I was so pleased with my house, but Mother was less impressed. 'To think my daughter has sunk to this,' she said. 'Who would choose to live in such a place?'

I opened my mouth to reply, and then thought better of it.

In fact, less than a year later, having created a beautiful home, I sold it at a substantial profit. I was mindful of wanting to protect the money my father had left me and become as financially independent as possible. The sale of the house was the first step towards that. The actor John Hurt, who had friends in the village, loved Vine House and bought it on sight.

From Nursing to Music

I saw little of Jennifer, but we were regularly in touch, as ever, by phone. Around the time our father had moved to the Isle of Man, she had given up nursing to study music, something she had wanted to do as a child. She concentrated on the piano and singing, and even taught herself to play the harp. She gained the Licentiate at the London College of Music and was later awarded a Fellowship. And so she was able to teach music and inspire many young people. She sang in choirs, travelling around England and Europe, and made a great many musical friends. So she began her musical soirées, to which she invited other musicians to play and of course any other music lovers she knew. She loved these events, and would show off her garden in the summer. Her boundless strength and energy, inherited from our father, never diminished. She went off alone for extended cycle rides in order to escape anything she did not like.

As always, she felt the need to help people less fortunate than herself. So she bought a guitar and was to be found with her girls at the blind club in Apsley, entertaining the residents, and then it was an old people's home in Watford, where she and the girls sang their hearts out. Of course, they went to the church regularly, and she continued in the vein of our early childhood, when she and I had sung duets (and I was a little breathy).

Jennifer was now settled in a large Victorian property in Boxmoor, Hertfordshire, which she had bought with money inherited from our father, called The White House. She was very proud of it, and thrilled to be moving out of Bennetts End at last. She had found it over a weekend of looking. It was a dilapidated house at the time, with an extensive garden.

Like me, she sorted out the house and gardens by herself. She was particularly proud of her raspberries and gooseberries, and a delightful pond. She was shocked that Philip, her husband, was not practical like our father, who could make anything happen. By the time I arrived, The White House was looking good. It was summer, the sun was shining, and as we walked around the garden I could see the joy she got from being there, her planting, the front borders and her wall. She had actually built a high stone wall along the front of her house without any help at all. I was so impressed. I had built a dry stone wall while living in Ascott-under-Wychwood, but had had to stop when it reached one metre high, as after that it began to fall down. Jennifer and I sat quietly in the garden sipping Earl Grey, listening to the birds and bees in the distance. All was peace.

She had a husband who was emotionally supportive, and two lovely daughters. In time she also brought Monica Merlin, an actress she had nursed and who had become a dear friend, into her house. Monica was ill, and needed some loving care and attention. She was funny, knew a great deal about the theatre, shared Jennifer's love of music and culture and became part of the family. She stayed with Jennifer for the last five years of her life, and left her half her house in Barnes. Jennifer loved her and really appreciated her thespian ways, which she enjoyed emulating. This period really enriched the Worth family life.

I sensed that Jennifer rather disapproved of me for ending another marriage – not that she said so in as many words. She did not need to. We each had an uncanny ability to know what the other was thinking, regardless of what was actually said.

After talking it over, Simon and I decided in 1977 that Dan should go to boarding school. We both felt that we had benefited from going away to school and we wanted Dan to have the same opportunity, particularly as we were living such separate lives. After I had looked at a dozen or so schools, I chose Abberley Hall in Worcestershire, as it was the only one sufficiently relaxed for me to feel able to send my son. He was only seven years old, and it really hurt to leave him there with only his favourite toy monkey for company. I need not have been concerned, as he settled in very well; the year before he left, at thirteen, he took the part of Portia in a school production of *The Merchant of Venice* and played in the finals of the tennis tournament, losing honourably. He had become an incredibly nice young man.

Louise had been diagnosed as dyslexic and we were advised by an educational psychologist that boarding at a specialized school was the answer. We sent her to St James and The Abbey in Malvern where she blossomed, appearing as the leads in many of the school plays, and playing in all the sports matches.

I missed Dan and Louise dreadfully during term time, but the holidays were a joy. Whatever the weather, there would be long walks through wide open fields, through woods and by rivers. We always seemed to be eating outside in the garden, or having delicious picnics where Dan would fish, Lou paint and Joanna read a book. I watched my children grow into themselves over the years, and I was more than satisfied. It truly was a peaceful time.

Joanna, although extremely bright, refused to stay on at school. At seventeen she organized for herself an au pair place in Rome. She certainly was at a rebellious stage.

Simon had taken on a partner, and his business was flourishing. He had moved into a flat in Greenwich, so I sat alone in my charming country cottage and pondered what I might do.

Mother's Death

In 1978, our mother was taken into hospital. It was an emergency. When I received the news I questioned the caller since Jennifer and I had had such a call before and had rushed to Dorchester, many hours' drive from where we lived, and, on arrival, found mother in bed, smiling rather sheepishly.

'Only constipation, dears,' she had said.

This time it was not constipation, but a heart attack. Friends had called on her and found her sprawled on the floor of her bungalow, and called an ambulance. Our father had died the year before following a heart attack, and I was still grieving for him. Surely not our mother now, so soon? I had been to see her only a month before, and she had looked so young and happy she could have been taken for forty-something, not sixty-four.

On this occasion I drove steadily, in contrast with the dramatic response of a few years before. She was in the same hospital in Dorchester, and I found her in the resuscitation ward with tubes in seemingly every orifice and various apparatuses monitoring her every move. She looked small and frightened. Jennifer was standing by her and they both seemed glad that I had arrived so quickly. She had had an acute heart attack, like Father, but was getting all possible medical attention. It was nothing like the affable cottage hospital on the Isle of Man where Father had been treated, and I felt confident she would recover.

'What are they doing to me, Chris?' she asked. I assured her she was in the best possible place. 'What can I do?' she said. 'I don't want to die.'

'All you can do, Ma, is to relax, and let the nurses and doctors do their jobs.'

I held her hand, as though she was a very small child, and she looked up, trusting me completely. Then she shut her eyes and went to sleep.

With my children back at Mother's house, and an assurance from the hospital that all was well, I left Jennifer beside our mother, promising to return at eight o'clock the next morning. I returned on a bright and sunny morning, secure in the knowledge that Mother's life had been saved by the miracle of modern medicine, asking myself why Father had not had such specialized treatment. I felt quite relaxed – until I saw Jennifer staggering down the hospital steps towards me, tears flowing, scarcely able to speak.

'She's gone, she's dead,' she whispered.

She was in pieces. I had never seen my sister in such distress. She was always the strong one, in my eyes capable of anything. Not this time. I put my arms around her, managed to help her into my car, and drove home on autopilot. My sister needed me now, and it was to her that I had to direct my energy. I would allow myself to feel all the sadness for my mother later.

During the days that followed Jennifer hardly spoke, disappearing into the Dorset hills and the surrounding seashore, not eating or indeed drinking much. There was much to do, and so I carried on without her. I rang Mother's immediate family and friends, wrote letters, saw the undertaker and the bank manager, registered her death. I met with the vicar, chose hymns and organized a funeral party in celebration of her life. Mother had always loved parties, and she loved her friends. I was also attempting to communicate with Jennifer, but she was completely withdrawn. I found I could not get through to her. Losing her mother had utterly devastated my sister. Never had I seen her so distraught. When I brought up the subject of food for the party, she became angry.

'Why give them food, when my mother has just died?' she said.

I explained that many people were travelling hundreds of miles.

'We don't need to feed them.'

'I can arrange it, I just thought you might want to—'

'Give them what you like,' she snapped, stalking away.

The day of the funeral came, the hearse and cars arrived. I donned the yellow dress I had bought from Fortnum's in London, which my mother said was her favourite. Jennifer could barely get herself ready. I helped her into the purple dress she had chosen, and then into the waiting car. We sat, two sisters, together and alone. The car took us on a short journey and stopped outside Puncknowle churchyard. On either side of the long path up to the church entrance were throngs of people who had not managed to squeeze inside. Jennifer clutched my arm.

'I can't do it,' she said.

She hung on to me, and I almost dragged her into the church. It was packed – hundreds of people, not an empty seat beyond the front row. Somehow, Jennifer and I got down the aisle with the music still playing. Still clutching my arm, she said, 'I don't know what to do.'

My tall, imperious, powerful sister looked small and depleted. My heart went out to her. 'Just do what I do,' I said.

She continued clutching my arm all through the service, in the walk down to the cemetery, through the interment, and back to our mother's home in the car. She seemed as helpless as a small child. We stood together in the front hall as hundreds of people filed past, all telling us of the wonderful things our mother had done. It was amazing: she was really loved by so many. Everyone who came in contact with her loved her, for she always left them feeling happier than when she had arrived. She had done so much, and made a real difference to the lives of these people – but we, her children, had been left bereft.

When all the family and friends had gone Jennifer looked at me, still unable to speak. We went into Mother's room. Neither of us wanted any of her jewellery, but we thought our children might. Of the grandchildren, Suzannah, Joanna and Louise had been at their grandmother's funeral, and we invited them to choose whatever they wanted from Granny's things. Shortly afterwards Jennifer departed, leaving me to sort out the debris after this wonderful party that mother would have loved.

I stayed on for a few days, sorting through things. In my mother's desk I came across a poem she had written. It was short and heartfelt. I was sure she must have written it after the death of my father the year before, as it seemed to me to perfectly express her feelings for him.

Although you have left me I shall not die
Nor shout my grief to reach the sky
I shall not ask for anything more

Than to walk according to natural law
One foot behind the other before
I shall wake at morning sleep at night
Tell unfailingly black from white
I shall use my brains to earn my bread
Snarl when I'm hungry smile when I'm fed
No I shall not die but my heart is dead.

I sat at the desk thinking about my mother, the love she had felt all through her life for my father. I was able to relate to every word. Their love story had endured to the end of their lives. The collapse of their marriage had been akin to detonating an explosive device beneath Jennifer and me, and yet I am not sure either of them ever fully understood the impact on us of what they had done.

While the death of my father had filled me with a grief that was to last for years, I found I did not mourn my mother to the same extent. I am not sure why. It may have been that I was still so raw over Father's death that there was simply not room to allow for any more pain; or it may have been that, despite his failings, my father always showed me love and kindness – never as much as I wanted or needed, admittedly – whereas, sadly, Mother did not.

It was not until many years later in 2010, when Jennifer's book *In the Midst of Life* was published, that I came to understand my sister's behaviour following the death of our mother. I had always thought my mother's health had deteriorated overnight, that she had simply passed away. In fact, the morning she died she had been in good spirits initially, having woken from a restful sleep, and had urged Jennifer to take a break from her bedside vigil and get some breakfast. Jennifer did so. It was such a wonderful day that my sister then decided to have a walk, and was gone for much longer than she had intended. She returned to the ward to find the door to the intensive care unit locked and our mother on the other side of it, having had a second cardiac arrest.

The nursing staff would not allow Jennifer to go in. She was forced to sit outside and wait. While she awaited news, she berated herself for having left Mother for so long.

'I envisaged her, weak and helpless, wanting me, perhaps calling for me, and I wasn't there. I had abandoned her,' she wrote in *In the Midst of Life*.

She hammered on the door. Still, her way was barred.

'I sat in numb grief for two hours. Self-reproach amounting to self-flagellation haunted me . . . Eventually, a doctor came and told me that my mother was dead. They had done all they could, he told me gently, but she had not responded.'

All this I discovered in the same way as anyone else who picked up the book. I read the account of those final moments feeling as if my heart was about to break. I had not known until then that my mother had suffered a second heart attack. I had known nothing of the resuscitation efforts, of the guilt and distress Jennifer had experienced that morning.

It explained so much. I only wished she had been able to tell me at the time.

I realize now that Jennifer was suffering from severe shock, and that the tears she shed when she stumbled from the hospital that day and into my arms were of regret. I pictured her banging on the door, begging to be allowed in, and being turned away. Poor Jennifer. So often she had said that the only thing she had in common with her mother was a total lack of mutual understanding. It might have been true, but deep down she loved her, fiercely loved her, despite the childhood Mother made us endure.

That she could not be there for her at the end of her life was so devastating a blow, she was hardly able to bear it.

St Martin's

For many years I continued to work in clay from observed models. I knew all about women and children, but men! I had nursed, been married, but never actually studied male anatomy as an artist. But I was determined, and looked about me. Adam was the answer – our strong, muscular gardener, a short, rugged Polish man.

He agreed to pose for me, rather proud of his new status as a life model, and happily stripped off down to his waist. When I got enthusiastic and wanted him to remove his trousers, he was not so sure. But I was paying him in whisky, and he liked whisky a lot, so he relented. In fact, as the sculpture grew he became enthusiastic at seeing himself immortalized, but he was seriously worried by its lack of good strong genitals. I told him not to worry: I would make them up. He was not happy – he did not want someone else's genitals on his figure, and certainly not any made up by me! Shyly, he sidled into the studio where I was standing working.

'Five seconds; you can see me for five seconds,' he said, and promptly dropped his pants, looked out of the window and started counting. Five seconds was enough! I was very pleased with the result – as was Adam – and got it cast, and when I moved to Idbury, decided to fix it to a very large stone outside the front door. Idbury is a tiny village, with only a dozen or so houses, and someone was offended by the sculpture. Adam was hacked to pieces in the night. I was so shocked.

Having turned Vine House in Ascott-under-Wychwood into a beautiful home and sold it on at a profit, I had bought another property, The Forge, in Idbury, the next village.

A close friend, Sir Charles Kimber, suggested I enrol on an art course. Working with Hydie Seton Lloyd had done great things for my confidence, and so I found what I thought would be a suitable course at the college in Banbury, applied, and was invited for interview. The head of the college had actually seen my sculpture on show as part of an Oxford Arts Society Exhibition. Over the following weekend he wanted me to do some drawings – one of the inside of my local church, one of my home, and a self-portrait. I was rather pleased with what I managed to produce, given that I knew nothing about drawing, and got a place on a one-year foundation arts course.

I didn't really know what to expect, but there was an opportunity to try out everything. I seemed to be the only one crawling about on the floor making things, since most people didn't like getting dirty. On the whole, I didn't mind. The sculpture master was young and enthusiastic, and gave me encouragement.

'You're rather good at sculpture,' he said one day.

'I do love it, but I don't know what to do about it.'

'Oh, you must go on, and the only place to do it is St Martin's. Nowhere else.'

At that stage I wasn't thinking about going on to another college, certainly not the prestigious St Martin's School of

Art in London – but at the end of the year we were all given a form to complete to say which university we wanted to go to, and the course we wished to do. I had no idea, but, remembering what I had been told, put down St Martin's as my first choice, and sculpture as my subject. I put a line through the space for second choice, since I had been told St Martin's was really the only place to consider.

I was called for an interview, and got together a portfolio to take with me. On the day, the car broke down and I missed my slot. Another appointment was arranged. I got lost in London, and again missed my turn. Third time lucky. So, I took the train. It broke down. I seemed destined not to get there.

'What shall I do? I really want to go there but everything seems to be stopping me,' I told Charles.

'Next time, my dear, I will take you,' he said.

He drove me up to London, dropped me on the Charing Cross Road right outside the college, and said he would wait for me round the corner. I was interviewed by a panel of three who looked through my portfolio and told me I was in. David Annesley, a senior member of the teaching staff, showed me around. He had exhibited at the Tate in London and the Museum of Modern Art in New York. I was very impressed.

I was singing with joy as I returned to find Charles. We were both thrilled with the result, and he took me out for a celebratory lunch and to Cork Street to see all the art galleries before heading home.

I had only just left Simon when I first met Charles. We were immediately at one. Charles and I both had regrets, but they didn't dominate our lives, and he encouraged me to do the seemingly impossible. Of course I loved him, but when he asked me to marry him I had to 'think on', in the words of a good old Yorkshire expression I had heard Joan, my mother-in-law, use.

I wanted to do the right thing for both of us. I was thirty-nine; he was sixty-six. I had got into St Martin's to do a degree in sculpture, and I doubted I could remain faithful to a man so much older than me. I wanted to go to St Martin's so much. Reluctantly, I gave him my reply. I could not marry him. He said he loved me hugely and would not mind me having lovers, but I knew that I would find such a situation impossible. I knew from my marriage to Simon what it was like to live a lie.

Charles and I remained firm friends all our lives, and he was the greatest influence on me and my three children. We all loved him. Joanna developed a long-lasting relationship with Charles, who became her adopted grandfather, and she named her first son after him.

He died at the age of ninety-three, and even at the funeral I was told by mutual friends that I should have married him. Perhaps I should; but I had no crystal ball to look into the future.

When I told Jennifer I was going to St Martin's to do a Fine Art degree, she thought it was wonderful.

'Of course, you're only going to get two letters after your name, dear – BA,' she said. 'I have so many letters after mine I can't even get all of them onto an envelope.'

I couldn't help laughing. Jennifer and I both had the same dry sense of humour.

On my first day at St Martin's all the new students gathered in a very large room and were welcomed. There must have been more than a hundred people there. Eventually, we all started to peel off into our various groups. I watched as the names of the fashion students were read out, then printing, fine art painting, and so on. Gosh, I thought, full of admiration for how good they looked, all wearing beautiful colours and flowing patterns. In the end, the only ones left were the sculptors, who seemed a serious bunch in rather dull, uninspiring clothes. We look like bank managers, I thought – I want to be with the painters!

Thus began three years of change and development, from being an upper-middle-class housewife into being a classless sculptor. I loved it. I was doing what I had always wanted to do.

It was very exciting going to St Martin's. It fitted in with the two younger children's holidays from school. Joanna had begun her nurses' training at the Royal Berkshire Hospital in Reading, the same place Jennifer and I had trained, and so was independent. The sale of my pretty house in Ascott-Under-Wychwood for a great deal more than I had paid for it, and the move to nearby Idbury, financed my time at St Martin's without my having to touch my father's money. Simon was paying the school fees and maintenance.

St Martin's was in the centre of London, close to all the main art galleries. It was so good to be part of this world. But my heart and home were in the country, to which I returned most nights and weekends. I suppose I missed out on the social side of the art world – which is important if you want recognition – but my children needed a proper country home, and so did I. Every day I had a journey by train of one and a half hours each way. I could work on the journey up, which proved a really good thing, but returning in the evening was not so pleasant, as I was tired and always uneasy about passing my station if I fell asleep. However, it was worthwhile, as I loved my cottage and could completely unwind there.

I passed my time in working at St Martin's by day, and seeing old friends at weekends.

Then one day, as I was standing alone at my kitchen window, a rather beautiful young man, tall and loose-limbed, passed by. On his way back some five minutes later, he looked directly at me and put out his tongue. How dare he! I returned the compliment, put my tongue out, put my hands to my mouth, wriggling my fingers, and made a horrible grimace at him – then collapsed with laughter as memories flooded back of Jennifer and me as children, teasing one another on the beach at Jaywick Sands.

The following evening there was a knock at the door and there was the beautiful young man, contrite, with a bunch of daffodils. William was American, lived at the other end of the village, and was a graphic printer. He came from Los Angeles, where his father had written music for films, and on coming to England for a holiday he had decided he had to live here. Formerly a musician and poet, he had trained to be a printer. England was short of printers then, and William ended up living in our tiny village in the Cotswolds.

Several weeks passed, and a couple who lived nearby – Alison and her architect husband, David – asked me to supper. I liked them a lot, and walked over to their house expecting a simple, quiet evening. It was snowing, and very cold. I threw on my gorgeous long fur coat, bought as a special present with my inheritance from my father. He had always appreciated well-dressed and attractive ladies, and would have loved to see me dressed up like this. Thank you, Daddy! I knocked, and the door was opened by William. Apparently, Alison had thought we would like each other.

The evening was a riot. David was pouring out more and more wine, and William had such a wonderful sense of humour. We left together, laughing and staggering in the snow, and holding on to each other for support. The next thing I knew, I was waking up in his bed with my fur coat clutched around me. I was horrified. William was still asleep. I left hurriedly, tottering home through the snow-covered village on my very high heels, feeling very guilty.

Thus began an exciting and torrid relationship, which inspired both of us for some few years. William was not only beautiful outside, but he had a deep inner beauty that recognized the essentials of life. He kept tumbling pigeons, very popular in the North of England, played music, wrote poetry, and was enthusiastically American. He totally disregarded any preconceived conventions, and cared nothing for money. I loved him; everyone loved him.

We shared so much in common in our attitudes to life and love. We spent idyllic times together in the Cotswolds, and in San Francisco. We wrote poetry to each other and made love. But he found London noisy, too full of people, everybody in a rush. It worried him. In October 1981, while I was at St Martin's, the IRA was setting off bombs in London. Two went off in the space of a few weeks in October that year: one at Chelsea Barracks, the other on Oxford Street. William was staying with me, and, being a gentle soul who liked to amble along in an elderly Morris Traveller, reacted badly to the danger and fast pace of the city. He could not fit in – and had no wish to. The capital was a scary place to start with, even without bombs going off at its heart, sirens and emergency vehicles tearing about. It was too much for him. He came to hate London, and everything and everyone connected with it.

*

What did I learn at St Martin's? How to offload many of my upper-middle-class habits, how to swear really well, how to make friends with people of any race, colour or age – and, most definitely, how to bat my own corner. St Martin's was a tough art college, no namby-pambying there. We had to know what we were doing and defend our actions to the highly critical staff. I had not been looking at my work closely enough, and learned to really examine what I was doing in great depth. It was never enough at St Martin's to say that you had made a piece because you liked it; when it came to your work, you had to be able to offer a considered view on every single decision you made. This has stood me in good stead.

I learned art history for the first time. In fact, I got a first for my art history degree. I learned how to read and consider books, to agree or disagree and to develop a new way of looking – and, as I looked, my looking became clearer and more developed. I really enjoyed myself. The tutor who remains the most memorable to me is Monty, a shambles of a man who seemed able to show us our weaknesses with consideration. The aggressiveness and rules of some of the other tutors did not affect him, and he carried on with the honesty he had always shown. Zadock Ben David, another tutor, became a friend, and David Annesley was always there, helping us to higher things. The bully boys, of which there were many, I will not bother to consider.

The final year was made difficult for me as the general consensus was that there was one way only of making sculpture and that was in the basement, mostly beating heavy metal over huge furnaces. It was incredibly hot and heavy. With my back to be considered and my questioning attitude, I opted out. This was generally frowned upon. The head of the department disliked me, and we had many altercations regarding my choices. I didn't like him much either, and certainly had little respect for him.

I spent my last year on my own in a huge open studio on the seventh floor, where I could order a model at will. I loved it, and learned to trust my own judgement. I constructed huge life-size figures out of clay which had to be fired at the Central School of Art, as the kilns at St Martin's were too small. I also made life-size figures constructed from wood and plaster of Paris. I learned that what worked for me was not to start making a figure from the bottom up, but to find the point of greatest tension and begin from there. I was not necessarily interested in making something realistic, and would exaggerate the areas I wished to emphasize, and I liked to see the tool marks in my work. I found it important to look and learn from my mistakes. It became important to me to demonstrate the movement and inner construction of the figure, and I have followed that path for the rest of my life.

When our mother's estate was wound up, Jennifer bought a flat in Brighton, where she was to write most of her books. It had few amenities and no TV or phone, but she loved it and valued the silence. It was somewhere she could escape to, to spend time alone beyond the reach of others. It suited her perfectly. It had been converted from the ground floor of a large Victorian house; the main room, originally a billiard room, had high ceilings and was oak-panelled. It was very impressive. Apart from that there was only a simple bedroom and a rather inadequate kitchen. But for Jennifer it was heaven. She could be herself and only herself; nobody's wife, mother or grandmother, and she was free from all media interference – no television, no phone and no newspapers.

She had always had a need to disappear, and in Brighton, she did as she pleased. She was truly at peace. And she was by the sea, her first love – and if she got there early, the long beaches of Brighton were empty and she would run along these wide empty spaces, collecting shells and debris from ships, brought in on the tides. I know how she felt, as our happiest times as children were spent on the beach at Jaywick Sands, and I too live by the sea and feel at one with the elements.

A narrow terrace ran along the side of the flat. Here Jennifer had large pots of bright red geraniums, and when I was with her we would sit sipping Earl Grey in the late afternoon sun, talking of our children and their blossoming lives.

Much of the time in Brighton, she was writing. 'And you should be too,' she would say to me.

I had no idea what she was writing, or that one day she would become a bestselling author.

I bought a tiny flat in London, in Pimlico, not far from the Thames and the Tate Gallery. Like my sister's bolthole, it had few amenities – no TV or phone – and I spent much of my time there during my final years at St Martin's, valuing the comparative silence of a neighbourhood in the centre of the city, waking to the song of birds from the garden square nearby. I loved it. I also rented a studio in Railton Road, in Brixton – a very dangerous district at that time – which I shared with another artist, Barry. I wonder what he's doing now, that nice man from the North.

Lady Temple

My life at The Forge in Idbury was always a joy, apart from many unpleasant spells of back pain. The surgeons had fixed the breaks in my spinal column, but not the pain associated with them, and of course this was noted by my friends and neighbours. I was often at the osteopath in Oxford, who helped a bit, but never cured me. Where could I get relief?

Opposite me in the village of Idbury lived Lady Temple, in a rather grand, forbidding house. My first encounter with her was not a success, when she complained that from one of her windows she could see my washing on the line in the garden, which really would not do. I swiftly took it down and set up a line inside the barn, out of sight. I had no intention of falling out with the neighbours. Fortunately we were able to get beyond this awkward beginning and, although I didn't see a great deal of her, she occasionally asked me to dinner parties (with uniformed waiting staff).

On one such occasion, when the subject of my back pain came up, she suggested I try going to her acupuncturist. I hated the idea of needles, but went along out of desperation and with some trepidation. Mike McIntyre, a gentle, kindly man, explained that I would need to have the acupuncture three times to give it a chance – so I did. The first time, no change; the second time, no change; the third time I walked away from his cottage pain-free, and without my limp. Unbelievable! I asked the McIntyres to dinner. Unexpectedly Joanna arrived, and we all had a fascinating time, as she was obviously intrigued and amazed to see me running around. She was disillusioned with nursing and immediately decided to do a degree in acupuncture, which would take up the following three years of her life.

Lady Temple asked me to make a piece of sculpture of her grandchildren to give to her daughter for Christmas. I was rather pleased, went to London to do drawings and take photographs, made an enchanting piece in clay and delivered it to a recommended caster, who agreed to have the bronze cast made by the end of November. My artist friend, Barry, made the base for me to my design, and I thought all was well. December came, and no contact from the caster. I rang several times: no reply. I eventually went to look for him at his home address – he had moved. I spoke to neighbours who told me he did his work at a foundry in the East End. More investigations, and I began to panic. It was a week before Christmas when at last I walked into the foundry: they were all closing down, and the men leaving. My work lay in a corner, untouched. I spoke to the owner about completing it.

'It will be impossible to finish in time,' he said.

'You must help me,' I said.

'The men have gone home.'

'I'll help,' I said, desperate.

He studied me for a moment. 'Do you think you can?'

'Of course!'

So the two of us worked non-stop for the next two days. I limped home, utterly exhausted, with the sculpture I had promised, only two days before Christmas. The next morning, greatly relieved, I walked over to Lady Temple's house with it. It was very beautiful, and I felt proud of myself for getting it done.

'No, I don't want it,' she said. 'It's too late. I've bought my daughter another present.'

I was horrified. I took a deep breath. 'That's all right,' I said. 'It's beautiful and I am happy to keep it.'

'What will you do with it?' she asked.

'I may sell it, or I might keep it,' I said. 'I like it very much.'

'You cannot sell the grandchildren,' she said. She shrieked for her husband. 'Dicky, she's trying to sell the grand-children!'

With that, she swept out, and I waited in silence in the huge hall. In time she returned, said nothing, simply took the sculpture and paid me. I crossed the road, opened my front door and burst into tears.

Some time after Christmas, Lady Temple arrived with three dozen perfect pink roses. Apparently 'The Grandchildren' had been on display at her daughter's highly desirable London house all over Christmas, and everyone had loved it. Ann Amos, her daughter, even sent me a note. Sadly, the experience had soured our relationship. Nevertheless, I have her to thank for introducing me to acupuncture, which I still use. Like a car, I have a service regularly. The after-effects of having an anterior spinal fusion have been considerable, and I have had to cope with periods of excruciating back pain all my life. Yet the operation was a success, and I'm very grateful not to be in a wheelchair.

Changing Faces

I enjoyed living in Idbury, and after finishing my BA (Honours) Fine Arts degree at St Martin's, I set up my studio in the old forge attached to my house. I was working well on large pieces in blocks of wood and plaster of Paris, twice life size at least. I had my first exhibition in Bampton and was thrilled to sell a couple of pieces, and get a wonderful write-up in the local papers. Both Charles and his best friend, James Bramwell, were at the opening, and sent me such encouraging letters. Much later I discovered that Charles had bought one of the pieces, but he never told me, or indeed showed it to me at his house.

Joanna needed somewhere to live while working on her acupuncture degree, so I handed over my flat in Pimlico to her for much of her three-year course. Both Dan and Louise were now at Bryanston School, which meant a great deal of travelling for me from Oxfordshire to Dorset for plays and so on. They were doing well, and looked set on being at Bryanston for some years to come, so I decided to move to be much nearer the school. I found a beautiful thatched house with a large barn in which to make my sculpture on the Cranborne Chase, only five miles away. This signalled the end of my relationship with William. He dreamed of us setting up a tumbling pigeon business, something I could not see working, although his birds were so enchanting. When released from their cages these tiny birds would soar high into the air, performing exhilarating aerobatics, returning to the ground in ever decreasing circles. Wonderful to watch. Why did I have to be so responsible? I am my father's daughter. We were both hurt. With real pain, I had to tell him no and let him go.

When Dan arrived at Bryanston we found he had a house-master he and I really could not like, but although I complained to the headmaster, there was nothing that could be changed and Dan soldiered on. Louise, however, after much reflection, decided to leave Bryanston early. It left me with a problem of what to do. By this time Joanna had finished her degree course in acupuncture and, in 1983, I decided to sell the London flat and the beautiful thatched house in Dorset and move to London to give both of them a suitable home. Jessie, our greyhound, and Toby, our Jack Russell dog, moved with us into a charming house with garden in Battersea, near the park. Thankfully, Louise was accepted at the Heatherly Art School across the river, so that problem was resolved. I worked at making the house straight, having little time for my sculpture. My family needed a full-time mother.

Fundamentally, as a family we were all country people, so it was quite an experience to live in London full-time. I thought that living by the park would solve our problems, but Battersea Park was not the country; the air was polluted by car fumes, the grass was trodden down by numerous feet and of course there were so many people everywhere. The first casualty was Jessie, our wonderful greyhound, who hated the park and even when let off the lead would not leave my side, returning home miserable and depositing her faeces on our newly laid carpets. She had always been scrupulously clean in the country. I felt so sad, and quickly realized that I could not inflict on her a life in Battersea. She was a dog who belonged in huge open spaces with the scent of wildflowers in her nostrils. So I got in touch with Greyhound Rescue, and she returned to her rightful place.

Toby was much less sensitive; he really liked the park and the sociability of the other dogs. But he was quite shocked one day, on going into a dry cleaning shop, to see himself for the first time in a large, long mirror. He had believed in the country that he was a king of dogs, and had bossed Jessie around unmercifully. In London, in a shop crammed with people, he had to recognize that he was really quite small, quite insignificant.

A Sculptor Again

In London, I found myself a great studio in Tooley Street, south of the river, overlooking Tower Bridge, and started work again. It was quite a revelation to me. At that time the area was pretty rough, with most buildings in a sad state of disrepair and the only shop a small sandwich bar that sold delicious sandwiches on the cheap. My studio was on the first floor over a taxi and motorbike delivery business, and endless phone calls and revving motorbikes could be heard through the thin floorboards. Most of the buildings were locked up – the whole area was pretty deserted – but the studio was large, and after I had painted it white all over and scrubbed the floors it was beautiful, a wonderful space in which to work. After completing my degree at St Martin's and studying with the painter Cecil Collins, I was drawing and painting. My goddaughter Juliette came to stay, and I did some very powerful drawings of her in charcoal. When Jennifer came to the studio and saw them, she loved them so much that I gave them to her.

'They're wonderful,' she said.

She was thoroughly impressed when she saw the work I was producing. 'It's so good, Chris,' she said, gazing about her.

I don't think it had really sunk in until then quite what I was doing, or was capable of.

Jennifer put up the drawings of Juliette side by side in her drawing room. I was touched to think she had given them prominence in the most important room in her house, where music prevailed and which was considered the heart of her home, and where they still live today.

I went for an interview at the Royal Academy, as I was being recommended for one of their postgraduate courses. There were two male interviewers, one my age and one very young. It was going along very well and I thought I was there, until the very young man asked me what I wanted from my sculpture. I replied that I did not want only to make interesting pieces – I wanted my work to have an emotional impact on the viewer as well. My answer obviously appalled the young man, and my interview was quickly terminated. I knew my response had blown it. For many years sculpture in the art world has been merely interesting, and more about commercial fantasy. Beauty and balance and honest emotion have been obliterated; their place in the modern world is anathema – so I work alone.

Jennifer, as always, was still short of money, and thinking of ways to generate income. Although Philip was earning, a junior schoolmaster's remuneration could never pay for the upkeep of a large house as well as a wife and two children. My sister began to encourage him to write a book; but this was not to be a success. Her next attempt to influence her perplexed husband was in the early 1980s, when she bought him a set of oil paints and boards and decided he was to be a great artist.

'Any fool can be an artist,' she stated when she told me of her latest idea.

I was stunned. Had she not realized the enormous amount

of work and effort and sacrifice that had gone into my years of training? For a moment I was utterly lost for words, and then decided there was no spite in what she said; my sister could simply be supremely tactless.

'There might be rather more to it than you imagine,' I ventured.

'Really?' she said. 'I don't see why, when so much of what passes for art today is so ghastly.'

I sympathized. Jennifer had a very poor opinion of modern art, and I could see why. A lot of it is about ideas and not much else. She explained to me that in a year's time, in 1984, it would be the fiftieth anniversary of the death of the English composer Gustav Holst, famous for *The Planets* suite. Philip was to produce a series of oil paintings to complement the music, and Jennifer would arrange for them to be exhibited. I was doubtful this would succeed but, ever determined, Jennifer went out and bought canvases, set Philip up in a room that was little more than a cupboard off the kitchen, and he began painting.

I had underestimated my sister, who put her considerable energy into arranging for the – as yet unpainted – series to go on show. Various galleries and concert halls were contacted regarding an exhibition to tie in with the Holst celebrations, and there were several takers, among them the Royal Festival Hall and the Royal Albert Hall in London, Manchester's Free Trade Hall, St David's Hall in Cardiff, the Dome in Brighton, and the town halls in Leeds and Birmingham. It was certainly inspired on her part. Once Jennifer put her mind to something she was able to make it happen almost by sheer force of will alone, although afterwards she told me the paintings had not actually sold.

Politics and Pimlico

It can be isolating to work on your own all day, so I applied to the Wandsworth Day Centre to set up art classes once a week for people with mental health issues. I ended up teaching painting, sculpture and woodwork there for two years, two days a week, until the government disbanded the Day Centre and my poor vulnerable pupils from every walk of life were thrown to the 'wolves' found lurking around the streets of London. This was called Care in the Community, but there was no care. I also saw the pain on the faces of the mostly black youths whose running track in Battersea was enclosed by high wire fencing. They could no longer build up their athletic powers. They had nothing else to do, and wandered off disconsolately to kick their heels in frustration and join the gangs already hanging around the streets. There were too many people there who *had*, and too many who had *not*; a difficult mix – I found it very uncomfortable.

It was about a year into our life in Battersea when Dan came back from the park, pretty upset. Three youths had collared him and trodden on the backs of his shoes as he tried to walk. He was frightened.

'Do we have to live here?' he said.

'No, we don't,' I responded, and immediately set out to find somewhere else I could afford on the other side of the river.

I settled on Pimlico, a lovely area with its large white stucco houses and wide roads. I bought a delightful, dilapidated freehold house there, which I quickly turned into a sort of palace, and we all loved it. Louise got into the Slade School of Fine Art, Joanna married a rather charming Irishman and moved into nearby Fynes Street, and Dan remained somewhat reluctantly at boarding school, coming home on the train for his exeats and holidays.

I applied and was accepted to join the Chelsea Arts Club, which, with its heavenly garden, billiard tables, great restaurant and like-minded people, became quite a focus for our lives. I put on an exhibition there, and also put pieces in Dolphin Square. Joanna started up an alternative health centre in Westminster and began a course in psychotherapy at Spectrum in North London. I admired her initiative, but found it almost impossible to communicate with her. I had no idea what she was talking about, so I joined the same course some months later. This was brilliant for me and indeed my whole family, but perhaps less so for my daughter. I learned a lot at Spectrum, particularly about giving feedback, which proved helpful to me. Giving information to another person on how their behaviour is affecting you, can help form new perceptions that can be used to modify behaviour in future. I tried to talk to Jennifer about this, but found that it annoyed her. She thought it rubbish – mumbo-jumbo, she called it – so I gave up.

One good thing about moving to London was that it was easier to see my half-sister Frankie, who now had three children and seemed content in her marriage. I saw less of my other half-sister, Pat. I recognized that Jennifer lived in a world of her own and in order to keep in touch I had to drip-feed myself into the veins of her life, and not the other way round. She never missed my birthday, however. A card always came, and I was sure to send one to her each year without fail. I loved her and generally smiled at her idiosyncrasies, even if I was a bit frosty at times.

Every day I would take Claud and Jelly, my dogs, walking in either Green Park or Battersea Park. In Battersea we watched the Pagoda being built, appreciating the great care the monks gave it, and every time we were in Green Park we watched the ducks, swans and pelicans. It all appeared much smarter than Battersea, until one evening when we arrived late. It was turning dusk, the park was empty of people and so very still. We quietly walked around towards Buckingham Palace when I noticed a dark cloud in front of us. Claud, my Jack Russell, saw it too. He was gone right into the middle of it, snapping and snarling ferociously. The dark cloud comprised rats, thousands of rats, moving as one out of the bushes across the path and into the lake beyond. I was terrified for Claud, for Jelly and for myself. The dog would not come back until he had broken enough necks to satisfy him. It appalled me to think of so many rats running under my feet – within sight of Buckingham Palace!

Christmas in central London is essentially quiet. Everyone seems to disappear, and the streets are empty. Our Christmases began when we walked in silence to Midnight Mass – then it was back home, excited that it was Christmas Day, hugging each other and eating mince pies. I would get up early to put the already-stuffed turkey in the oven, put the pudding in the steamer and rapidly make brandy butter and bread sauce, before laying the table for breakfast. It was always boiled eggs, coffee and hot rolls, as I'd had at Wycombe Court. Who was there, that memorable first Christmas in Pimlico? Joanna and Jeremy, her future husband; Louise and her boyfriend Andy; Dan and me; and, of course, Claud and Jelly, resplendent in huge bows made from wide red ribbon. They certainly joined in the fun. Lou had also brought her parrot.

We exchanged presents beside the Christmas tree and sipped champagne, and all the world was good. The table was laid for our Christmas feast with silver candlesticks, crackers and table decorations of holly. In fact, the whole house smelt of the country with so much holly and fir everywhere. The turkey was perfect, as were the roast potatoes and parsnips, tiny sausages wrapped around with streaky bacon, and sprouts with chestnuts and gammon on the side. The smell was wonderful and I was overwhelmed to see so many joyful happy faces. But the smell had also overwhelmed Lou's parrot – and the huge bird shocked us all when he swooped down onto the turkey and grabbed a leg in his beak. There were shrieks of laughter, and chaos ensued as we all tried to catch the bird. It was such fun, and everything was so good that year.

Every year on Christmas Day Jennifer would phone me, always calm and considered; someone else had to be doing all her cooking! And every year we would contact each other by phone on New Year's Eve. She loved New Year, and would allow herself to be outrageous and have fun.

Jennifer was fond of our half-sister, Pat, and for many years after Pat's divorce, they shared Christmas. Jennifer would ask Pat and her children to come every year, and every year Pat would ask what she could contribute, and every year Jennifer would say the same thing: 'Anything you like, darling, you know I'm a terrible cook.' So Pat, remembering the previous year, would arrive with turkey, pudding and everything necessary for a Christmas feast. And of course she cooked it, and everyone was happy.

It was around this time, in 1987, that Jennifer's great love Nevill Harrow died. She had been in close contact with him all her life, and when she learned he was dying she was almost hysterical and desperate to go to him; but her best friend Wendy, fearful of the effect it might have both on my sister and on Nevill's family, strongly urged her not to stir up old feelings after so many years. What if Nevill did not wish to see her? Reluctantly, Jennifer agreed to stay away, although the decision caused her huge heartache.

Wendy's sole concern was for Jennifer. She had memories of the two of them training together at the Royal Berkshire thirty-something years before, and seeing her friend turned inside out over Nevill – wanting him to marry her, hoping for so long that he would, finally accepting it was not going to happen. What Wendy never knew was that all along Nevill had a wife. Even so many years later, as he was in the final stages of his life, Jennifer kept this detail from her best friend.

It was as if she could not admit to anyone the truly impossible nature of the relationship.

Invisibility and a Hasty Decision

On my fiftieth birthday, in February 1988, surrounded by my very independent children and eating wonderful cake made by Louise, I realized that my serious mother role would soon be over. I had friends around, but no close friend or partner of my own. For the first time in my life I felt horrifyingly lonely.

I had never wanted the easy option in life. After all, I had left two husbands when I felt redundant; now I felt redundant in relation to my children, who had their own lives. Having brought them up to fly the nest, I recognized that this was healthy, but at the same time I felt bereft. I also began to feel as if I was somewhat invisible and at odds with my own life. It was not nice, and I am sure many women experience this at a similar age. My parents were long gone, and although Jennifer and I spoke on the phone every few weeks and met up in London occasionally, we no longer spoke the same language. I found that she was unwilling to engage in any discussion relating to problems. If anything difficult was mentioned, she would cut me short.

'Go with God,' became her stock answer to everything.

It had been the oft-repeated phrase favoured by an elderly and rather eccentric Sister at the convent who had made a lasting impression on my sister.

'Her constant phrase, "Go with God", puzzled and annoyed me a good deal,' Jennifer wrote in her book *Call the Midwife*. 'Suddenly it became clear. It was a revelation – acceptance. It filled me with joy. Accept life, the world, Spirit, God, call it what you will, and all else will follow.'

Jennifer spent much of her time in prayer and listening for God's word. If I tried to engage her in anything important to me, this reply, 'Go with God', blanked out any further communication. I felt so frustrated. And if it was not that, she would say, 'Listen, just listen' – but I wanted to listen to my sister, not God. I had to accept that my sister Jennifer had chosen Christianity, and would stick to these dictates all her life.

Being alone at fifty led to me doing something incredibly stupid. In 1988, one thing I looked forward to enormously was a trip to Russia I had booked with Swan Hellenic Tours, through the Tate Gallery. I was going on my own and had been advised there would be other single people on the trip. I absolutely loved Russian art, and looked forward to meeting the others on the tour. At the airport on the day of departure an elegant, rather eccentric-looking man in a huge Russian fur hat attached himself to me. In a very short space of time I learned that he was a diplomat with the Commonwealth Secretariat in London, and was recovering from an operation.

On arrival in Moscow our group embarked on a train journey of more than 600 kilometres to Leningrad (now St Petersburg). I had never been on a train quite like it. At the end of each carriage was an elderly lady making tea in silver pots set on trays with exquisite china. As a lone traveller I was sharing a berth with another single woman, and I was restless, so I got up and made my way along the corridor in search of tea. There I ran into the eccentric friend from the airport. John had been put in with a man whose snoring made it impossible for him to sleep and, like me, was in need of tea. For most of the night we drank our tea and chatted.

Halfway through the trip John told me that some weeks earlier a huge cancerous growth had been removed from his stomach, and that he had only months to live – six at most. I was bowled over, my defences down in an instant in sympathy for this poor man. I could not help admiring his spirit and good humour in the face of such shattering news.

Two days before returning home, he asked me to marry him. He needed me. I was surprised, but on consideration, it did not seem a bad idea. He had a good job, a flat in London and a cottage in Lewes in Sussex, three children and a good income. Why not? Our incomes matched, and I was becoming increasingly lonely. The picture he painted of our life together was certainly tempting. We would have little time to enjoy it, but I could care for him in his hour of need.

'Our children won't like the idea, so why don't we do it straight away?' he said.

I can see now that I was swept up by the romance of it all, as well as the enormous compassion I felt for him.

'Yes, let's do it,' I said, ignoring the part of me that knew such a hasty decision could not be wise.

When we got home, I came down with flu and was very ill. I broke the news about the wedding to the children, and their reaction was total horror. I was too ill to take much notice. I cannot remember what Jennifer said. I don't think I actually told her until after the wedding had taken place, when she simply shrugged and gave me a look that let me know she thought I was crazy. I'm sure it was yet another nail in the coffin, in terms of her view of my behaviour.

Three weeks after returning from Russia, John and I exchanged our vows in the familiar setting of the Old Marylebone Town Hall, where Simon and I had been married. On this occasion, I wore a green alpaca greatcoat and a huge white cashmere stole. Afterwards, we went for a meal at John's favourite Italian restaurant in Soho with my children and his daughters. The atmosphere round the table was strained. I really had not thought things through. Looking at our mismatched families, I was filled with remorse.

'My God, what have I done?' I thought.

In the back of my mind, however, I felt that John had little time left, that I could take care of him and nurse him, and make his final few months happy.

We went down to Lewes to his cottage for a week's honeymoon, and on our return he moved into my house in Pimlico. On remarriage I had given up my maintenance from Simon, but my new husband was not prepared to contribute more than fifty pounds a week to run the entire household. I had always been generous and found this restriction intolerable, particularly when he demanded that my children pay for any food they ate.

'I can't stand this,' Louise said, and moved out immediately, while Joanna kept away.

John wanted us to have a joint account, and took me to see his solicitor to discuss our wills. I was reluctant and, when the paperwork came through, did not want to sign. When his solicitor called to ask what the hold-up was, I explained my reservations.

'Surely you trust your husband?' he said.

It seemed churlish to make trouble when John had so

little time left, so I signed, and in doing so virtually signed away my house. I found it almost impossible to do any art-work with him around, and was suffering greatly from my ill-considered decision.

Things got worse. I came home one night to find Dan had returned from school, helped himself to an avocado, and was in huge trouble with John. My poor son was in a state of shock when John rounded on him and demanded he pay for it. What had I done? The eccentric, cheerful man I had known on holiday had become a mean, didactic husband and stepfather. Had I really managed to create the sort of atmosphere in my home that had prevailed during Judith's tenure at Sonamarg when I was a child?

I spoke to Jennifer.

'What sort of cancer does he have?' she said.

'It was like a very large balloon in his stomach, and was getting bigger,' I said.

'So it was an encapsulated cancer, then?'

'I suppose it must have been.'

'Well, he's probably got a good amount of time, in that case. He may not be about to die at all. You could have him for a very long time.'

I considered my options. We had bought a cottage in Parracombe in Devon, with the intention of selling the Lewes house, and I went down for a few days to get the new place habitable. Louise and her boyfriend came too, and worked in the garden. When John arrived, he blew his top.

'How dare you let *your* children touch *my* garden?' he said.

I had to leave him. No way was I going to inflict this man on my children or myself for a moment longer than was necessary.

I moved out of my lovely house in Pimlico and into the cottage in Parracombe. It had not been lived in for some time and was almost derelict, freezing, with an ancient stove. I had very little furniture, and it was hard work to live there while sorting things out, but, after the crushing life I had with John, I loved it.

It seemed to me I was in an impossible situation financially. I had no income, as John had somehow managed to prevent my getting access to our joint bank accounts. I sold my lovely car and bought a tiny Subaru Justy, thinking I would in that way save money. But a Subaru Justy was not a good idea, and not really man enough to do the long journeys to London to see the girls, or across Devon to see Dan at Bryanston. My ready cash was fast running out. I needed some advice, so I crawled up the M5 motorway in the inside lane and across the M4 to Wantage to see my friendly bank manager, Haydon Jones, who had known me for many years.

'You have nothing to worry about, my dear; you actually have more collateral than most people. You have always made money and always will make money, so come out to lunch.'

We drove to my favourite Italian restaurant, and I enjoyed a really good lunch, fast beginning to feel more human again. I told him of my concerns about my tiny car, and on returning to the Bank I found myself outside a super-smart garage, full of wonderful sports cars. He took me inside.

'Try one,' he said.

My confidence was so low, I felt too intimidated to even touch one. 'Go on, you can afford any one you like and when you decide, get the manager to phone me and I will arrange things for you.'

He left. I tentatively tried out several of these exotic beasts and, half an hour later, left the garage driving a shiny new black Porsche. The journey up to London was amazing, as my confidence returned by the minute, and I cheerfully faced the reality of my hasty decision to marry husband number three. But how was I going to get this man out of my house? He loved the place, and had taken over my bedroom. Joanna came up with the answer.

'Pack up all his suits and shirts into cardboard boxes and put them in the spare bedroom, that's all.'

I quietly packed them up and counted sixty-seven shirts. I cleaned and aired my lovely bedroom, locked the door, and waited. John came in, surprised by my reappearance, and asked why I was not in Devon.

'I went to see my bank manager, bought a new car, and arrived an hour ago,' I said.

'What do you need a new car for?' he said. 'I thought a little clapped-out one was eminently suitable.'

I swallowed my anger.

'So what is it you've bought?' he asked.

'It begins with P,' I replied.

'Is it a Pinto?'

I shook my head.

'Is it a Peugeot?'

'No,' I replied, shaking my head again.

'Well, what is it, then? Some sort of *pedal* car?'

I absorbed this insult as I watched him. 'No, it is not a *pedal* car,' I said, lingering. 'It's a *Porsche*.'

He strode to the window and looked out at my shiny new monster, and without speaking, left the room. Going upstairs, he immediately saw the situation; no more beautiful bedroom for him, only a tiny box room at the back. He strode out of the house in silent anger, slamming the front door behind him. I was jubilant, the relief enormous. The next morning a very large removal van arrived and his few possessions, amounting to three or four boxes, mostly containing shirts, went off with it.

I had my home and my family back, although my children found it difficult to forgive me. They could not believe my irresponsibility. Neither could Jennifer. When word reached me that she had said, 'Chris seems to have made a career out of getting married,' I was so hurt.

What tore me apart was the impact of this brief, unhappy marriage on my family, the way my children withdrew from me and remained distant for a while. I well knew I had been irresponsible, and felt dreadful about it. Only recently I have realized that what I did, in marrying John, was exactly what my mother had done with Jock. Like her, I rescued a man in a terrible plight, in need of love and care, only to end up trapped in an abusive marriage. We were both lonely, and had wanted a relationship so much it led to an impulsive decision.

The only difference was that I put up with the situation for six months, while Mother tolerated Jock for twenty-five years.

Parracombe

I stayed in Devon for some years, dividing my time equally between there and London. I put on exhibitions of my work in the Pimlico house regularly, and sold quite a bit to private collectors. Frankie borrowed my London house for her fortieth birthday party in 1989. I forgot to ask about numbers – there were so many people, the house heaved. I met her youngest son, Sam, for the first time. He was absolutely gorgeous. I felt I recognized him as one of my own – certainly a Lee boy. Anyway, he got together with Dan on the balcony and together they consumed half a bottle of champagne, getting quite drunk. They then decided to go for a walk with the dogs, and got lost. Panic ensued until they were found singing in a churchyard nearby.

I also remember taking a sick chicken, an exotic bantam, back to London with me and installing her on that same balcony. As she did not improve, I took her along to the Blue Cross animal hospital. She was the star of the waiting room, everyone crowding round to have a look. They had never before seen a chicken that was alive. Even the vet could not believe that I would pay his fees to help a chicken. But she was not just a chicken – she was *my* chicken. I had nurtured her since she had come out of her shell, she had given me countless eggs over the years, and I loved her. In the country, she would sit quietly on my lap, and I would gently scratch her head while she cooed. When she eventually died of old age, I missed her.

Devon is a magical place, particularly in the summer, and all the children and their friends would come down to stay. The good thing about the Parracombe house was that it had a huge barn. I turned it into a great studio, and really enjoyed working there. I found myself painting large canvases and making so much sculpture, all motivated by the countryside and my newfound peace. My life as a sculptor had taken a big knock when I married John – his domination and mean-ness overtook all my creativity. It was only when I realized this, and walked away to set up home in north Devon with only my Jack Russells for company, that the sculptor in me could re-emerge.

My three children came down a great deal during this time. The house was spacious, and there was room for them and many other friends. It was such a good time. I loved being with these young, enthusiastic people with so much of their lives to look forward to. We walked for miles over the hills and down to the sea. We stopped for meat and fish in beautiful Lynton, and when we needed more we drove down to the Barnstaple covered market. And at home it was so good to collect eggs from the chickens and dig up potatoes, pick vegetables and cook huge, delicious meals. We would eat by the range in the kitchen in winter or picnic in the garden in the summer, leaving wild flowers to dry over the kitchen range; everything was very beautiful.

We had a hammock strung between two old apple trees, and garden chairs and tables in various parts of the garden, so in the summer, breakfast outside was spread-eagled every-where. And what breakfasts – bacon and eggs and sausages and tomatoes and mushrooms and black pudding, and quantities of fresh coffee, and huge hunks of buttered toast with home-made jams and marmalade. I love cooking, and I loved feeding these young people with their hungry appetites and huge appreciation. And when they were with me, they shared my studio and helped me paint the lounge in vibrant colours. Their very presence made me idyllically happy.

Joanna was running an alternative health centre in Westminster, and I was looking for ways of showcasing and selling my art. She suggested I meet Brian Stevens, who had an antiques shop opposite her premises and was planning to open a gallery in the basement. We met, and he invited me to lunch. On the appointed day I arrived late, casually dressed in jeans and a jumper, my white and tan Jack Russell on the passenger seat beside me. Brian, in an immaculate pin-striped suit, was waiting on the pavement outside his shop.

Winding down the window, I said, 'You're not going to love me, the passenger seat's covered in dog hair.'

He just smiled, returning to his shop. Moments later he came out with two silver hairbrushes and proceeded to sweep out the car as best he could, while my little dog sat on my lap. He got in and took the dog from me.

'Well, that's lovely,' he said, and off we went.

As I followed him through the large elegant restaurant I saw that the back of his suit was smothered in white dog hair. I said nothing but couldn't help smiling. This man was so refreshing, walking round completely oblivious to his extraordinary resemblance to a snowman from behind, and it was not long before we became lovers. It was an incredibly enriching relationship.

Brian lived with his two huge Saint Bernard dogs on a longboat on the Thames, moored opposite Dolphin Square.

He took me to the Savoy for breakfast in their wonderful dining room overlooking the river and we ate quantities of eggs and bacon, lots of toast and strong black coffee. A good breakfast was always Brian's first essential of the day, and it is certainly mine today. On Friday mornings he would come down to Devon, full of good humour and with baskets of wonderful things to eat. He loved nothing better than wandering off alone for hours at a time – I never knew where, and never tried to find out. He was a gentle Buddhist and took me along to many meetings in London; I loved the chanting, and the ethics. He also took me to Switzerland twice a year, where we stayed at the fashionable Hotel Verenahof in Baden with its incredible thermal baths, returning to England completely rejuvenated.

My studio in Devon, with its open fire in the middle, was warm even in the winter months. Work was almost a process of recovery after what had gone on with John. I asked Jennifer to come down, knowing it would do her good. I could give her nourishing food and the silence she craved. I very much wanted to see her.

'I couldn't possibly,' she said. 'It's just too far.'

I knew from the tone of her voice that it was pointless to try and persuade her. I put down the phone and walked into the garden, appreciating its beauty, and breathed in the air, so pure and so healing. Little Pushkin, my baby duckling, was waiting for me on the lawn, quacking away and happily rushing about.

The only nasty element in this state of bliss was the prospect of an extremely unpleasant divorce. John had survived well beyond the six months he had been given to live – as Jennifer had predicted – and seemed determined to make me suffer. Philip Druce, my valued solicitor from Witney, presided. The only time I saw my third husband after his departure from my house in Pimlico was in the High Court of Justice in the Strand, where our divorce was settled some years later. The outcome was that I had to sell my home in London. This was tough, since I had loved the house; but I had been foolish to marry in haste, and was to repent at leisure. It had been a painful lesson and I had lost a lot. With my share of the proceeds I decided to treat myself again, and bought a white Mercedes sports car with red leather interior. After all, my Porsche needed replacing. I thoroughly enjoyed scooting around the countryside and up to London in my new beast.

It was 1994. I was keeping exotic bantams, ducks and guinea fowl. I had Claud, my King of Jack Russells (who seemed to have sired the whole of North Devon), and Jelly, one of his puppies, and two cats. I had become pretty self-sufficient. It was all very beautiful and I was at peace. I seemed to be living in an identikit of my grandmother's house, with chickens in the yard and dogs at my heels, but there were differences. Inside the house, the colours were outrageous – strong, happy, childish colours – the chickens were exotic rare breed bantams, not Rhode Island Reds, and the vegetable garden was set out in wild patterns. My mind soared upwards and outwards, chasing new things to make and create. The kitchen range was always burning, the smell of baking permeated the house and log fires crackled. Outside, the garden beckoned and the robin waited. I seemed to be moving in a preordained pattern.

Still, there were black times when I was alone.

In Worcestershire, heading home after a weekend with Joanna, I had a horrible accident. An old sack blew into the road and onto the windscreen of a car coming towards me. Blinded, the driver crashed through the central reservation at speed and hit me head-on.

Ears blocked by noise, metal on metal, five chickens in the back flapping around me, Claud and Jelly barking, as if in the distance – and then all became suddenly quiet. I realized I was alive. I looked around and saw the driver of the other car, utterly still. In time, an ambulance arrived. Somehow the paramedics kept the flapping chickens inside the car, and got the dogs out. In hospital, I waited. Doctors examined me; I was X-rayed. Nothing was wrong, other than severe whiplash. I was in pain, weeping uncontrollably, and was dismissed and sent away.

Uncertainty

November 1994. There was a real nip in the air and my toes were cold, despite sitting in the snug – which, by the way, was not snug at all, just small. The fire smoked and gave off little heat, and the winter sun belied the sub-zero temperature outside. I stopped to change out of my smart Swiss shoes into my treasured fur-lined boots, bought from Harvey Nichols many moons ago. They are a bit scruffy now and have a toggle missing, but no matter. I made up the fire with more coal collected from the metal feed bin. Having no shovel, I had to open it up and pick out the coals by hand; they were freezing. I noted the sprinkle of snow on the hard ground, the tree no longer in leaf, and the pub beyond, dazzling in the winter sunshine. I made some artichoke soup.

I was comfortable now; the fire had really got going, and my feet were warm. The dogs lay peacefully on their dark brown sheepskin by the fire. Claud was now ten and got arthritis in the winter; he needed his creature comforts, and so did I. I was not potty about animals, but was used to having them around me and would feel bereft without them. Anyway, Claud did deserve the best, after being with me for ten years and putting up with the change and upheavals of my life with fortitude and great courage. He was truly magnificent, and I valued him more and more. He and his daughter Angelica were squat, chunky, smooth-coated Jack Russells – white and chestnut, when not grubby from rabbiting.

I was a white woman, English of middle-class origins, whatever that means, and of an uncertain age. Uncertain is how I felt five per cent of the time, although it used to be a lot more. Uncertainty was a horrible feeling. It manifested in a raw lump in the bottom of my chest and pressed down into my abdomen, making me feel sick and breathless. I hated this, and recognized it immediately when it came over me. I knew I had to ride this tiger for as long as it takes – usually it passes with the night. I saw little and heard little at these times. I knew I had to walk the dogs, put on Radio 4, and clean the house. I wanted to scream. I felt isolated, alone; very, very angry. I just had to wait for the day to run out.

A good day. I awoke with a smile on my lips and felt able to consider the wreckages of yesterday. I knew the remedy. I needed contact, I needed help. I rang my children for comfort, but only managed to alienate them. I must have sounded horribly tight and artificial. I resolved not to phone them again when I felt like this – I had dumped too much on them already, and they had their own weights to carry. Anyway, today was a day of hope and happiness.

I picked up the phone to my sister.

Jennifer sliced into my consciousness. She was glowing with pride at the success of her exceptional daughter, Juliette, and talked of her play *Brave*, written out of the ashes of a questionable relationship. Put on in Birmingham, it was inspiring and humorous.

I asked Jennifer to come to Devon. She would not, yet

wanted to organize my garden for me. I admitted that it did look like a builder's yard at the back, and certainly needed attention I could not give. She had a lodger, a landscape gardener, who would love to do it for me on the cheap.

'Has he agreed?' I asked.

'No, not yet, but he will,' she said.

'Ask him, then, but do explain my circumstances.' I had virtually no cash. 'I cannot spend £3,000 on a fish pond. He can stay here and I'll feed him, but he will have to make do with all the stones and bricks lying around, and only peppercorn wages.'

Silence.

Jennifer returned to the subject of her creative daughter, an unmarried mother, then on to her divorced sister-in-law. She finally came to me.

'There are two types of women,' she stated, 'as you must surely know from Greek mythology. One sat embroidering and waiting for her man, Ulysses, to return from the wars, putting an extra knot in each year to signal the passing of time.' She paused, allowing her words to sink in. 'This is the man's woman, and she is never alone, as the man is always by her side to the end.'

I sensed where this was going.

'The other type of woman develops herself, and uses a man as a stud. She ends up by herself, with only her dogs to pet.'

'Yuck,' I said, and somehow restrained myself from saying more, muttering something about restricted vision.

'You should write your autobiography,' she said, raising her voice.

'I can't remember it,' I shouted back.

'You should write it, anyway.' The line was taut with

tension. After a moment, she said, 'I will ask the landscape gardener.'

The line went dead.

I was stung by her words. I was flawed, as we all are, and while I had made mistakes, I was not alone in doing so. The conversation played again inside my head. I had never used a man as a stud. *She ends up by herself.* In the end, surely, we are all on our own.

Claud ambled over and sat at my feet, pressing his body into my legs. He seemed able to pick up on my feelings. I put a hand on his head, and felt greatly blessed to have a dog to pet. My dogs and I really speak to each other and they give me far more than I give them.

The room was quiet. From the mantelpiece in the sitting room came the soft chime of the clock. My children did not hear me, my sister did not hear me. Perhaps I would, as Jennifer suggested, write it all down, as much as I could remember; and perhaps someone would read it one day. At least writing would give a voice to my world, and my much-criticized life.

Perhaps Jennifer, like me, felt that we were too different to find much common ground. In my frustration, I felt like giving up, letting go; and yet even as I had the thought, I knew I never would, for I had no doubt about her love for me or mine for her. Our love was the thread that tied us to one another. Flimsy, seemingly in danger of snapping under pressure at times, but unbroken.

Claud lay down, his chin on my foot. For a moment I tried to picture Jennifer and what she might be doing. The image wouldn't come. How much did I know of what was really going on in her life? How much did she know of mine? When I needed her, really needed her, and laid bare my true feelings, all that ever came back were the three familiar words: 'Go with God.'

I wanted to rail at her – I don't want to go with God. I want to speak to my sister and for her to hear me!

Reality

In 1996, I realized I needed to return to the real world and earn some money. I could not live in my idyllic haven in Devon forever. I took out the map of England, picked up a pin, and stuck it in. It landed on Stratford-upon-Avon, Shakespeare's country. If it was good enough for the Bard it would be good enough for me. I set about putting the Devon house on the market and finding out about Stratford and its environs. It was quite depressing; properties in Warwickshire were so much more expensive than Devon. The agents' particulars came in thick and fast, and not one was remotely suitable. We had been used to so much space, and I was beginning to lose faith in my original intention.

One day details of a property arrived by post. It was derelict, with a tree growing out of the drawing-room window. It looked like an impossible undertaking. Peter, my builder and sculpture assistant, came in to see me. I showed him the particulars of this latest house.

'This is all I can afford,' I said, feeling dismal.

He studied the photo on the front of the brochure at length.

'Well, it's got straight walls,' he said.

'So I see, Peter, but it looks too much for me to take on,' I said, a touch terse.

'Oh, me and the boys could sort that out in a month,' he replied, sagely.

I chose to believe him, drove straight up to Stratford-upon-Avon and agreed to buy the wreck of a house, which was in the beautiful village of Armscote, a few miles south of the town. A few weeks later, I moved up there with Peter and 'the boys' – five of them. The tree in the drawing room came out, a damp-proof course went in, and Rentokil sprayed. Floors were repaired, walls knocked down, fireplaces renewed and plastering and painting done. All completed so quickly, and so well. The outside was rendered, windows repaired, two bathrooms and a kitchen fitted and plumbed in. At the end of the six weeks it was ready and the boys, who had slept happily on my sofas, returned home to Devon, content that they had done a good job. I can never thank them enough. It had been fun, I had prepared splendid food for them all day, and Dan and a friend had come down as labourers and sorted out the garden. How could I be so blessed?

Brian loved Stratford and its environs, and our delightful relationship continued to flourish as we spent weekends and holidays together. Yet when his sixtieth birthday was imminent he began to feel really unhappy. He did not like the prospect of being sixty at all. 'You must marry me before my sixtieth,' was his constant refrain.

'You are not the marrying kind. You would hate it,' I replied. But I loved this crazy man and eventually I relented, saying 'yes' just before Christmas. The effect was catastrophic. He went into severe panic and left me on Boxing Day. It was a shock, but a part of me was not surprised as I really understood this gentle man. The following month, after sending me huge bouquets of flowers, he rang to say that he had been diagnosed with a brain tumour, and died some time later.

He had a beautiful Buddhist funeral with candles and chanting and I said my goodbyes knowing how much I would miss him.

I was still searching for a spiritual home. I attempted Buddhism, but found chanting on my own a problem, so when I came across a Quaker Meeting House, I walked in. I enjoyed being a Quaker for about three years. I felt a deep appreciation of their quiet values and would have stayed, had not a large, loud and rather controlling man joined the group, with the consequence that the peaceful atmosphere disappeared. It was at this time that I felt the need for a father figure, and with this in mind I sussed out the Catholics and made my way to the Catholic church in Ilmington. Mike, my first husband, was now dead, and I realized that in the eyes of the Catholic church I was no longer a reprobate for having divorced him. I chatted to Father Tony, a truly remarkable human being with a wonderful sense of humour. He was a broadminded ex-Marine, and I felt accepted by him. He did say that I was something of a heretic, and I have certainly been a questioning Catholic ever since.

On talking to Jennifer about my religious convictions, she said she could never become a Catholic as she could never accept the infallibility of the Pope. As the original doubting Thomas, I am happy to leave this question open. I value the time I spend in church, any church, as it gives me space to consider my family, my friends, myself and my death.

Eczema

Early in 1996, Juliette, Jennifer's younger daughter, was married. I had not seen Jennifer for some time, and was utterly appalled at how ill she looked. She was dressed in a white sheet that she had fashioned into a loose-fitting kaftan over a white petticoat and white cotton plimsolls. Her face was red and swollen, and she was painfully thin.

'Jennifer, what's happened?' I said.

'It's eczema,' she said. 'I can't wear colours next to my skin. Everything hurts.'

She had first complained of eczema in 1990, but had made nothing of it to me. I had also experienced bouts of eczema, no more than minor flare-ups over the years and, from what my sister told me, I had thought she was suffering the same thing. She had developed a couple of inflamed patches of skin on her legs, she said, and initially thought they were insect bites.

Going by what she had told me in our phone calls, I had no sense it was anything serious. Thinking back, I should have probed more; but I doubt it would have made any difference, as Jennifer only ever told me as much as she wanted me to know.

At Juliette's wedding there was little opportunity for my sister and me to talk, but she did tell me her whole body had been affected and that, at its worst, the eczema made her skin red and rough – almost like bubble wrap.

'I can't even wear a bra,' she said. 'The straps are just too painful.'

My heart went out to her and yet, as it turned out, I still had no real sense of the scale of her suffering. As was so often the case, my sister was not willing to let me in on what was really going on in her life.

Jennifer had always had what I considered to be odd eating habits. I understood that she did not want to consume meat or fish, but her diet generally was very limited. Mostly, all she wanted to eat was bread and cheese, or cakes. At the wedding that day I cannot remember her eating anything. Now I know that she was on an extreme eating regime, in an effort to rid herself of her debilitating skin condition. Another year would go by before I finally realized the extent of her suffering and its impact on her life.

Living in Armscote was truly lovely, and being so near to Stratford-upon-Avon a delight. I had a studio at the back of the house, and happily worked there. I was following my original intention of living a creative, independent life, unrestricted by the bounds of convention and marriage, with a free mind and spirit, valuing nature, where everything is possible.

All the houses I have lived in have looked the same inside. I take all the furniture, rugs and memorabilia with me. Joanna says I'm like a Bedouin moving around the desert: I move around the country with my essentials, things that define my life. And as I work, making sculpture and painting, there is always the same atmosphere around me. I had not intended to move so often, nor indeed to have so many husbands and partners. The biggest challenge for any artist in this day and age is how to financially support themselves while they create. Historically, 'wealthy patrons' would support 'young talent'; but even so, history is littered with artists who lived in poverty, paying rent in drawings and dying before they are 'recognized'.

I trained as a mature student and single parent with a family to support, so I made the decision to fund myself through buying and renovating houses. On reflection, it would have been easier to have a home and then a 'renovation project', to avoid moving so frequently. However, I also needed a big workshop space in which to create sculpture; therefore I used to buy a bigger place in need of renovation, live and work in it, and do it up over a couple of years or so, then sell it on.

It is true that rolling stones gather no moss, for I have few very old friends now; but it is also true that I have no heavy weights weighing me down. I love life, and I love people, and they are everywhere – in the country, in towns, on trains, in shops, everywhere – so I am never, never alone or lonely. Why have so many men wanted to marry me? It is certainly because of my love of life.

I revelled in the plays and the awareness of the theatre industry throughout Stratford. I was working happily there making very simple pieces that encapsulated all that I had absorbed from the past few years. I began drawing huge pieces on paper fixed to my dining-room walls, as my studio was too small for them. I worked with plaster of Paris and wood, mainly on birds; and I had some cast, ranging from eighteen to twenty-four inches in size. But I wanted to do something really big – hence the drawings in the dining room, and hence my walking up to a boat builder.

Nigel the boat builder had all the equipment I needed to make really large birds, and was pretty enthusiastic about my project. So I went home, made huge paper cut-outs of my design, and returned to see him a week later. Nigel was a genius with steel, and made my first large steel birds exactly as they were drawn, not changing anything. It was wonderful.

But Stratford was a desert then, for artists, and we needed an arts club, so I gathered together half a dozen interested artists, and held discussions in my drawing room. We needed a professional project manager. I can't remember how or when Jackie Nixon appeared. She was attractive, pleasant, had all the organizational and administrative qualities I lacked, and we worked together at promoting the arts club along with sculpture for stately homes. For the next three years, this proved very successful, although on reflection, I don't think we valued each other enough. I needed to spend more time on my own work, and I don't think Jackie felt sufficiently appreciated. We based the arts club at a very cool restaurant on the edge of Stratford, held exhibitions there, and had delicious lunches on Sundays with a beautiful harpist and great conversation.

Our first sculpture park was held at Ragley Hall, a stately home near Alcester. Many important sculptors contributed, and I really enjoyed placing the pieces around the beautiful and impressive grounds. My large stainless steel piece graced the entrance, and looked incredible. We had invited many local dignitaries to the opening, including the Mayor and other council members. The Earl and Countess of Yarmouth played their part to perfection and gave a delicious tea. It was a really wonderful day.

As I left, the Mayor, Councillor Mrs Joan McFarlane,

asked me to phone her. The following week, as we sipped tea in the Mayor's parlour, she asked me to make a fountain to mark the 800th anniversary of Stratford's Royal Charter in 1996.

'We all admired your piece outside Ragley Hall, and we want a local sculptor to do the work. Would you be interested?'

I could hardly believe my ears. 'Yes, of course,' I said, barely able to contain my excitement.

She asked if I would be ready to discuss the matter with the relevant committee the following week, and I said I would. I spent the weekend alone working on huge drawings and cardboard cut-outs, made a maquette and showed it to the Council. The *Stratford Herald* reported this the following week, and a number of artists and sculptors then began shouting for an open competition, resulting in the Council withdrawing its instructions to me. The proposed fountain was subsequently advertised as an open competition. I was so disappointed – yet the day before the final submission date, it dawned on me that there was no reason why I could not put in my original proposal again, and so I did.

A week later, I was informed I had won the competition. There was one tiny problem. The Council had only a limited budget, certainly insufficient to make a fountain of any size. So I sat down one night and wrote four identical letters to four millionaire businessmen of the town, asking for their financial backing. One of them, for whom I had worked before, came back to me. Richard Cooper, founder of Country Artists, a prosperous and well-known firm in Stratford, agreed to fund us to the tune of £40,000. The Council would contribute the balance. Richard was a tremendously nice man and we seemed to speak the same language. I was not at all surprised that he had developed such a successful business in just ten years. So began a period of incredibly hard work.

The Fountain –
Factors for Consideration

All of my energy went into the making of the fountain. The site was to be Bancroft Gardens, next to the Royal Shakespeare Theatre, and there was much to consider. How would it relate to the surrounding period buildings and gardens? What size, and what materials?

It needed to be modern, but it was important that the general public would be able to relate to it. This was a monument for the people of Stratford, and had nothing to do with the town's famous theatre or its connections.

I spent quite a while on site, taking notice of how the local people related to the area in general. Without exception, they gravitated to the river and watched the swans gliding almost regally along. Swans it had to be. It was important that the piece be uplifting and so the swans needed to be placed high up: one male, one female.

I decided to make them out of mirror-polished stainless steel to reflect the surrounding areas and therefore be part of the whole, and to place them in a brass bowl to add variety and texture. I also wanted the water to shoot up from the base, hitting the brass bowl underneath and giving the impression that the entire sculpture floated on the water from the elevated bowl. I also wanted another small fountain to project water directly under the swans, to form a lacy surround when overflowing the edge. The fountain would be ever-changing as the day changed from morning to night, summer to winter. I wanted people to reflect on it and feel uplifted.

Roger Abbott, my creative architect, and I could always find a way out of the many difficult situations that arose. We had a very good team, all local, and goodwill prevailed. The only exception to this was the welder, Brian Harrison, who helped me with the third-size model. I found working with him almost impossible and became determined not to let him anywhere near the development of the fountain itself. The ramifications of this decision were to colour my life for quite some time.

Her Majesty the Queen was to open the fountain on November 8, 1996, a Friday, and we all had to work flat out to meet the deadline. Scaffolding was erected, and the whole structure was covered ahead of the big day. The week before, the various sections arrived on the back of a lorry and eight men struggled to lift them into position. It was quite a job. I was up a ladder giving instructions, feeling a sense of pride and some nervousness as it all came together.

Our biggest difficulty came only three days before the opening, when the water engineer could not be found to test the fountain. He was in America, running in a half-marathon! It seemed unbelievable, and yet we overcame it. The day before the inauguration, as the scaffolding was being taken down, a pole fell and struck me on the head, sending me crashing to the ground. I had no hard hat, and was briefly unconscious before the ambulance arrived and took me to Stratford Hospital, where I was X-rayed. The pain was immense, but nothing was broken – however, they said I should stay for observation.

'I've got to go,' I said, getting to my feet. 'There's so much to do, and the Queen's coming tomorrow. I can't miss any of it.'

The doctors looked at me as if I were mad. They may well have thought I was rambling. I discharged myself.

There was another drama looming. That same day, still dazed from the blow to my head, I took a call from a reporter who said he had heard that there was a dispute regarding the ownership of the design of the fountain and that the Queen would not, after all, be performing the opening. This was not true. There was indeed a dispute in the offing, but the opening was to go ahead as scheduled the following day.

The fountain was up and running, and ready for the Queen. To meet Her Majesty was a privilege not to be forgotten, and I was thrilled at the prospect. My son Dan was my partner; Jennifer was there too, and to my great joy she looked well and happy, with not a trace of the eczema that had been plaguing her. Philip was with her. My half-sisters Frankie and Pat also came, with their spouses. It was unusual for all four sisters to be together, and that added to the occasion for me. My best friend, Wilhelmien, was also there with her husband Terry. I had also invited a wonderful neighbour from my village, ninety-nine-year-old Mildred, whom I had grown to respect and love.

We had to be ready for the Queen well in advance of her arrival. It was a bright winter's day and I was wearing an emerald-green floaty skirt and black fitted jacket. At the last minute I made a doughnut of a hat, and covered it in a green and black silk scarf. As we waited and time passed it got very cold. I was frozen. Dear Terry was wearing a lovely soft tan cashmere overcoat, and kindly lent it to me. And so I met the Queen wearing a borrowed overcoat several sizes too big.

She seemed very pleased with the fountain, and spent some time asking me about the idea behind it and its construction, before unveiling a commemorative plaque.

Afterwards, I went with Dan to the town hall, where the Queen was to have tea. We rushed, thinking we were late, and in fact arrived early. As we wandered onto the balcony, a huge cheer went up from the crowd below. Dan, delighted, began waving. He spotted his girlfriend Corina in the crowd, waving and laughing, and he vigorously responded. After several minutes of this I decided enough was enough, and tugged him back inside the room.

Later, once the formalities were over, all those who had worked on the sculpture crammed into a room above our favourite pub where we had food, drinks and speeches. It was hilarious. Everyone was so happy and relieved that it had all gone so well. That night, I had arranged another celebration at my own home. The centrepiece was a cake I'd made, decorated with a replica of the fountain.

Jennifer was very proud of me. 'You are a *genius*,' she kept repeating.

We were both so happy that day, and it felt as if we had really connected again after so many years. My sister was glowing with pride, and absolutely thrilled for me. I felt great love for her.

The morning after, all those of us involved were exhausted. I was still somewhat dazed from my bang on the head, as well as all the excitement of the opening and subsequent celebrations. I then discovered that Mr Harrison – the welder of the third-size model – had put in a writ the day before under the 1988 Copyrights, Designs and Patents Act, claiming breach of copyright and the right to be identified as 'joint author' of the fountain design. The *Stratford Herald* ran the story under the headline: 'Fountain to be a one-day wonder?' According to the report, the fountain might have to be dismantled. All this had created mayhem for the Council, our small band of workmen, and the Palace.

Dealing with a local solicitor was obviously not going to solve this appalling travesty, so I approached the Arts Council. They advised me to go to Taylor Joynson Garrett, who specialized in copyright disputes. I was under intense pressure from solicitors and the public alike, and letters descended on me almost daily. I could not work, and indeed felt like giving up altogether. It was a terrible time. This dispute was ruining my life. Financially, I was getting close to being broke. Emotionally, I was extremely low and physically totally exhausted. Was it worth it?

In 1997, as the dispute over the fountain rumbled on, Jennifer's first book was published by Merton Books. She sent me a copy of *Eczema and Food Allergy: The Hidden Cause*? I had not even known she was writing it. On the first page I read that my sister had been almost driven to suicide by what she called the hideous skin disease that had covered her entire body. I reeled. The words swam in front of me. What horrors had she been going through?

I thought back to our phone calls. Why had she said nothing? I felt awful, as if I had been knocked out. Throughout periods of terrible suffering she had kept me in the dark, and yet now every detail of her illness had been laid out for general consumption.

It struck me that on the many occasions I had wanted

Jennifer to visit me in Devon, she must have been battling eczema, seeking help from various specialists, undertaking the most extreme of diets, which at one time consisted solely of meat – an indication of how desperate she must have been, since she had been a confirmed non-meat eater for many years.

She must have been in the most dreadful state. I had had no idea.

'The itching, day and night, like a million tiny insects crawling around under the skin, biting and nibbling beneath the skin surface. It is impossible to imagine the horror of it, if you have not experienced it . . . I quite calmly thought I would die,' she wrote.

I read her account in utter shock.

'I think that if I had not met the doctor who eventually cured me, I would have committed suicide.'

No wonder she had looked so wretched at Juliette's wedding. Of course, she could have told me then at least some of what was going on. I would have understood. She *could* have. She chose not to. I cannot say why. I was so hurt, I could not bring myself to ask her. Like so much else, it lay between us, never to be spoken about.

While the chasm between us had widened, Jennifer had become ever closer to my daughter, Joanna, and I realized I was jealous. I wanted that same closeness. Jennifer had also grown increasingly fond of our half-sister, Pat. I was glad about this, but it did hurt to hear her express her support for Pat when, if I sought the same, I was brushed aside with the familiar, 'Go with God.'

Jennifer and Joanna

While Jennifer was proud of her children, she felt she didn't quite understand them, as they were so very different to her. She was full of energy and stamina, loved the outdoors, and never seemed to see any danger in her activities, or worry what anyone thought of her. Her sensitive daughters may perhaps have felt somewhat cowed by the sheer force that was their mother. She may have found it difficult to tell Philip anything that might make him worry and, as she did with me, just kept things to herself. Whatever her feelings, however, she had an immense determination to keep her family together.

Over time, Joanna became the person in whom Jennifer confided her secrets. When she was due to spend three days in hospital for a heart procedure it was Jo she told, while her husband and children were kept entirely in the dark. Joanna was also something of a helpline to Jennifer, who suffered from allergies all through her life. She would take to her bed, wheezing, feeling dreadful, and turn to Jo for dietary advice. For a while she would eat only what she called her safe foods – pheasant, rice and pears – until she felt better again. Once she started eating all the things she really enjoyed again, like cheese and puddings, her health would begin to deteriorate once more.

For Joanna, her aunt was a tall, commanding figure, impatient in crowds, liable to go to the front of a queue and round the back of a shop counter to help herself, oblivious that such behaviour was not 'the done thing'. Jennifer did as she liked. She thought nothing of walking down the King's Road in overt diamonds and pearls. When I suggested that this was not a good idea, she raised her eyebrows and looked down her nose at me. 'No one would touch me,' she said imperiously, and I believed her. She never did respect physical barriers – did not even see or feel them – which I'm sure was why she loved plunging into cold seawater and walking barefoot. That way, she actually felt something. Later on, in her seventies, she thought nothing of walking about in flimsy kaftans or stripping naked in front of people on the beach in Brighton when she changed into her swimsuit – invariably one that became transparent when wet. Her behaviour was certainly unconventional. It was during the writing of this book that my daughter told me of much that she and Jennifer had shared, and so I finally came to learn the painful truth.

Much of what my sister had felt, I simply never knew. She never told me. When Joanna revealed that all through Jennifer's life she had felt eclipsed by me whenever I walked into a room, I was utterly horrified. Simply by virtue of my being the person I am, and looking as I do, my sister had felt diminished. My mother had planted this seed when we were children. Hearing this made me feel unbearably sad. Learning that my oldest daughter had also at times felt this way compared to her younger siblings was equally sad to me.

For years, I had wondered why I could not get near my sister, and had never felt able to ask her. The wall she constructed around herself was too solid to breach. Now

I understood why she was so remote. She was much too proud to ever have told me how she really felt. I wish we had managed to have the conversation. It might have made things easier. We shall never know now. What I can say is that even knowing what I do now does not change the way I feel about her. I loved her, and I know that she loved me.

While I didn't understand Jennifer at this time, I did feel as if I had resolved some of my complicated feelings towards my mother. For a long time I had been judging her, and now I realized I wanted to put that aside and think about the good things. I sat down to write her a letter.

> *Hills View, Devon*
> *Summer, 1998*

Dear Mummy,

And I mean dear, dear to me – a big, generous real person. But not until now can I unreservedly be a real person with you. It has taken me fifty years to get to this stage, fifty years to see clearly. As a child I saw as a child and loved you unreservedly, seven years of as near bliss as I can imagine. I have those seven years in my heart for ever – THANK you – then seven years of torture – I blamed you for everything. Now I know that you too were a victim of circumstance, a child of your generation. I do not blame you now.

What I need to say to you is that I now really appreciate your unbelievable innocence and goodness. No one taught you that in this world there is a necessary other side to the coin, 'a bite'. I now have a bite which I use when I remember and I am now in control of my life and my destiny. But most of the wonderful parts of me come from you – the great

GREAT *love of life, and being part of the natural world, the grass, the flowers, the birds, the trees, the wind, the sun and the sea. And the need to share it all with others in poetry and paint, the celebration of who we are, the seasons of our life and of knowing the unknown. For all that and so much more I thank you.*

I would love to share my work with you now it has moved on so far since the first piece I made in your shed in Devon. I would also love you to know that your time living in Dorset still lives with the people there. They still play your harvest hymn at their harvest festival – they call it their hymn. Only a few months ago you were talked about on television, your poetry, your realness and your hymn. And wherever I go where people know you they clamour to talk to me about you and because I'm your daughter they want me close to them.

I weep that you are no more, and I miss you.

With overwhelming love,
Christine

Marriage Number Four

It was around this time that Douglas came into my life. Charming and very clever, a Michael Heseltine lookalike, he had been in his day the Jeremy Paxman of television, grilling and annoying Margaret Thatcher and other notable political figures. He was also the chairman of sixteen different media companies simultaneously. I met him at a party and he invited me to lunch at Charingworth Manor in the Cotswolds. My friend Sue told me I had to look my best, as it was a very smart hotel, so I put on a pale green silk suit I hardly ever wore, silver stockings and silver shoes. As I swept up the driveway to the hotel in my sports car I saw Douglas standing on the terrace in the sunshine, looking rather glamorous. A Greek god, I thought!

We had a fabulous lunch that went on for three hours, during which we talked and laughed non-stop. All of a sudden I noticed the time and had to leave in a hurry to make a business meeting in Stratford. Later, Douglas told me the sight of my silver legs and shoes emerging from my low-slung sports car had knocked him sideways.

As a former journalist he knew about the law of copyright, and was therefore the perfect man to take over the legal battle I was going through. The pressure on me changed, and I soon began to realize that another man wanted to marry me.

'You do know I've been married several times before?' I said, when he brought the subject up.

He was determined. I was feeling weak and vulnerable and I needed someone to care for me. I wanted to be altogether out of what felt to me to be the rat race of sculpture. But marriage number four?

Meanwhile, the court case over the copyright dispute about the Country Artists Fountain came to fruition at Birmingham High Court on June 30, 1998. I had great support. Douglas was there, as were my son-in-law David and the architect, Roger. We travelled up by train to Birmingham, me wearing borrowed clothes again (Lou's best business suit) and feeling pretty apprehensive. After all, the legal team had only given me a seventy-five per cent chance of winning the case, and that left twenty-five per cent uncertain. I don't like 'uncertain'.

As we filed into the courtroom I looked across at Mr Harrison. It was the first time I had seen him since we worked on the model in Stratford. This man, with men either side, was grinning at me. All dressed in black, they looked like the Mafia, and I felt very uncomfortable. The judge, Mr Justice Jacobs, was impressive. After only three hours he stopped the case which had been scheduled to take up to three days. The design was deemed to be my original work, and I was entirely vindicated.

When I returned home to the peace of Armscote I wandered round to see a friend, who also happened to be a solicitor. She was delighted by my news. When I told her the whole case had hinged on whether or not I had made the fountain templates on my own, something that was hard to prove, she was incredulous.

'But don't you remember breaking off from your work to

give me and my mother tea, and then showing us the fountain model you were busy making? We could have vouched for you.'

It all came back to me. If only I had remembered their visit, it would have saved me many, many months of hell.

Douglas and I were married by candlelight on November 28, 1998, in a delightful ceremony at Ilmington Catholic Church. I had filled the church with white and pink lilies, and it looked lovely. Louise grabbed a bunch for me to carry as I walked down the aisle, since I hadn't thought about a bouquet. I wore a long dress and jacket in dark lavender, and in my hair a tortoiseshell and marcasite clip, a gift from Dan.

We held the reception at my house, and it was a great event. Jennifer came and, again, as at the opening of the fountain two years before, she seemed well and happy. I remember, though, that as ever in a large social group, she seemed a little isolated, declining offers to dance and preferring to observe. Wilhelmien, my oldest friend, was there, as were four out of the six children Douglas and I had between us. Douglas had filled a dustbin with ice and bottles of champagne. I am not a fan of fruit cake, so had arranged for a wedding cake that was a copy of something I had seen in France. It was made of thin layers of sponge, fruit and meringue, and had two oblong tiers, one slightly smaller than the other. When it arrived the night before the wedding, to my dismay, it was plain and white and boring. I rushed upstairs and drew lots of different types of birds, painted them different colours, attached them to sticks and dotted them all over the cake so that they seemed to be in flight. Everybody took one home.

Jennifer felt it was a very good thing for me to marry Douglas. I think she felt we were well suited and, like me, really believed that this time it must surely last.

At one point during the reception I found her wandering round looking for Philip.

'Oh, he's in the smoking room, having a jolly time,' I said.

'But he does not smoke!' Jennifer said, quite put out.

I ran upstairs, found him, and told him that Jennifer was looking for him. He looked alarmed, and quickly put his cigarette out.

Douglas was fond of Jennifer, but it was only on the day of the actual wedding that he first encountered her un-conventional side.

'Father Tony was due to come—' he was saying.

'No, he can't, he's much too busy!' Jennifer burst out, interrupting his speech.

Poor Douglas was thrown completely off his stride. Then, having already had two slabs of wedding cake, Jennifer ate the one remaining piece, which I had put aside for him. He was the only person not to get any cake, and was most displeased. I doubt my sister even noticed.

Douglas took me on honeymoon to Rome and we stayed in the Picasso Hotel (which boasts original works by the artist), went to the Vatican, saw Pope John Paul II at Sunday Mass in St Peter's Square and generally devoured Rome.

It could not have been a more perfect start.

Once Douglas and I were married Jennifer invited us to stay with her at Boxmoor, where she played some of my favourite pieces on the piano and we had a really relaxed time, talking about music and books. It was the first time I had been asked there with a partner, which was a sign of how much Jennifer liked Douglas.

Back to Devon

Douglas was keen to move to Devon and so, with regret, I left Stratford-upon-Avon. We bought a lovely house on the edge of Ottery St Mary. It had delightful gardens running down to a stream, and huge barns in which I could start work again. I loved it there. In the evening I would cook and set a table with candles beside the river, and we would eat outside, enjoying the peace and beauty of our surroundings until well after the sun went down.

I valued being able to work again, even taking a stand at the Chelsea Flower Show, which was exciting. I was creating large pieces in stainless steel and inside my studio had set up a space exactly like the one I would have at Chelsea to show my work. I had an Australian assistant working with me. Every day I disappeared into the studio, and every day Douglas would come in, tell me what to do and generally interrupt my way of thinking.

Unfortunately, I was no longer used to living with a husband, and found the closeness of the relationship and what I felt was the controlling side of Douglas very difficult. He was not used to a working wife. Whilst I was happy to emerge from my studio at five in the evening and cook and spend time with him, it was not enough for Douglas, who, most days, was on his own, walking the dogs and having lunch at

317

the pub. I was wrapped up in my work but, looking back, I can see he was unhappy and wanted more from his wife. He later said how lonely he was. Sadly, I think my nature and work ethic probably made me a somewhat distant wife – and indeed mother.

When plans were unveiled to build a supermarket close to our house, Douglas decided we must move. I had only just got settled, and really did not want to move. We went to look at many houses, none of which I liked; then Douglas found a farmhouse on the edge of the village of Cadeleigh, not far from Tiverton. The property was set down a long drive and as we approached I thought it was wonderful, set in a valley with open views all round. The house itself was in a dire state. No kitchen, no bathroom: just a tap on an outside wall. There had been chickens in the bedrooms, and pigs at one end of the house. It was damp, the few windows that remained were cracked, and it didn't even have straight walls. I thought, this is the worst of the worst.

It was up for auction, and we got it. I did some lovely designs, and the builders came in. Almost at once, there were problems. Everything I asked the builder to do, Douglas changed. The poor builder did not know where he was. I wanted us to live on site in a caravan while the work was being done, but Douglas refused, and instead we stayed in a bed and breakfast. I could see the bills piling up. Douglas and I were constantly at odds.

'I've done this kind of thing dozens of times before,' I said. 'Just let me get on with it.'

'No, I'm in charge,' my husband insisted. Total impasse.

We arrived one morning to open up. Everything looked as we had left it the night before, but the dogs took off round the back of the house to the barn, where our furniture was stored. I went after them and saw that the doors had been forced open, and all our furniture had been trashed or taken. So many precious things were gone. Most painful was a handbag that had been a gift from Joan, my ex-mother-in-law – it was exquisite, made of delicate gold chain, with a heavy gold chain handle and a clasp of sapphires. It had belonged to her grandmother, and inside bore the inscription *Mrs Cooper, North Cave, Yorkshire.* As she gave it to me Joan had said, 'This is for you for being such a wonderful daughter-in-law.' She may have been difficult at times, but I had really loved her.

Douglas arranged for the insurance assessor to arrive. More bad news followed: our cover would not extend much beyond replacing white goods. I was horrified. All my beautiful Georgian furniture collected over the years had gone, and I could never replace it. What Douglas was most upset about was that his Victorian desk, which had been with him since he was a reporter, had been smashed. I arranged to have it repaired.

The burglary proved the final straw for Douglas. In 2001, with the house still unfinished, he went off on business for a few days and on his return said he was starting divorce proceedings.

'You're the worst-tempered woman I have ever met!' he said.

I don't actually think I was bad-tempered. I just didn't want Douglas telling me what to do all the time – particularly telling me how to make sculpture, when he didn't know how to make it himself. I was shocked by his words, but at the same time immensely relieved that I no longer had to fit into the 'wife' box. It had taken me years to realize that I am no longer wife material, and that my work is of paramount importance to me.

In time, we sorted out our differences, became legally separated and remain the best of friends – although he refused to accept the Victorian desk I had gone to great lengths to have restored for him, and I still have it.

Once Douglas had gone, I still had to somehow finish the house and sell it. I had a great deal of money invested in it, and very little ready cash, so I applied to the technical college in Tiverton for teaching work. They were desperate for someone to teach watercolours. Although I hated watercolours, I needed the money, so we compromised and renamed the class 'Drawing into Colour'.

I was driving back from my first evening class in Tiverton when, on the way through Cadeleigh, I saw someone I knew from the village, Chris Middleton, standing in the middle of the road. I had no choice but to stop.

'Where are you going on your own at this time of night?' he said.

'I've been teaching at the technical college, and am totally exhausted,' I said.

'You don't need to teach – what's that about?'

'Douglas has left me. He said I'm the worst-tempered woman he has ever met.'

'Oh, you need to come into the pub for a drink.'

I was so exhausted, both from teaching and from trying to get the house finished, that I said no.

'No, you must come in and have a drink,' he said, insistent.

I parked the car, and went with him. From then on we were inseparable. The next few months were ones of great joy and great pain. He was the sweetest man I had ever met, and impossible not to love. I felt the same about Chris as I had about Ronnie all those years before – that there was an instant connection. Not that Chris was without his problems. He was an alcoholic.

'I want to live with you forever,' he said.

'I can't – you're an alcoholic.'

'Well, I won't be an alcoholic, then,' he said.

'Ask me, then, in a year's time.'

He decided to stop drinking, just like that. I don't think he realized what he would go through. It was a dreadful experience, sweating and shaking, going through the agonies of withdrawal. He managed it, though, and the pride he felt seemed to make him grow somehow.

We were so happy. I should have known it was too perfect.

We had a trip away planned, and en route we spent a night with Joanna on the Welsh Borders. In the evening the three of us went for a long walk with the dogs into the countryside, and that night Chris stood in the sitting room with his back to a roaring fire, looking so well and happy and strong. I was convinced he had grown taller, and felt so proud of him. He radiated happiness.

When I asked Joanna where we could sleep, she put Chris in a bedroom in the attic and me elsewhere. Poor Chris was cross. He didn't want us to sleep apart.

'I'm sorry; you'll have to put up with it until tomorrow night,' I said.

The next morning, March 9, 2002, I went to wake him, but he was in such a deep sleep that I tiptoed away. A second time I went in, and again, left him to sleep. As it got to ten o'clock and we needed to go out, I went up a third time and leaned over him, intending to wake him gently. He was still, unmoving, not breathing. He had suffered a fatal heart attack during the night. I was devastated, utterly.

Joanna was kind, and put me to bed in her room. I could not move, could not get out of bed in my shock and grief. I was afraid I would forget – forget the sweet man, and all the times we had shared. Joanna gave me a small note-book so that I could jot things down. 'So much laughter, so much *sweetness*, so much love, so much caring one for the other. So much,' I wrote. 'I'm nine years older. When he asked me I said "I'm older than you but can't quite tell you at the moment." "You will," he said. I could now. It's not important.'

Pages and pages I wrote, of all I felt for him. The love we shared is still with me.

After his death, Jennifer wrote a heartfelt letter to me. She understood, knew too well, the pain of losing a loved one. Reading between the lines, I knew that Chris's death had stirred in her memories of Nevill and a love she had never quite let go. Losing him had been a kind of bereavement for her, long before his death. She wrote that she was there for me if I needed her. It meant so much.

Dear Chris,

   I do hope you are beginning to feel stronger now after the terrible shock you must have sustained last week. It doesn't bear thinking of what you must have gone through, especially as he was a dear friend. I am so glad that you have other friends around who are helping and supporting you. Poor Jo must be as much shaken as you are, and I feel for you both.

   Please ring if you want to, but I won't trouble you, in case I should ring at a bad moment or something.

   Much love,
       Jennifer

Psalm 46, which Jennifer and I had learned by heart when very young, saved me in the aftermath of losing Chris. I would say it in times of trouble. Eliza, our grandmother, had it framed on the wall near her favourite chair.

> God is our refuge and strength a very present help in
>   trouble,
> Therefore will we not fear, though the earth be
>   removed,
> And though the mountains be carried into the midst
>   of the sea.

Grandmother had many framed writings on her walls. 'If' by Rudyard Kipling was one of them. It influenced both Jennifer and me. What I did not like was the framed piece in my grandmother's bedroom that read:

I went to bed, and dreamed of beauty
When I awoke my life was duty.

I did not want a life like that: I wanted beauty in my life. Jennifer was different, and wholeheartedly embraced a life of duty.

With nothing to lose, I finished the house in Cadeleigh, sold it, gave Douglas his share, and in 2003 moved to Devon with only my two Jack Russells for company. Before moving to Devon I'd been delighted to sell my large steel birds to Ettington Park Hotel. I had organized the placing and the lighting, and the manager and I were both really pleased with the results. But six months later I had not been paid. I wrote to him: no reply. I wrote again: still no reply. A year passed. I really felt that it was just not good enough, so I went to Ettington Park, only to discover that the manager had changed. This new manager said that he liked my piece a lot, but was not prepared to pay for it – it did not fit in with his budget. How could he treat me, or this beautiful piece of work, so shabbily? Did we have no value? I was very angry, and was not prepared to be treated as so much trash.

I arranged to have the sculpture dismantled and delivered to my new home in Devon. It was large – seventeen feet in height – but nonetheless just fitted into the small garden in front of my house, where it has been much admired by passers-by over the years – all, that is, but one. I was quietly weeding the garden outside the front of my house one day when a small black sit-up-and-beg car screeched to a halt. A very small old lady in black, her head only just visible over the window sill, pointed at the sculpture and shouted at me, 'That yours?'

'Yes,' I smiled in return.

'You've ruined our village,' she barked, and haughtily drove off at speed.

As a sculptor, I'm quite used to being ignored or other less-than-pleasant reactions, but never before directly in my face. I found myself smiling, hugely smiling. I really liked the directness of this feisty old lady.

PART 4

To Be Fully Known

I began writing this book and making the
sculpture of The Sisters in 2011.

My Angels sculpture in Exeter cathedral, 2014.

A Free Spirit

I kept busy with my sculpture, and Jennifer remained deeply involved with her music. She enjoyed singing in choirs and travelled frequently with them, even coming to the cathedral at Exeter, almost on my doorstep. Of course, as was typical of my sister, she didn't tell me until afterwards. When I asked her how her voice was holding up now she was in her sixties, she admitted that it was no longer what it had once been.

'It's not a problem,' she said, of singing with choirs. 'If I can't manage something, I just "fish" it.'

'Whatever do you mean?' I said.

'I open and close my mouth, and that's it.'

'You don't sing?'

'Quite.'

I had to smile.

She was also writing. For many years she had disappeared to her flat in Brighton, which was where she wrote *Call the Midwife*, the first of what would become a bestselling trilogy. Jennifer had always had the ability to write fluently and creatively, but she did not think of writing anything for commercial reasons until an article by Terri Coates in the Royal College of Midwives' journal posed the question: 'Why does no one write about midwives as James Herriot has for vets?' Jennifer was pushing seventy and, as always, was short of money, so she decided to take up the challenge, and *Call the Midwife* was born.

Although I knew she was writing, I did not know precisely what the book would be about until it was published in 2002. Once again, my sister had taken my daughter into her confidence, and Joanna gave her feedback on the manuscript.

'Not so much religion,' Joanna advised.

I also encouraged Douglas, who had remained close to me despite our separation, to support Jennifer's writing and he was an enormous help when it came to editing her manuscripts. The book was turned down by thirteen different publishers over the course of a year, until in desperation Jennifer turned to Pat Schooling at Merton Books, who had published her first book on eczema and food allergy. Although the company specialized in health titles, Pat agreed to publish it and they were on their third printing when Orion took it on. We all thought *Call the Midwife* was good – a fascinating and intimate social history. I was very proud of Jennifer. It also made mention of the love she had felt for Nevill.

'I was so in love with a man I couldn't have, and for whom my heart ached more or less all the time,' she wrote. 'We had met when I was only fifteen. He could quite easily have used and abused me, but he didn't, he respected me. He loved me to distraction, and wanted only my ultimate good. He had educated me, protected me, guided my teenage years.'

None of us, Jennifer included, had any inkling that her tale of being a midwife in London's East End would capture the public imagination in the way it did. Despite the success the book began to bring her, she remained unchanged, and was always uniquely herself.

In 2005, with her career as an author taking off, she came up with an unusual way of marking her seventieth birthday. She would, she announced, cycle and walk 1,000 miles to raise awareness, and funds, for Action Against Allergies. Jennifer's own experience of asthma and eczema meant she knew how debilitating such conditions could be and that there were many others suffering. She was determined to help. The day she phoned to say what she had in mind for her birthday, I was taken aback. I think I asked if she couldn't think of an easier way to raise money. That was the point, of course. Jennifer never took the easy, conventional option. The walking and cycling marathon was far more in keeping with her character. On consideration, I never take the easy option either. I agreed to sponsor her, yet with some trepidation.

In typical Jennifer fashion, she undertook the challenge without fuss or fanfare, quietly clocking up the miles. One day, I received a magazine in the post, which she had come across in a hotel in Chipping Campden, in the Cotswolds, during one of her cycling stages. She thought I would like to see my swan sculpture on the cover. She was so proud of it, she said, that she had bought three copies. In the end, she notched up more than 1,400 miles, both on foot and in the saddle, and in the process raised £1225 for AAA.

Around this time, I remember going to a concert with her and Philip at the Royal Festival Hall on the South Bank in London, and coming outside for some air at the interval. We strolled onto the walkway beside the river with our drinks. It was teeming with people out walking, skateboarders showing off their skills. Without warning, Jennifer lay down on the pavement in the middle of it all. I was alarmed, and turned to Philip.

'What should we do?' I said.

'Let's walk away,' he said.

We stood at a distance watching as people went up to her, stopped, and walked on. More people came and went while Jennifer lay flat out, unconcerned. It occurred to me that Philip had witnessed such behaviour many times before, since he seemed not a bit worried.

'She'll come back when she's ready,' he said.

She did, too: simply got back up and returned to the auditorium in time for the second half of the concert.

The last outing we had, a few years later, was to the English National Opera.

'I've got us wonderful seats,' Jennifer had said.

I arranged for us to have lunch in the garden of my club overlooking Green Park that day. Jennifer was with Philip, and I had taken a close friend with me. After lunch we strolled through the park, returning to the club for tea. It was a lovely day, and Jennifer seemed happy. As she always did, she dressed up for the opera that evening, in a long frock with a train and some of her remarkable jewellery.

As we were about to set off, she said, 'Oh, I decided those seats were far too expensive so I returned them and found us cheaper ones.'

At the London Coliseum, in St Martin's Lane, we followed her up the stairs as far as we could go, all the way to the gods. Jennifer somehow managed to accommodate the train of her evening gown in the cramped row of seats. We all squashed in beside her, our knees up to our chests. All around us were students, everybody in jeans. We could see very little, but Jennifer did not seem to notice.

We were close enough to my club to walk back afterwards, and I suggested to Jennifer that she and Philip take a taxi to Euston to catch the train to Hemel Hempstead. She would not hear of it.

'We're going on the tube,' she announced.

I left her to walk to the underground station in her evening dress, with train and diamonds.

Goodbye

Early in 2011, in one of our regular phone calls, Jennifer mentioned that she was having difficulty swallowing. I'd had the same problem and had been prescribed Omeprazole, which had helped, and every so often I had to have my sphincter stretched. I thought perhaps it was a hereditary problem, and advised Jennifer to go to the doctor. Instead, she went to Brighton on her own and told her family she was working and did not want to be disturbed. As was always the case with my sister, she was more concerned with what was going on inside her head than her body, and ignored her symptoms. When Philip went down to see her for a weekend he found that she had not been eating, and had lost weight. He was worried by her appearance. She finally acquiesced, and saw a doctor.

In March 2011 she was diagnosed with cancer of the oesophagus. It had already gone too far, and was inoperable. The only treatment she allowed was to have a stent put in to help her swallow water and manage light foods.

When she broke the news of her cancer, she made little of it.

'I'm not letting them touch me,' she said. 'I've made a great big DO NOT RESUSCITATE notice, which I'm putting above my bed – and I'm going to make quite sure nobody does.'

I knew from all that she had written in her book, *In the Midst of Life*, that she was opposed to keeping people alive at any cost, and wanted to die in peace.

'To be allowed the space, the time, and the silence in which to know that I am going to die, to contemplate death and to come to terms with the inevitable, and above all to become friends with and welcome the Angel of Death, is what I pray for,' she wrote. 'All dignity will go as control of bodily functions goes, and I will become totally dependent on others, but if peace remains, that, for me, would be the perfect end.'

She had told her consultant she was delighted with her diagnosis. 'Now I can get on with the next part of my life,' she had said.

I arranged to see her, arriving at Boxmoor on April 20, 2011, spending several hours at her bedside. I had driven up from Devon slowly, considering our lives as I went. We had been such different characters and chosen such differ-ent paths in life. I wondered how I would find her, and whether she would be pleased to see me. When I arrived at two in the afternoon she was expecting me, and was full of enthusiasm.

'Come in, come in,' said this childlike form from the bed. She looked uncomfortable – not quite lying down, not quite sitting up.

'Let me help you up,' I said, and puffed up her pillows, re-arranged the bedding and lifted her so that she was propped up.

'How wonderful to have you here, a proper nurse,' she said, a smile stretching across her face.

I had picked cowslips for her that morning from a friend's garden. Jennifer and I had loved picking cowslips together, whole swathes of them in the meadows beneath Chardellows. I can still smell their sweetness.

She clasped the little yellow flowers to her. 'Take those dreadful orchids out of this room. I hate orchids,' she said. 'Put these in a pot.'

I did as I was bid, and can still see that jar of cowslips on her chest of drawers and the smile on her face as she looked at them, utterly content.

We could not stop talking – there was so much to say, so many years to cover in a few short hours. It was easy between us. Once again, we were children playing on the beach at Jaywick Sands, two sisters who related to, and loved, each other.

Her books were by now enjoying huge success, and a BBC television series was being made.

'One good thing,' she said with a wry smile, 'now that I'm ill I don't have to go to America to do all that promotional stuff. That's something.'

We were silent for a moment.

'I would have liked a few more years, Chris, but it was not to be,' she said.

She had put her faith in God and accepted His will. Beside the bed, as she had said there would be, was a large notice fixed to the wall: DO NOT RESUSCITATE. She was eager to get on to the next stage of her journey.

My sister was open and honest with me that day, as I was with her, in a way that we had not been in years. Why had we had this forced relationship, I wondered? How had it developed? For both of us, love had been withdrawn all of a sudden, and the impact had stayed with us for the rest of our lives, a wound that had not healed.

She did not want me to leave, and I did not want to go.

The pain of knowing I was losing her was indescribable. Outside, in the car, I sat and wept. I drove a little way down the road and stopped and wept some more. I knew I would not see her again.

A few weeks later, on May 31, 2011, she died.

Her funeral was held at St John's Church in Boxmoor. It was packed with hundreds of people. Jennifer had left instructions for the service she wanted, one that was deeply religious and followed by a burial which the family attended. At the time my crying was uncontrollable and, irrationally, I did not want to leave her alone in the burial plot, surrounded by the remains of strangers. Jennifer had specified no flowers, and where she lay seemed so very bare. Back at the house, a large wreath had been delivered and was in the sitting room. It had come from my daughter, Louise. Someone took it and placed it on the grave, which gave me some comfort.

I came home, and started making clay figures of the children we had been. As I worked, I tried to understand our relationship. The figures took shape as I lost myself in the work and two little girls emerged, almost of their own accord, kneeling, one with her arms outstretched, the other bent over, head bowed. They really did look like my sister and me.

I placed them on a stand and stepped back, looking at them with a questioning eye. Something was not quite right, but I couldn't work out what. I kept thinking, 'What is it – what's wrong with them?' Every day, I studied the figures and waited for inspiration. Suddenly I knew what I had to do: I jammed them together, the larger one protective, yet wary, the smaller one held in her arms, shielded from the world.

Our childhood had come to an end at the moment our mother had a stroke and our father departed from our home. From then on, Jennifer had been placed in the impossible position of having to be a parent to me, her sister. In some part, the protection she gave me as a child has meant I have been able to enjoy what has been on the whole a very good life, and for that I shall always be grateful.

Compassion

Today I still live in Devon. I continue to work on my sculpture, and I write a lot, constantly overwhelmed by the incredible beauty of the countryside around me. My work continues to show me the way, and it is good to see my three children and ten grandchildren successful and happy.

As I write this, three years have passed since Jennifer died. I feel her presence as strongly as I ever did. She is with me in spirit, always. I light candles for her in churches all over the world, and have prayers said for her. I find myself wanting to pick up the phone and have one of our frustrating conversations in which, very often, so little of any importance was said.

After making many pieces of sculpture inspired by my relationship with my sister and our childhood, I turned my hand to making angels. My final angels are loving and close, yet separately relating to each other. This was how our relationship developed over the years – close genetically, with a shared family background; both strong and creative, and yet apart. My last piece of sculpture, made in black American walnut in memory of my sister, is called Compassion, and stands some eight feet tall. It is placed opposite the Lady Chapel in Exeter Cathedral.

Jennifer created a loving, stable family, although she had

had no experience of such a thing before. She wrote books that touched millions. She was fierce, no-nonsense, brisk and kind.

I now realize that all too often I did not understand my sister. The wall she put up around herself was utterly impenetrable, and so I withdrew, when what she really needed was for me to somehow find a way of breaking through. Knowing this, and having to accept that I will never have another opportunity, is extraordinarily painful.

When Jennifer was alive, I wanted to cry out to her to talk to me. Perhaps she felt the same.

Or perhaps she understood – as I do now – that it was what was unsaid, rather than any words that passed between us, that mattered the most. A deep and enduring love.

ACKNOWLEDGEMENTS

I'd like to thank Patricia Schooling of Merton Books,
a true friend and inspiration to myself and Jennifer.
And all those family and close friends who
have remained with me along the way.

extracts reading groups
competitions books new
discounts extracts extracts events
competitions extracts reading groups
books new discounts
events books reading groups
extracts new reading groups
new titles reading groups events
interviews
events extracts extracts events new
discounts books
new books events interviews new books extracts
events new events

www.panmacmillan.com

extracts events reading groups
competitions books extracts new books